Steve McGraw   4¢ —

D0429072

CLINICAL KLEIN

CLINICAL KLEIN
From Theory to Practice

R. D. HINSHELWOOD

 BasicBooks

A Division of HarperCollins*Publishers*

Library of Congress Cataloging-in-Publication Data
Hinshelwood, R. D.
  Clinical Klein / R. D. Hinshelwood.
  p. cm.
  Includes bibliographical references and index.
  ISBN 0-465-09531-3
  1. Klein, Melanie. 2. Psychoanalysis. 3. Child analysis. I. Title.
RC438.6.K58H56 1994
616.89'17—dc20   94-16624
                                                                        CIP

94 95 96 97 RRD 9 8 7 6 5 4 3 2 1

*For Anna, who has patiently
let me indulge in these interests.*

CONTENTS

ACKNOWLEDGEMENTS

I am deeply grateful to Muriel MacIver for her time, concentration and unsullied 'innocence', generously given to reading my manuscript. And those readers who do in fact find this book a serviceable entry into Kleinian psychoanalysis have a similar debt of gratitude to her and her persistent questions.

I have had important comments from Ann Scott, Bill Barnes-Gutteridge, John Gordon, Bob Young, and Gérard Bléandonu, which have helped and challenged my thinking, and spurred me on.

I am very grateful to Eric Brenman, Michael Feldman, Betty Joseph, Donald Meltzer, Irma Brenman Pick, Hanna Segal and John Steiner for their willingness to let me use their published material here. I want to acknowledge especially the help and support of Elizabeth Spillius as Secretary of the Melanie Klein Trust, and also Betty Joseph, the Chairperson, for permission to use the case material from volumes of *The Writings of Melanie Klein*. I have been in touch with the literary executors of a number of authors, and wish to thank them for the permissions they have given: Mrs Francesca Bion for her husband, Wilfred Bion; Donald Meltzer for Roger Money-Kyrle; Mrs Lottie Rosenfeld and Angela Rosenfeld, wife and daughter respectively, for Herbert Rosenfeld; and Margaret Tonnesman for Paula Heimann. I have to thank them all not only for their willingness but also for so many well-wishing comments. Curiously, after considerable enquiry, I have not been able to trace the literary executors of Susan Isaacs.

I have also been granted permissions by the publishers of the quoted authors: Routledge and Tavistock Publications; Cesare Saccerdoti of H. Karnac Books; Random House; W.W. Norton; International Universities Press. Many pieces of material were first published in journals, which have all given their permission: Alex Holder, currently editor of the *Bulletin of the European Psycho-Analytical Foundation*; Hermi Däuker of the British Psychological Society, which owns the *British Journal of Medical Psychology*; Josephine Shapiro, currently managing editor of the *Psycho-Analytic Quarterly*; and – by no means least – David Tuckett, current editor of the *International Journal of Psycho-Analysis*, has patiently dealt with my requests for permissions for the many quotations from the cases originally published in his journal.

Above all I want to thank Ann Scott, who has supervised the mounting tide of paper to which these permissions gave rise. But also, I have to thank her for her support in so many other aspects of getting this book ready to be read, as she has prodded it step by step through the publishing machine. Finally, Gillian Beaumont has worked on the later stages of editing with her usual meticulous care.

Dr Tonnesman has asked me to mention that Paula Heimann left the Klein group in 1955 and material used in this volume was all written before that date.

EXAMPLES

Introduction: A Guide to the Baffled Reader

When I was reflecting on the *Dictionary of Kleinian Thought* in 1988, I remarked how unusual it was to write about Klein from a theoretical point of view, as I was then doing. The present book is a clinical one. It is therefore complementary to the *Dictionary*, to which reference should be made for theoretical expositions of Kleinian concepts; and it attempts to complement the admirable *Introduction to the Work of Melanie Klein* by Hanna Segal, a classic which in the past has served to bring so many to their understanding and enthusiasm for Klein's work. It is not an investigation of specific cases or conditions; it stands merely as an illustration of how concepts emerge from the clinic.

Despite the heavy clinical emphasis by Melanie Klein and her followers, however, clinical writing is not the rule in psychoanalysis. Rather, it is top-heavy with theory. Nevertheless, my method in this book is to look at *published* clinical material. Clinical writers have tried to show us what their own psychoanalytic work has discovered by giving keyhole glimpses of their work. The success of the vignette method is variable but Kleinian writers, especially, have tried to demonstrate their concepts in the detailed record of the processes in their clinical work. Their writing is an indicative method. This book returns to those clinical indications of the concepts to extract their meaning in the terms of personal experience. I chose published records deliberately; they are available for you to go and consult for yourself in any particular instance to check my version and my views. So the book tries to guide the reader through these selected bits of recorded clinical practice. They show my bias. Go and balance it with your own.

I do not claim the book as a proof that Melanie Klein's discoveries are true. Rather, I attempt to indicate practically and clinically what Kleinian psychoanalysis is. Its correctness or otherwise is something that readers must ponder for themselves – or with the help of their own psychoanalysis. I claim that you are guided best if you look first at what Klein and her followers were putting before us. You will not find more than an occasional glance in the direction of other schools of psychoanalysis. I am not practised in any other psychoanalytic tradition than the Kleinian, and am not qualified to make a reliable comparison with the way other psychoanalysts would generate their concepts out of their (or this) clinical material.

This book is not an easy read for people coming to Kleinian writing for the first time. It is not light reading. As with immersion in any system of thinking, it takes time before you can swim. It requires persistence and a willingness to go on in the dark until light begins to dawn. One of the difficulties in mastering psychoanalytic language, and especially the Kleinian variant, concerns the different vantage points: on the one hand there is an objective approach, as if one is standing outside looking on; the other is the subjective, as if one is trying to get 'inside' the experience of another person, of their life and of themselves. These vantage points have given rise to quite separate psychoanalytic languages, and that has created confusion. If one says: 'The infant is struggling with an experience that his tummy is being gnawed away by nasty beings in it, and he comforts himself by constructing the phantasy that his thumb is a good ally that he can take into him to fight off these bad things', this stance, from within the infant's subjectivity, sounds different from the more objective language: 'He is defending against frustration by regressing to an oral level and using the mechanism of introjection.'[1] These languages run side by side in psychoanalytic literature. For the novice, this creates a degree of confusion which has to be faced and overcome. To some extent the confusion could be clarified by defining our terms more accurately, but in this book I have resorted to a method of 'pointing out', the *indicative* method. You cannot define what red is to someone who has never seen it, you can really indicate it to them only provided they are not blind. It is like the old story that if you described an elephant to a blind man, he would not believe you. It is the same with psychoanalytic ideas: they are not believed unless they come from experience.

Psychoanalytic thinking is not easily contained in a linear argument: premisses leading to conclusions. It is a particular way of thinking. At first this may be disconcerting. The means of arriving at what are held to be psychoanalytic truths may seem unconvincing at first. Debate and argument, though vociferous, play little part in the actual progress of the ideas; it is not like an academic discipline in that sense. So comprehension does not arrive like a light being switched on, it grows slowly – often irritatingly slowly; and only with hindsight will you notice that something has become familiar and acceptable to the extent that you are already using it for yourself in your own way.

To understand the material in this book, you need to fall back on your own experiences simply as a human being. To get *inside* these experiences, you may find access through your own: having children; the vagaries and perplexities of ordinary social interaction; your own introspection and subjectivity – at some time in our lives we all have to be confronted with relationships that appear irrational. Some readers may have experience in professions in mental health, or education, or other related work where they have again been challenged by the irrational and childlike nature of human beings. Finally, you may be undergoing your own psychoanalysis or psychotherapy.

The ideas and experiences we will address are often very remote from consciousness; and unfortunately, psychoanalytic writing has not been as plain and lucid as it might be. Psychoanalysts are not necessarily picked for their literary abilities. This can be a problem, and it is true of Melanie Klein herself. Her descriptions of her patients are often extremely vivid, but the manner of her writing is off-putting, sometimes positively alienating. Klein was writing for psychoanalysts. She did not spell out her clinical intuitions and deductions in detail. Often she took it for granted that other psychoanalysts would follow her use of terms, and would accept the meaning of certain kinds of symbols, without the need for laborious explanation. For the newcomer, though, this gives a rather densely textured account of her cases, and her conclusions often appear to be alarmingly arrived at with minimal evidence, as intermediate steps may be omitted, leaving you floundering if you are not familiar with the psychoanalytic method of working with the evidence. My intention, therefore, has been to try to select and elaborate many steps which, it has seemed to me, might appear obscure.

In addition, and even for trained psychoanalysts, Klein has a rather didactic way of introducing the most difficult or, perhaps, deepest ideas. Some have therefore written her off as wild in her views, or as dismissive of alternative points of view. And sadly, people often give up and resign themselves to the conclusion that without going into their own psychoanalysis, or even into training to be a psychoanalyst, they will never understand her. It is undoubtedly true of course, that having a personal psychoanalysis will considerably enhance the possibilities of gaining from this book – as well as, of course, from life itself.

Because one so often hears that Klein's writings are baffling, we might be led to the conclusion that we should not use them for the expositional purpose of this book. However, I think that to overlook her writings robs us of extremely sensitive and detailed clinical observations. Her case descriptions are often very clear, despite their occasional tendentiousness. Therefore, I am including many of her case examples – in fact, about a third of the examples I have chosen. I have tried where I can to use a clinical session where as much of the evidence as possible is presented. However, there is not always a worthy consistency in this respect. Instead, at times a reversion to more discursive accounts results in conclusions without advance precise clinical evidence. The recourse to theoretical debate, albeit rather less prevalent among Kleinians, is still prominent, and many of the examples I have selected have suffered from that clinical tentativeness. I would have liked to be more rigorous. I would have liked to present only session material that was process-recorded in exemplary manner to give the patient's confirming (or otherwise) response to the psychoanalyst's interpretations. Despite limitations of this choice, some of the material is quite exemplary in this regard, and I have tried to emphasize this in my comments. Overall, the material I use gives a sense of how the psychoanalyst's thought works in detail, both its limitations and its meticulous observational achievement.

Whatever the general standards of clinical reporting, however, we retain a problem of access to the deeply unconscious human material. There is a curious irony: this is all about human beings; it is about us. It ought to be accessible to all of us who are the very thing being studied. Yet there is so often such an experience of obstructiveness to the material that it seems remote, unrelated to any already known thinking – you feel that you are not party to the basic tenets, and that they are obscurely withheld from you. I think this is a struggle you have to engage on with yourself rather than with the book. But here it is crucial to understand that some aspects of the human mind have been discovered only through probing the psyches of highly disturbed people, particularly psychotic patients. It is rather like groping for knowledge of the stars at the other end of the universe, with the eventual result that it presents back to us something about our own corner of the universe. Confrontation with severe mental disturbance is always challenging, yet the effort to overcome the worries of a close encounter with it does open an understanding on to the wide new horizon towards which Klein pointed.

To all these difficulties I can only say: 'Push on'.

I write as a psychoanalyst who is now familiar with all these ideas, and with this form of practice. It has been an effort to try to return to that moment when the beginner first encounters this new world. I decided, after collecting the material I wished to include, to prepare drafts to be read by people who were closer to that moment: people whom I thought of as 'qualified by innocence'. I have tried to be alert to the difficulties of entry into this body of knowledge, and I hope that despite bafflement, an enthusiasm will lead you on. I have written as a Kleinian psychoanalyst, and no doubt my own enthusiasm and commitment show through. I hope they are in some measure infectious, but this should not lead you into accepting more than your own judgement allows. In the end you must make up your own mind whether some, all or none of this book carries conviction. Those of you who come to this for the first time should make your innocence a telling instrument for questioning what I and my sources have written. Many other readers, however, will start with their own particular commitment for or against Kleinian views. I can only ask that, whichever it is, you use this book to re-examine any of those convictions with which you come.

PART I
THE FOUNDATION

1 THE PSYCHOANALYTIC BACKGROUND

Melanie Klein's contributions are so rooted in the basic Freudian discoveries that they cannot be comprehended without some understanding of Freud. However, Freud's fundamental discoveries of the nature of the unconscious, infantile sexuality and the long history to the ideas about transference cannot be dealt with systematically in this book. Nevertheless, I think it is necessary to point towards some aspects of the fundamental ideas which are especially relevant to the developments which Klein eventually made herself. Chapter 1 is therefore a scene-setting exercise; it may perhaps be passed over by readers who are familiar with Freud's work. My elucidation of Freudian concepts is selective – confined to those upon which Klein especially depended – and also rather cursory. Those who need a sounder basis, or want a greater depth, should consult Sandler, Dare and Holder (1973) and Laplanche and Pontalis (1973).

When Freud started his research (in the 1880s) into the symptoms of neurotic and hysterical women, the dominant mode of psychotherapy had been developed, principally in France, out of Mesmerism, known in medical and scientific circles as 'hypnosis'. Although its value was disputed, a number of French physicians persisted with developing this kind of therapy, a development which culminated in the methods and ideas of Pierre Janet. The general thrust of the French method was that the contents of the mind could be changed by suggestion. Unwanted thoughts and troublesome feelings could be eradicated; attitudes could be changed. However, this depended upon the patients being pliant and willing to accept the suggestions. Some physicians used hypnosis to induce the patient into a particularly suggestible state of mind, while others attempted to accomplish their aims with the patient in the normal waking state; but all variants of this therapy had in common the fact that the doctor took over control of the patient's mind and changed its contents.

Freud's line of approach was different. He had studied these hypnotic and suggestive therapies in France, but in the end he abandoned them. Instead he took up the ideas of a Viennese medical colleague, Josef Breuer. Breuer had found something different: if he brought his patient into a hypnotic trance, then got her[2] to talk about her symptoms and associated feelings and thoughts, he noticed that a strong emotional response developed during the trance. Then, after the emotional release, the symptom abated. Freud became more attracted to this *expressive* method, in contrast to the didactic (or corrective) methods of French suggestionists. And this has remained a fundamental difference between psychoanalysis and certain other forms of therapy – expression of what is in the mind versus correction of it.

Thus Freud's research led him to a method for exploring the patient's psyche rather than controlling it. It is now well known that these explorations led to his discovery of the dynamic 'unconscious', a part of the mind which is active in influencing thoughts, feelings, relationships, attitudes and behaviour in a way which is completely unknown to the person.[3] He sought to give *expression* to what is not under control, rather than to control it. In the process he discovered that the contents of this unconscious mind derived from childhood upsets, traumas and frightening phantasies; and in particular he pointed to a troubled childhood phase dominated by worry about sexual matters, especially a set of fears and longings connected with the parents' sexuality, the emergence of babies from mother, and anxiety about sexual violence of various kinds. This intense, troubled sexual life of the child came to be known as the Oedipus complex.

In later chapters we will see how Kleinian analysts have developed the notion of expression (as opposed to suggestion) in terms of containing, and the therapeutic effects of simply knowing, becoming aware, and thinking thoughts.

SYMBOL INTERPRETATION

Because Freud was not a very good hypnotist, his use of hypnosis gave way to simple encouragement of his patients, in the waking state, to remember their childhood past – he called this the 'pressure method'. Eventually he developed the method of free association, when he had made another discovery – the way dreams can be decoded as sets of personal symbols. In effect, dreams are a kind of secret communication with oneself. Why would someone communicate in secret with themselves? It sounds a bit odd. However, once it is recognized that an unconscious part of the mind is kept in some way out of that person's conscious awareness, then the issues which remain in the unconscious, and are active in influencing them, must be represented in some way which is not at all apparent to the conscious person. Thus dreams represent an *unconscious* thinking about the secret thoughts and phantasies which have to remain unknown. So Freud thought that this mental activity, which is not consciously appreciated, could partially break through, as it were, into consciousness when the mind is in the unconscious state of being asleep. But the contents are obscured by being represented in disguising symbols. Freud worked out a method for translating those symbols. It was not a dictionary, or a 'dream book', of which there were many at the time; it was a method of unravelling the idiosyncratic symbol system developed by each individual person. Each person (indeed, each dream) develops unique symbols for the immediate purpose – to continue concealing the unconscious contents of the mind.

Freud found that if he took his own dreams, wrote them down, broke them up into individual elements, and allowed his mind free rein on each element (free association), some theme repeatedly emerged. He jotted down notes of the sequence these thoughts took. What emerged was a cluster of specific issues, memories and wishes. They began to cohere together with clearer, and more meaningful, links between them than in the manifest elements of the dream itself. A certain theme came up like a photographic plate in the developer. Although it was not explicitly contained in the dream, he believed that such a recurring theme was an underlying (and disguised) content – the *latent* content of the dream. It was in this way that Freud thought he could crack the code of the dream and reveal its hidden meaning. He contested the view that the symbols of a dream were universal. Instead, each symbol is chosen idiosyncratically by each individual – that is to say, on each occasion the symbols and the code must be interpreted anew. He interpreted a number of his own dreams in this way, and then increasingly those of his patients; he revealed a full subterranean life of memories and wishes, and a whole unknown 'grammar' which arranged the symbols – the processes of condensation and displacement. Most troubling was the fact that these hidden mental activities so often concerned sexual thoughts and wishes. He became very unpopular for these ideas in his own prudish times, and today they still remain very challenging on first acquaintance, even though many of them are now quite familiar in our culture.

The method of free association entailed getting the patient to relax and to say whatever came into their head. The stream of consciousness that was then produced could be dealt with like the elements in a dream and the associations to them. The psychoanalyst would gather the recurring – albeit hidden – references to the past, and to childhood sexual preoccupations. Those items in the patient's thoughts which came next to each other in the time sequence were deemed to have a linked meaning. Thus associations are meaningful links, even though the meaning may be obscured, just as the dream conceals through the use of obscuring symbols. For the rest of his working life Freud relied mainly upon his method of symbol interpretation to bring out the patient's expression of hidden issues.

TRANSFERENCE

However Freud's understanding of symbols, and the way the unconscious uses symbols, was gradually superseded by another approach. This too was initiated by Freud himself – in fact, by a disastrous failure he had with his well-known patient Dora. He had intended Dora's case, begun in October 1899, to illustrate his method of dream interpretation in action with a patient. Dora broke off her treatment a couple of months later, at the end of December, in the middle of Freud's work. He delayed publication of this case for some five years before he presented it, with a discussion of what had gone wrong (Freud, 1905). It seems that he had been so intent on interpreting the details of the dream symbols and following them up through the associations that he completely overlooked another occurrence. That occurrence came to be known as the 'transference'. It consisted of a particular development in the course of the treatment – not a verbal presentation of symbols, but direct wishes towards the psychoanalyst himself. Freud's reading of this was that Dora developed a particular wish to frustrate him and leave him disappointed. This she did by terminating the treatment. Freud did not realize this important development in Dora's relationship with him until it was too late. Her wish to frustrate Freud and take revenge on him by disappointing him was connected with Dora's own frustrated disappointment in relation to her father. Frustrations that belonged to her relationship with her father had been taken out on Freud.

Ever since his work with Breuer ten years before, Freud had known that patients may fall in love with the psychoanalyst. However, it was not Dora's love which took him unawares – it was her hatred and revenge. The transference is striking because of the intensity of both love and hate; they betray its unacknowledged origin – in childhood. Freud learned from this that he needed to interpret more than the symbolic content of the patient's dreams and other verbal material. He had to attend to and interpret the meaning of these unusual – and unexpected – aspects of the relationship with himself. So he came to distinguish two ways in which patients produced their memories of the past: one was by recollecting in words; the other was by repeating, in some form, actual past events or phantasies. Repetition (or re-creating) in the relationship (the transference), as an expressive act revealing contents of the patient's unconscious, has become a cornerstone of psychoanalytic technique. It could be argued that this is perhaps the most important development in the clinical practice of psychoanalysis – more important than any of the multitude of developments in psychoanalytic theory, because the transference is the tool by which all the evidence and testing of the theory take place. As we go through the material in later chapters, the increasing importance of transference in Kleinian practice will emerge.

Jung was a psychiatrist; Freud was a neurologist. This, among other differences, created strains when Jung and his Zurich group joined up with Freud and the Vienna group in 1906; and one of the strains was that Jung had considerable experience treating psychotic patients, while Freud did not. There were a number of other strains too, but Freud's experience of psychotic patients was that he could not analyse them. In particular he found that schizophrenics do not relate to the real world, only to an imaginary, constructed one. They live in a world of their own delusions and hallucinations. As a result, Freud's method, depending as it did on the patient co-operating in a relationship with the psychoanalyst, failed.

Freud attempted to understand schizophrenia by analysing the written autobiographical memoirs of Judge Schreber (Freud, 1911): he 'psychoanalysed' the book! On that basis he developed a theory of why psychotic patients could not be analysed. In the process, in 1914, he developed his theory of narcissism.

NARCISSISM

Freud took over the term 'narcissism' from Havelock Ellis, an English doctor. Freud had taken a interest in Ellis because both studied sexual disorders; so Ellis, in turn, had taken a keen interest in Freud. The narcissist is deeply – even exclusively – self-involved; so Freud thought that the schizophrenic, who was so wrapped up in his own world constructed with voices, hallucinations and delusions, deserved the term 'narcissistic'. However, he explained this in terms of the theories he was using at the time.

LIBIDO

At the beginning of his research Freud wished to make his descriptions as rigorous and as scientific as possible, and to give the impression that he could measure 'psychic forces' (mental energy) just as Galileo or Newton could measure physical ones. He used the idea of mental energy, which he called 'libido'. The libido is directed *towards* an object – that is, it is invested with a person's interest. He then described the object as 'cathected' with the libido. The terms 'cathect', 'cathexis' and 'libido' were Latinized scientific-sounding words invented, in fact, by Freud's English translators to try to impress a medical readership. They were not Freud's own terms in German, which were actually more down-to-earth. 'Libido' and 'cathexis' refer to the interest or fascination that someone has in some topic or some other person.

The narcissistic person is self-involved; the object of his greatest interest is himself. In the case of the psychotic patient, interest in the world around has been completely lost. In the scientific terminology, the patient has 'decathected' all the objects in the real world; instead, the libido has been directed towards the self – it has cathected the ego. So Freud described the self-involvement of the schizophrenic as a withdrawal of libido from the world; as a result, mental energy ('libido', interest) has been invested in the person of the schizophrenic alone, or some part of the schizophrenic.

Freud discussed the complicated relations between the narcissistic state, when the libido has been withdrawn and directed towards the self (ego-libido, he called it) and the more usual state when the world of real people and things remains within the person's interest (object-libido). The term 'object' also needs a little explanation. It is used in the sense in which the term 'object' is used in grammar – 'subject–verb–object': the object upon which an action is performed by a subject. Freud likened this process, in which interest in some other person or object can be withdrawn (and later possibly returned), to the process in which an amoeba puts out a thread of protoplasm (a pseudopodium) towards things in its environment to test them as potential food, and so on, and can withdraw it if it is not interested. He saw the withdrawal and redirection of the libido (interest) as a fluid situation, one which explained many occurrences in normal psychology as well as in the schizophrenic. Going to sleep, for instance, entails a withdrawal of interest in the outside world and an investment in the internal dream world of the night. Then, in the morning, awakening involves the redirection of the libido, or mental energy, outwards again to the world and the people and things that interest the person. Similarly, in illness or in pain there is a withdrawal of interest into the self, or into the particular organ that is diseased and in pain; a toothache becomes the only experience for the sufferer, and the rest of the world pales into insignificance while the tooth throbs.

Freud's bewilderment with the seriously narcissistic conditions, the psychoses, led him to call them the 'narcissistic neuroses'. The beginning of the way out of the problem of investigating them psychoanalytically will be the focus of the next chapter, and the discoveries made in those attempts are the roots of psychoanalytic thinking which became identifiably Kleinian.

2   INTROJECTION AND PROJECTION

In this chapter and the next we will consider certain aspects of the development of psychoanalytic ideas mostly before Melanie Klein started her work. This concerns the attempts, particularly by Freud and a colleague in Berlin, Karl Abraham, to understand certain psychotic symptoms and patients. In describing primitive defence mechanisms and unconscious phantasies I shall draw at times upon the fuller understanding that was contributed by Klein and her colleagues, but these notions were deeply embedded in the thinking of Freud and Abraham, explicitly described by them, and received from them by Klein and her followers.

During the time (around 1910) when Freud was concerned about his failures with psychotic patients, Karl Abraham started a new line of thinking in which Freud collaborated closely. Abraham was a German psychiatrist who had trained in psychoanalysis with Jung in Zurich, but returned to Berlin in 1907 to found the Berlin Psycho-Analytical Society. He was one of the foremost psychoanalysts in the first generation of Freud's followers, and he was an outstanding clinical observer of patients and their mental states.

Abraham had an important idea: if it is impossible to investigate schizophrenia directly, then perhaps psychoanalysts should start elsewhere. In manic-depressive psychosis the patient has intermittent psychotic phases with lucid, apparently normal, periods in between, so Abraham attempted analysis of these psychotics during their periods of 'normality'. He produced a series of papers on his discoveries between 1911 and his death in 1924. In 1917 Freud produced a major theoretical paper on the same topic:

'Mourning and melancholia'. That paper became significant, because it took his theory of narcissism a step further forward.

INTROJECTION

The idea of the withdrawal of the libido (interest) can explain the extreme self-involvement of manic-depressive patients – the libido has turned from the object to the self (ego). In that process the patient's interest becomes invested solely in him- or herself, invested in that patient's own world of ideas, feelings, memories, worth, and so on. In this way such patients are similar to schizophrenics. Depressives spend a major part of their time reflecting on their own actions, worth, moods, and so forth. Freud developed this point in his paper.

But something else happens too. With the loss of interest (withdrawal of the libido) the depressive comes to feel different about him- or herself, and feels towards someone else as if he or she *were* actually that other lost person. It is as if not only has the libido been withdrawn, like the amoeba's pseudopodium, but the object too has been drawn back inside the self (ego) with the libido. This is a very peculiar process leading to a peculiar state of mind – in essence, a mad one. Such a process appears to have, said Freud, some similarities with another – and this time quite normal – state of mind. He compared the melancholia of the manic-depressive with the state of mourning of someone bereaved. Following a bereavement, there is a withdrawal of involvement; the interest in the lost one has to be given up. Freud recounted how emotionally hard it is to give up interest in a dead spouse, or parent, or child, for instance. It requires a prolonged period of active psychological work to detach one's interest, and this entails great pain over many months, at least. He described how this is a step-by-step process, as if every memory of the loved one has to be brought out and, bit by bit, relinquished. Gradually, over time, interest in the world is re-established. Other interests become more lively, and the capacity to love slowly turns towards others. In this Freud thought he saw an analogous process to the narcissistic states – for example, sleep or illness. The amoeba's pseudopodium withdraws, and slowly another one is put out again elsewhere.

In the case of the depressive, the whole process is problematic.

The depressive has a particularly strong ambivalence towards loved ones; that is to say, she or he not only loves but also hates them. Freud thought that the component of aggression and hatred, inevitable in any relationship, is particularly strong in this pathological condition. Even the slightest rebuffs or slights, hardly noticeable to others, will make depressives feel that they have lost their loved one and have only a hated one; as if the loved one has actually been lost. Attention then turns rapidly towards the self – and stays directed there. This results in a particular quality to the *relationship with the self*, which resembles the way the person once related to his or her loved object – that is to say, ambivalently, with a special intensity to the hatred. This, then, is self-hate. When depressives ruminate upon their worthlessness, this is the hatred that was once focused upon the object, turned now towards the self (ego). In Freud's view the same reproaches that the depressive once directed against the object are now directed against the self.

Because of the excess of hatred, it seems, the patient becomes absorbed with that same kind of relationship with him- or herself, stuck in a hostile self-relationship. In mourning, in contrast, the love for the object is stronger than the hatred, and this leads to a very different course, which allows the eventual turning out again to objects in the external world. Depression seems to be a process of mourning which has gone wrong because of the especial strength of hatred towards the object.

Thus Freud spelled out in this paper a very curious occurrence: it is as though the object is moved from outside the person, literally, to the inside, to join the identity of that person. This is peculiar, even mad. The loved one, who was once hated (as well as loved), has been relocated inside the person, and the hatred continues to be directed against the ego of the person, inside which the object is now *believed* to be located. It becomes real for the patient that the object has been moved inside to become an actual part of his or her own personality. Not only has the libido been withdrawn, but the object itself is also drawn inside. The person's identity becomes disturbed: it takes on the characteristics of the loved (and hated) one. Freud called this process 'identification': the 'object' is absorbed into the identity of the 'ego'. Later, with Abraham, this process came to be known as 'introjection'.

Many of Freud's later theories come directly from this idea of a process of internalization ('identification', or 'introjection'). In 1921 he used the idea of 'identification' as a basis for a revision of his theory of social groups. The solidarity in groups, the 'glue' that sticks people together, is an identification which they have in *common*. They all introject the same person (or idea) as a central part of themselves (their egos). Christians, for instance, are joined in their central belief in Christ, and they each 'carry' him in their heart. In this later view, however, Freud has taken a new step: the odd manoeuvre of introjecting an object is no longer the particular oddity of the depressive – Freud is now observing its regular occurrence in ordinary people in ordinary groups.

Later, in 1923, Freud based his structural theory of the mind – id, ego and super-ego – upon the idea of introjection. At some point a child, in the phase of the Oedipus complex, has to give up mother, or father, as their loved one (sexual loved one). Freud thought that this was accomplished through the same slow process of identification, similar to that in melancholia – that is, the parent is withdrawn (introjected) into the ego. The super-ego, he said, is 'the heir to the Oedipus complex'. The super-ego is the special bit of the ego into which this is absorbed, and it becomes thereby somewhat separate and apart from the rest of the ego. The super-ego represents the standards of the parents which the person, from then on, honours and loves in the way that the parents were loved and honoured. The super-ego becomes an *internal* object. It is the result of an internalizing movement (introjection) of an object into the inside of the personality. This process gives rise to a new category of objects, 'internal' objects (or 'introjected' objects; or sometimes 'internalized' objects). The only internal object with which Freud concerned himself was the super-ego.

Abraham, however, took these ideas in a different direction. Whereas Freud's development was a theoretical advance – the structural model of the mind that integrated the Oedipus complex as well as painful states of unconscious guilt (and masochism) – Abraham's work remained clinical, and his theoretical conclusions were more limited. His clinical discoveries did in fact suggest profound theoretical developments, but these were left to others to make – notably Melanie Klein. We will now look at some of Abraham's meticulous clinical reports.

THE LOCATION OF OBJECTS

The fullest expression of Abraham's views was written in 1924, just before his early death: 'A short study of the development of the libido, viewed in the light of mental disorders', where he richly specified the clinical manifestations of introjection and projection. Abraham concentrated a special interest upon the fate of the object; this contrasted with the more usual emphasis on the vicissitudes of the instincts. In Freud's theory of instincts each instinct, and each component instinct, has a source (in the body), an aim (to do something), and an object (the thing or person upon which the aim is carried out). Abraham changed emphasis: from Freud's emphasis on the source and the aim to an emphasis on the object. Or rather, he was driven to take this step by his psychotic patients' interest in their objects. It was *their* anxious interest in what happened to their objects that led him to emphasize the importance of the 'object'.

Abraham illustrated the concreteness of phantasies about moving the object in and out of the self. He established a centrality for introjection and projection. (A word of warning: this material, coming from psychotic patients, may seem emotionally disturbing.)

Example: Anal holding on

One patient, who had had several periods of depression:

> began his analysis just as he was recovering from an attack of this [depressive] kind. It had been a severe one, and had set in under rather curious circumstances. The patient had been fond of a young girl for some time back and had become engaged to her . . . [But something] caused his inclinations to give place to a violent resistance. It had ended in his turning away completely from his love-object . . .

You will note that the patient turns away from his loved one – this amounts to the 'withdrawal of the libido from the object'.

> During his convalescence a *rapprochement* took place between him and his fiancée, who had remained constant to him in spite of his having left her.

Abraham is indicating to us that the patient's mental state (the clinical depression) recovered with the rediscovery of his love. With the recovery the patient's interest (his libido) turns outwards to the object again.

> But after some time he had a brief relapse, the onset and termination of which I was able to observe in detail in his analysis.
>
> His resistance to his fiancée re-appeared quite clearly during his relapse . . .

Abraham uses the term 'resistance' to indicate an anger towards the fiancée; the patient seems to resist his own love. In this sense he loses her. The loved object is lost, or felt to be lost, because she has turned suddenly into a hated one. Freud's theory expresses this in objective terms, the 'direction of the libido'. But Abraham now emphasizes the patient's concern with the object; it is this kind of subjective description of loss which he was beginning to discover. Then he reveals a link between this relapse and a particular kind of activity with the object:

> . . . . and one of the forms it took was the following transitory symptom: During the time when his state of depression was worse than usual, he had a compulsion to contract his *sphincter ani*.

The symptom is a bodily one – holding fast to the contents of the bowels. In linking it with the patient's depressive phase, Abraham is implying that from the patient's point of view the faeces in the bowel represent his hated ('shitty') fiancée, who is slipping away from him. He attempts to hold on to that object as if it is physically located inside him.

Abraham uses Freud's description of the melancholic's loss of the object; but in addition he specifies the melancholic's anxious attempts to restore the object that has been lost. He then describes another version of the patient's attempt to hang on to the object by putting it inside him:

> A few days later he told me, once more of his own accord, that he had a fresh symptom which had, as it were, stepped into the shoes of the first. As he was walking along the street he had had a compulsive phantasy of eating the excrements that were lying about.

This is a repellent notion. However, it is of great significance; the patient has, in his strange way, substituted another preoccupation with faeces, an attempt to put them inside him. Again we are asked to consider that the faeces are equated with his loved (though also hated) fiancée; and so, with the phantasy of eating the one, he is internalizing the other (introjection):

> This phantasy turned out to be the expression of a desire to take back into his body the love-object which he had expelled from it in the form of excrement. We have here, therefore, a literal confirmation of our theory that the unconscious regards the loss of an object as an anal process, and its introjection as an oral one.

Abraham thinks this kind of material conveys the very primitive ways in which the mind of a psychotic patient may connect the outside world with a phantasied world inside the body (or inside the self, as it is felt). It does so through a bodily activity – eating. In addition, loss may, in this patient, be experienced bodily as defecating.

These are uncongenial notions, which often seem far-fetched. They are, however, the attempts of that time (the 1920s) to capture the incomprehensible experiences of the psychotic patient. Abraham repeatedly emphasized the processes of losing and regaining loved ones in terms of losing and regaining substances and things from and into the body. The importance of objects believed, in phantasy, to be inside the body led to a special importance for the bodily processes that bring things (objects) inside the body, or lose them out of the body. These objects are believed to be quite real at some primitive level for these patients, and are handled just like bodily, physical objects. Loss of one of these objects is experienced, unconsciously, as just as real as the expulsion of faeces out of the body through the anus.

Abraham's descriptions differ from Freud's paper on melancholia in certain fundamental respects, particularly the extra stress he places on the complex to-and-fro motion of the object in and out of the body; the very explicit experience of concrete internal objects (e.g. just like the bodily experience of something, faeces, in the rectum); the relation of these phantasies to oral and anal instincts (sucking and excreting); and thus a clear link between bodily instincts and active relationships with objects. Abraham describes these actual phantasies, in disguised form like the narratives of dreams, as very primitive processes. Love, loss and restitution expressed as phantasies of bodily activities are a

considerable amplification of Freud's theories about melancho-
liacs. They diverted from Freud's theory of the super-ego, and were
to lead psychoanalytic theory in a new direction.

In summary, Abraham described how his psychotic patients
were preoccupied with very primitive processes which have
important characteristics: the concreteness of the phantasies about
the personality and its make-up; the belief in a physical presence
of entities *inside* the body; the connection of phantasies of oral
incorporation with the mechanism of introjection, and those of
defecation with projection. However far-fetched these ideas seem
at this point, they can hardly be more strange than the minds of
psychotic patients. I want to turn our attention in the next chapter
to the idea of 'unconscious phantasy', which Freud – and especially
Abraham – were debating in the early 1920s. I shall repeat the
attempt to illustrate this fundamental root of unconscious
meanings, experiences and activities in phantasies connected with
bodily sensations.

3 UNCONSCIOUS PHANTASY

A further illustration from Abraham's 1924 paper reveals the extraordinarily imaginative, and often desperate, quality of phantasies that unconsciously underlie and give meaning to experiences. Bear in mind that in Chapter 2 we saw how these phantasies are rooted in the experience of the body and its activities. In the next example these occurrences are not merely the mad processes of psychotic patients. Now the discovery is that the introjection (and the underlying oral phantasies of incorporation) appear as part of the familiar process of mourning *as well as* in melancholia. The following illustration refers to 'cannibalism'. The notion comes from the idea of introjection – people, loved or hated objects, may be taken in, through the mouth and in the activity of eating. This is a bodily expressed notion, or 'phantasy', which underlies the 'mechanism' of introjection.

Example: The bereaved analysand

Abraham's example is a non-psychotic man whose wife became very seriously ill while she was expecting their first child, which was eventually born by Caesarean section:

> My analysand was hurriedly called to her bedside and arrived after the operation had been performed. But neither his wife nor the prematurely born child could be saved. After some time the husband came back to me and continued his treatment. His analysis, and in especial a dream he had shortly after its resumption, made it quite evident that he had reacted to his painful loss with an act of introjection of an oral-cannibalistic character.

> One of the most striking mental phenomena exhibited by him at this time was a dislike of eating, which lasted for weeks.

Our attention is drawn to a link Abraham has spotted between the patient's emotional state of bereavement, and a bodily symptom – not feeding. His example will reveal that this link lies in an unconscious phantasy which underlies the emotional state. Such a phantasy is not known by the patient consciously; instead it is experienced in bodily terms. This phantasy concerns the mouth. It is more complicated than the example in the last chapter; there the phantasy of ingesting faeces represented retrieving a loved, albeit hated, object by locating it inside the subject's own body. In this example the activity of the mouth represents two different activities at the same time – both a destructive (sadistic) biting, and also a poignant loving act.

> This feature [dislike of eating] was in marked contrast to his usual habits, and was reminiscent of the refusal to take nourishment met with in melancholiacs. One day his disinclination for food disappeared, and he ate a good meal in the evening.

The symptom has abated; does this bear on the bereavement, and anticipate a recovery from it? And if so, of what does this process consist? How is feeding involved? Abraham discovered answers because they were revealed in a dream the night after the patient had had the meal:

> That night he had a dream in which he was present at the post-mortem on his late wife. The dream was divided into two contrasting scenes. In the one the separate parts of the body grew together again, the dead woman began to show signs of life, and he embraced her with feelings of the liveliest joy. In the other scene the dissecting-room altered its appearance, and the dreamer was reminded of slaughtered animals in a butcher's shop.

Freud had discovered that two scenes in a dream put side by side like this signify a connection between them, some closeness of meaning. This is also disclosed in some of the associations which the patient gave to the dream:

> The dreamer's association to the dream in analysis brought out the remarkable fact that the sight of the dissected body reminded him of his meal of the evening before, and especially of a meat dish he had eaten.

Remarkably, his wife's dissected body seemed to be linked to the meat from the butcher. At some level, it seems, the meal could not be eaten because it *was* her body. The dream connects eating the meal with butchering (operating upon) the dead body, and suggests destructive phantasies involved in eating and biting. At the same time as the dream conveys a butchering of his wife, the patient's dream also means something else –

> Consuming the flesh of the dead wife is made equivalent to restoring her to life.

The dream connects the introjection (phantasy of putting her inside him through eating) with the joyful reanimation of the dead body. The resurrection was accomplished by establishing his lost wife *inside him physically* by eating the object. Abraham invites us to accept that the symptom – not eating – occurred when the patient was preoccupied more by his fearful phantasy of biting/dissecting/butchering his wife;[4] and that eventually a different phantasy came to the fore – lovingly devouring his wife to restore her as a living presence inside him. Abraham invites us to share this view: as the second of these phantasies (the loving restoration) begins to take precedence over the butchering, the patient's more usual attitude to eating returns. This loving restoration, *inside him*, seems genuinely to indicate some recovery from the bereavement – he recovers his loved one but he now has her inside, as a loved internal object.

Abraham's view of the dream suggests answers to our questions about the nature of recovery from the bereavement. The recovery *is* represented in the dream. It is accomplished by bringing the loved one, the patient's wife, to life again; but now she is alive as an *internal* object, and brought to life specifically by the bodily process of eating. The bodily process of eating allows (or is coupled with) a mental taking in, an introjection. Both the bodily activity and the psychological phantasy seem to be joined. The effect of the phantasy on the mind is as strong as the effect of actually eating food on the body.

The way Abraham analysed this dream typifies the kind of evidence that psychoanalysis has available. It is based on Freud's method of decoding dreams through the linked associations (quite brief in this case). Connections are expressed by contiguity in the dream. In Abraham's hands this method showed that a narrative or *phantasy* about an object is unconsciously active. In this case the unconscious phantasy seemed so real for the patient that it determined a symptom – not eating. Recovery involved a new phantasy: that eating could restore his wife and bring her back to a kind of life again. These unconscious phantasies are a profound way in which psychoanalysts represent the activity of the unconscious mind. They convey the striking equivalence between bodily experience and activity (e.g. eating) and relating to people.

Unconscious phantasies have played a supremely important role in the theory of psychoanalysis and its clinical practice for certain schools – pre-eminently the Kleinian. The fact that these phantasies are active indicates a curious self-awareness – not, to be sure, a conscious awareness. This patient's mourning process seemed to involve these primitive unconscious notions of what his own mind was doing. The idea of eating an object as a process of restoring it is extremely remote from consciousness, but it appears from his dream that this is indeed an 'idea' that is around in this patient's mind. These phantasies, if consciously indulged in, would appear quite mad. Perhaps these primitive phantasies are not as remote from consciousness for psychotic patients as they are for the rest of us. And, clearly, in the example in Chapter 2 (*Anal holding on*, p. 21) they are not necessarily encoded in disguising symbols, as in dreams, nor channelled usefully into socially acceptable activities (like becoming a actual butcher, for instance).

THE MIND AT BIRTH

Unconscious phantasies like the one just described are so close to the biological make-up of the person that they represent the very earliest, and therefore the most primitive, functioning of the mind. In this view, unconscious phantasies of relationships with objects constitute the mental activity of the newly born infant. These are the primary experiences from which the rest of life, mind and development starts. They are of fundamental importance. Although they are displayed within psychotic symptoms (as in *Anal holding on*), psychoanalysts argue that such phantasies compose the baby's experiences maybe as far back as birth, and underlie the ordinary dream life as in *The bereaved analysand*.

Intuitively, we would mostly regard an infant as aware of its sensations in a psychological way, as well as simply reacting mechanically with cries, struggles, and so on. The question is: to what extent can we, as adults, know them; or, given our reliance on words, describe them? There is often a widespread general scepticism about knowing the infant's experiences before the age of speech. The infant cannot convey experience directly. It requires a stretch of the imagination, as adults, to get a feel of what it must have been like at that early age when perceptions and bodily experiences were so much more primitive, not yet coated with the meanings that family and society apply. Here is Joan Riviere attempting to convey something of such experiences:

> if the desired breast is not forthcoming and the baby's aggression develops to the limits of its bodily capacities, this discharge, which automatically follows upon a painful sensation, itself produces unpleasure in the highest degree. The child is overwhelmed by choking; its eyes are blinded with tears, its ears deafened, its throat sore; its bowels gripe, its evacuations burn it. The aggressive anxiety-reaction is far too strong a weapon in the hands of such a weak ego; it has become uncontrollable and is threatening to destroy its owner. (Riviere, 1936a, p. 44)

The bodily parts are suffused with active suffering. In this description there is more than mere mechanical reaction: neurological reflexes and a suffering infant are one. This seems to be almost as far as we can go in understanding the way biological make-up and psychological experience interlock. It is generally understood within psychiatry that in the psychoses a very fundamental biological flaw in the brain is linked with a developmental cul-de-sac in the psychology. At some early level of infant development the physical and the psychological converge, and the distinction between them blurs. The serious psychological defects in psychotic patients represented in bodily terms in unconscious phantasy seem to point to a hangover from that very early psychophysical functioning. In a sense the primitive quality of the psychotic has some resemblance to the primitive quality of the infant mind. In Chapter 7 we will encounter other specific aspects of the psychotic which are not represented in the early life of the infant.

Example: The little girl and the shoe

As well as extrapolating back from clinical evidence, there is another method of tracing the developmental age at which these phantasies first came about. This method is used by Susan Isaacs in this example; the symptom, the fear of a broken shoe, had been observed at an early age (twenty months), even though it could be *understood* only later:

> . . . a little girl of one year and eight months, with poor speech development, saw a shoe of her mother's from which the sole had come loose and was flapping about. The child was horrified, and screamed with terror. For about a week she would shrink away and scream if she saw her mother wearing any shoes at all, and for some time could only tolerate her mother's wearing a pair of brightly coloured house shoes. The particular offending pair was not worn for several months. The child gradually forgot about the terror, and let her mother wear any sort of shoe. At two years and eleven months, however (fifteen months later), she suddenly said to her mother in a frightened voice, 'Where are Mummy's broken shoes?' Her mother hastily said, fearing another screaming attack, that she had sent them away, and the child then commented, 'They might have eaten me right up'.

The child's later comment clearly identified a primitive oral phantasy which must have been active at the preverbal stage when the phobia started (one year and eight months). She saw the sole of the broken shoe as a dangerous mouth. It was quite real to her, entailing at that earlier age a fantasy that felt completely real for the infant. The little girl's memory was not one of words, nor was it mediated by words: it was a memory of an experience (at a time before she could speak) of a fear of being eaten up. Only later could it be given verbal expression. Without words the expression is very crude – screaming. But the phantasy itself, it seems, was quite formed and coherent.

As words developed, however, the fear eventually came to be overlaid by verbal thought, and the underlying 'unconscious phantasy' changed from feeling completely real to find calmer expression as something more symbolic. This change from a reality to a phantasy is a crucial step represented in the infant's development by this example, but it is a step which falters in psychotic mental functioning and features centrally in this condition (see the section on symbolization in Chapter 11). Usually these unconscious phantasies are, to all intents and purposes, forgotten. However, certain cases like *The bereaved analysand* suggest that this non-verbal, primitive level of phantasy life, concerned with bodily activity, is never given up, but always remains a potential, unconscious presence.

However far-fetched these ideas may seem, they have found pragmatic use in greatly extending the range of people who can be analysed, and in significantly deepening the psychoanalysis of all patients. In the next chapter we will examine how these remote layers of human experiences were explored by Melanie Klein, and what understanding she drew from them. Some readers may prefer to skip the hypothetical descriptions in the Appendix to this chapter, and go on immediately to the clinical material in Chapter 4.

APPENDIX
EARLIEST OBJECT RELATIONS

Fundamental to the later thinking of Kleinian psychoanalysts is the idea that the mind is a vast composite set of phantasy relationships with objects. Much of this will be illustrated with indicative clinical material. Before proceeding to that, however, I will briefly sketch some of this theoretical development. This is a résumé of those 'unverifiable' experiences of the earliest moments of life as a Kleinian psychoanalyst might construct them.

When a baby is born, right from the start, it has a suckling reflex. Thus if its cheek is touched by mother's finger, the baby will turn its face towards the stimulus, and its lips start sucking movements. This activity is present immediately after birth. It is clearly innate, and is designated so by the term 'reflex'. However, can the infant actually *experience* the stimulus, the touch on its cheek? Can the activity of muscles and lips form an experience of what has stimulated it? On the whole, most people, on intuitive grounds, would tend to believe that the infant does have some kind of experience of the components (active and passive) of the reflex.[5] In later life, sensations that cause hunger, for instance, certainly derive from biologically pre-formed features of the body, but are clearly psychological experiences. If we grant experience at birth, it seems that we must accept that it has some biological (i.e. innate) roots – innate meanings. So: biological activity comes with pre-formed psychological meaning. And if it is true at the very early stage, it would seem to be right that meaning must be in terms of bodily activities. 'Phantasy is the mental corollary, the psychic representative of, instinct' (Isaacs, 1948, p. 83) . . . 'Unconscious phantasies are primarily about bodies, and represent instinctual aims towards objects' (ibid., p. 112).

For those who do not grant the possibility of an infant psychology, the phenomena under discussion will remain a mystery. For those who do, there are still other formidable mysteries; if the infant has an experience of what happens in the sucking experience, we have to ask: *what sort of experience* is it? The infant can have no adult conception of what a breast actually is, or of what feeding is for, or of what really happens in sucking or hunger, and so on. Yet if these things are experienced, they must have characteristics that are psychologically appreciable by the infant. What are those characteristics, and how can we gain access to such experiences?

Susan Isaacs's paper (Isaacs, 1948) was a landmark in trying to define and catalogue the characteristics of unconscious phantasies. Her long survey can be condensed as follows:

1 Instincts, arising from somatic stimulation, are psychologically represented as unconscious phantasies of relationships with objects.

2 Unconscious phantasies have an innate form involving a subject; an object which has supposed intentions; and a relationship in which the subject wishes to do things to the object on the basis of the object's intentions.

3 There are certain innate and primitive discriminations: (a) the object is located inside or outside the subject; (b) the object's intentions are felt to be either malevolent or benevolent towards the subject.

4 Different objects and relationships are discerned according to the bodily sensations which are aroused: e.g. hunger and feeding, warmth and cold, a full bladder or an emptied one, etc., etc. (note – these are paired according to the discrimination in (3a) and (3b) above).

5 Unconscious phantasies are experienced in the first instance as bodily sensations, later as plastic images and dramatic representations, and eventually in words.

Consider, for instance a baby assailed by the bodily sensations of hunger, arising perhaps from the stomach walls rubbing together, producing an unpleasant sensation. This will be represented in the most primitive way as an object somewhere inside the tummy which is malevolently intent on causing painful sensations. The supposed malevolent intent on the part of the object is innately terrifying for the infant. This is what terror is – the experience of being attacked with malevolent intent (especially from inside, by something malevolent there). The infant is not capable of expressing those experiences clearly, yet through empathy adults do sense a baby's fears of malevolence; and these can then be formed into evocative words, as in Joan Riviere's vivid description, above, of the infant's terrified experience of its own sensations.

With pleasurable experiences, by contrast, the object is supposed to be lovingly intent upon making the infant feel safe, alive and blissful.

Despite the term 'unconscious phantasy', the infant experiences objects as completely real, not as an imagined phantasy at all. Their malevolence is the experience we may (later) call 'terror'; their benevolence is the experience we may (later) call 'bliss'. The point is that these experiences are innately formed notions of relations to malevolent or benevolent objects. These innate, primitive notions, called 'unconscious phantasies', are remote and inaccessible to us as adults. They are just about knowable – or at least inferrable – from psychotic patients' symptoms, from dreams, and from young children's conscious fantasies.

PART II

MELANIE KLEIN'S CONTRIBUTIONS

4 A Method for Children

Melanie Klein made continuing contributions which accumulated until her followers became a distinct school of psychoanalytic practice and theory from the 1940s onwards. A little more than twenty years previously she had begun to develop a remarkably effective method for adapting psychoanalysis to very young children – as young as three or so. Her brilliance derives from three things: realization of the effectiveness of the tool she had developed; then, like Abraham, her possession of an extraordinarily acute ability for clinical observation; and a vision of the far-reaching significance of her observations. In the next chapters we will consider the method she developed, then the practical and theoretical implications of her clinical work and her discoveries through it.

Klein called her method the *play technique*; she began to develop it as long ago as 1920.[6] We will begin by considering this contribution to the technique for 'early analysis', a term she adopted to emphasize the special requirements for analysing very young children:

> On a low table in my analytic room there are laid out a number of small and simple toys – little wooden men and women, carts, carriages, motor-cars, trains, animals, bricks, and houses, as well as paper, scissors and pencils. Even a child that is usually inhibited in its play will at least glance at the toys or touch them. (Klein, 1932, p. 16)

During treatment the child kept a set of toys for him- or herself in a locker provided in the playroom. Klein found that the invitation to play quickly produced the expression of acute anxieties. Often she was quite perturbed by the intensity of the anxiety the child demonstrated in the content of the play. The use of the toys, many of them small male or female figures, clearly pointed towards relationships with, and between, objects. She regarded these configurations and relationships in the same way as Abraham had looked at the material of his adult patients: they showed the unconscious phantasies active in the patient's mind. As we shall see, she linked the fate of the toy figures to the child's worries about what would happen in reality between the child and the important other figures in his or her life.

Klein talked to the child about his or her worries in a manner that is so direct that it might sometimes seem quite reckless. Often, intuitively, we want to help a child by reassurance, with soothing comments and telling him or her not to worry. Instead, Klein took the worries very seriously in the child's own terms, and on the whole she found that children were remarkably responsive to being taken seriously in this way – if she was correct in what the play meant, this would bring relief to the child: 'I was strengthened in the belief that I was working on the right lines by observing the alleviation of anxiety again and again produced by my interpreta-tions' (Klein, 1955, p. 122). By this she meant, in effect, that the child's worries signified something else. They were not realistic worries in grown-up terms, but still they had a logic of their own for the child – the kind of validity or truth that Freud had discovered in dreams and Abraham, as we have seen, discovered in the mad symptoms of psychotic patients. It was the child's own 'logic' that Klein sought to understand and to help with. She thought she could find a consistent *unconscious* content in the anxious play. Thus as she talked about the child's play she would relate it to what she thought were the deeper (unconscious) meanings in the child's mind.

The process in her work starts with the patient's play; proceeds to an interpretation, explicit and direct; and then results in a response of some kind in the further play of the child. We will see the sequence **anxiety–interpretation–response** repeatedly in the examples in this chapter.

We must now look at an example of the play technique and the process interpretation initiates. In the following example Klein's interpretations begin simply, and over the course of two reported sessions she works towards deeper anxieties. Initially this child's play was quite seriously restricted by an inhibiting level of anxiety, but it became freer as she worked on. The alleviation of anxiety and the immediate change in the character and content of the child's play were important markers for Klein in assessing the validity of her interpretation; and, indeed, of the technique itself.

INTERPRETATION AND RESPONSE

We can now start to look at what an interpretation is with the patient Melanie Klein discussed when she described her technique. We will concentrate on the 'anxiety–interpretation–response' process. Although in 1920 interpretations were conceived slightly differently from the way they are conceived today (developments in technique will be addressed in Part III), in principle they attempt to put into conscious words those ideas, emotions (especially anxiety) and relationships that are hidden, or part-hidden; in effect, to speak the unspoken to the child. With children there is much more of a sense of doing something together with the patient (or even *to* him or her); this contrasts with adult psychoanalysis, where there is a tendency to speak *about* things. It should be noted, however, that in latter years, as we shall see in Part III, there has been a realization that adult psychoanalysis is also a 'doing something' together with the patient.

Example: Inhibited play

Peter, aged three years and nine months, was treated by Klein in the early 1920s. Peter was very difficult to manage, and clung strongly in an ambivalent way to his mother; he was unable to tolerate frustration. Klein described him as

> totally inhibited in play and gave the impression of being an extremely timid, plaintive and unboyish child. At times his behaviour would be aggressive and sneering, and he got on badly with other children, especially with his younger brother.

She began her sessions with Peter as follows:

> At the very beginning of his first session Peter took the toy carriages and cars and put them first one behind the other and then side by side, and alternated this arrangement several times. In between he took two horse-drawn carriages and bumped one into another, so that the horses'

feet knocked together, and said: 'I've got a new little brother called
Fritz.'

Here is a child who seems to play in a quite innocent and 'ordinary'
way, but towards the end of this sequence we can see that some
concern enters in – about his brother. Klein could have asked him
more about his brother; instead she did something else. She focused
on his play:

> I asked him what the carriages were doing. He answered: 'That's not
> nice,' and stopped bumping them together at once, but started again
> quite soon. Then he knocked two toy horses together in the same way.

The description is beginning to give an impression of Peter's kind
of play. We should note the degree of repetitiveness. It is not really
very imaginative play, as you might get from some children where
there is a flowing of lively invention. Here toys are placed one
behind the other, or side by side, or knocked together; and this
arrangement goes on and on. This is what Klein means by
describing him as 'inhibited'. The inhibition is again indicated
when she asks him what the carriages are doing, and he says 'That's
not nice', and stops bumping them together. That process of
inhibition goes on under the very nose of the analyst. Perhaps there
is a connection between little Peter's feeling that something – we
do not know what – is not nice, and his ceasing to play. In fact, we
are invited by this material to postulate a causal connection – that
because something or other is 'not nice' (carriages bumping
together), he therefore becomes inhibited, especially at the point
at which the analyst has noticed the bumping together.

But what does this bumping together mean? Is the inhibition of
play in fact linked to the specific content of the play? Inhibited and
poverty-stricken though it is, the actual knocking and bumping in
the play may represent some actual *unconscious* aspect of the
inhibition. There are various candidates for an answer to that
question – for instance, some kind of aggressive activity, or perhaps
a sexual one.

An anxious child might be expected to choose to play, at the
outset of the first session, with what concerns him most at the time.
For Peter the worry (what is 'not nice') is represented, he says, by
the carriages 'bumping together'. With someone (an analyst) to
notice it, he might feel that he has an opportunity to do something
about it; but it also seems to worry him that she does notice – so

he inhibits his play. In this sense Peter may be in conflict between wanting to communicate his worries and wanting to inhibit them. The analyst picked up the wish to communicate, and asked what the carriages were doing. She reports that having stopped bumping the two toy horses together, he started again:

> Upon which I said: 'Look here, the horses are two people bumping together.' At first he said: 'No, that's not nice.'

The analyst is trying to develop some sort of dialogue about this bumping together, and starts by interpreting that Peter is preoccupied with people and with the relationships going on between them. That is, she suggests that the toys represent people, and the bumping represents the activity going on between people.

Now, Peter's response was interestingly familiar; first he said 'no'. Is this his inhibition again? It might simply be disagreement. But then he repeated his earlier anxious comment – 'that's not nice'. His use of the same comment would seem to be significant; but what is this significance? It occurred first in connection with Klein's comment on his play with the carriages; now it is connected with the people. That would seem to indicate a link between carriages, horses and people. Unconsciously, then, the similar response seems to link them, and would indicate that the interpretation is valid – that the play with carriages and horses does represent the bumping together of people. Thus we can look not so much at the conscious content of his words, as at their occurrence – where they occur, what they are connected with. What is his further response? Peter continued:

> . . . [he] added: 'The horses have bumped together too, and now they're going to sleep.' Then he covered them up with bricks and said: 'Now they're quite dead; I've buried them.'

And this ended the first session. It seems rather a meagre amount of play and activity in the course of a whole session, but this is an inhibited and repetitious child. There does, however, seem to be some progress from the initial repetitive and mechanical bumping together to a slightly more imaginative idea about the horses dying, and burying them. In fact it was after Klein's comment that the horses were people that there followed a moment in which the play went ahead. It was, in a small way, a momentary freeing of imagination.

The analyst, too, is cautious during this first session. She takes it slowly because of the meagre and uninformative play, and she has to be cautious, because when Peter agrees – 'Yes, that's two people bumping together' – we have to assess the significance of his agreement. We could say that he acquiesced, in the end, to an adult who may have appeared rather dominating, so conscious agreement is not really significant. What can decide the issue is the way the play continued. If the transitory release from his inhibitions is valid, it is more crucial than any conscious 'yes'. That release is some indication of a deeper response in him than mere acquiescence.

Klein was interested in that sort of change in the emotional atmosphere, but it was the content of the play which could point to the details of why the change occurred. The *content* of the play at this point concerned death. The next play material we hear about is from the next session, and it continued as in the first session – identical, inhibited, repetitive:

> In his second session he at once arranged the cars and carts in the same two ways as before – in a long file and side by side; and at the same time he once again knocked two carriages together, and then two engines – just as in the first session. He next put two swings side by side and, showing me the inner and longish part that hung down and swung, said: 'Look how it dangles and bumps.'

The paucity of Peter's play (his inhibition) varied slightly by the addition of the swings, and he pointed out something to be taken notice of, something that dangles and bumps. He seemed to be trying to indicate something specific. Klein was struck by how he actually tried to show her some aspect of the toy and what it was doing; significantly, it bumped! She then proceeded to interpret:

> Pointing to the 'dangling' swings, the engines, the carriages and the horses, I said that in each case they were two people – Daddy and Mummy – bumping their 'thingummies'[7] (his word for genitals) together. He objected, saying: 'No, that isn't nice.'

Klein's interpretation puts a hypothesis to the child. Having elicited the day before that the toys probably represent people, she now specifies which people – his mummy and his daddy. And because of this inner part of the swing which dangles and bumps, she thinks he is trying to talk about the genitals, and is preoccupied with their activity (bumping). This is the interpretation; now his response is

'No, that isn't nice'. This again is the same phrase which had come out the day before in response to her interest, and seemed to be associated specifically with the inhibition. It is very difficult not to draw the conclusion that her interpretation really does connect with something that worries him: something to do with his parents together; something very troubling which they do with their genitals. Perhaps he feels that it is a very aggressive kind of interaction which goes on between Mummy's and Daddy's genitals; that would be rather speculative. So, to look at his continuing response: he had first objected with his 'No, that isn't nice' –

> but went on knocking the carts together, and said: '*That's* how they bumped their thingummies together.' Immediately afterwards he spoke about his little brother again.

Again there is a conscious affirmation – which could be acquiescence – but there is a reference to the brother, and it does point to a significant link with his anxieties; a pattern which, in fact, Klein had noticed:

> As we have seen, in his first session, too, his knocking together of the two carriages and horses had been followed by his remarking that he had got a new little brother. So I continued my interpretation and said: 'You thought to yourself that Daddy and Mummy bumped their thingummies together and that is how your little brother Fritz came.'

This new interpretation suggests that Peter is preoccupied with exploring how the arrival of his brother happened, and has ideas that it came out of his mummy and daddy, out of their relationship with each other, and that it is to do with their genitals. This seems very troubling – it is a 'not nice' activity. Because of the link with death in the previous session, it seems probable that in his own mind their activity can cause them to die, and he will bury them. Again we must question: was Klein right in her hypothesis about his play? The litmus test is Peter's response. This is her report of his further play:

> He now took another cart and made all three collide together. I interpreted: 'That's your own thingummy. You wanted to bump your thingummy along with Daddy's and Mummy's thingummies.' He thereupon added a fourth cart and said: 'That's Fritz.' He next took two of the smaller carts and put each on to an engine. He pointed to a carriage and horse and said: 'That's Daddy' – placing another at its side – 'That's Mummy.' He pointed once more to the Daddy carriage and horse

and said: 'That's me,' and to the Mummy one and said: 'That's me, too,' thus demonstrating his identification with both parents in coitus. After this he repeatedly hit the two small carts together and told me how he and his little brother let two chickens into their bedroom so that they could calm down, but that they had knocked about and spat in there. 'He and Fritz', he added, 'were not rude gutter boys and did not spit.'

Peter's response to the last interpretations is a quite different playing, strikingly different from all the rest of the preceding play in the two sessions. The character is more like that of a child who is imaginatively getting up to all sorts of things, and has a variety of different kinds of relations going on between the figures in a much richer sequence. It is this development from inhibition to a much more imaginative play to which Klein draws attention; and she wants to show us that it is the effect of making interpretations of a very explicit kind about the child's worries. In this case she feels pretty confident that Peter worries about his parents in some sort of intercourse that produced his little brother. Perhaps also it seems that the parents are engaged upon a very aggressive and dangerous activity which will result in unpleasant consequences – death and burial.

The sequence **play–interpretation–response** is much in evidence in this play material. Klein thought that the kind of changes we have seen were rich evidence of the validity of her psychoanalytic technique for helping children. Peter's phantasy that his little brother came as a result of his parents bumping together was connected to considerable anxiety over frightening (i.e. 'not nice') wishes, probably towards his parents. However, by putting this phantasy into words, Klein enabled Peter to respond by expressing himself in a more vivid, direct and imaginative play; hitherto his play had been inhibited. It is clear that at this age he was very confused about the bodily activities associated with parents; he could conceptualize it only as 'bumping', 'knocking' each other, or 'spitting' together. I will come back to Peter in a later example, but I want to discuss these kinds of interpretations.

EARLY INTERPRETATION

Despite Klein's conviction that her results validated her technique, there were counterarguments from others. It was suggested that interpretations of deep, unconscious anxieties wrought a change in the child's play because they made him *more* anxious. It might be said that Peter's apparently freer play represented his greater anxiety bursting out of him. This debate became highly technical. By 1926 Klein had become embroiled in a heated and sometimes acrimonious dispute over the wisdom of making interpretations of the unconscious and the Oedipus complex to young children.

Anna Freud had also been developing a method of analysing children, and although she embarked on this at a slightly later date than Klein did, she had the backing of her father and the orthodox psychoanalytic establishment in Vienna. The substance of her argument turned on the way in which a child relates to the psychoanalyst. At the time, she, like all analysts, worked on the basis that the power of a psychoanalysis was the strength of the patient's positive feelings towards the person of the psychoanalyst. Love for the analyst overcame the resistance to the pain of becoming aware of the unconscious. The idea was that the patient could take the psychoanalyst's painful interpretations seriously only if she or he loved the analyst enough. Psychoanalytic writing from the first quarter of this century describes this manoeuvring of the transference love on the psychic battleground, often with metaphors that have a strong military ring about them. The strength of this love derived from the transference of past experiences and longings when the person was a young child. 'Transference' – this term had come into use since Freud's difficulties with Dora (see Chapter 1) – indicates that the feelings were transferred from another person and from another developmental stage. Thus, for instance, the psychoanalyst is loved as a father would have been in childhood; he becomes a new father-figure. This had vital implications for practice. The transference of strong positive affections had to be built up before interpretations could be accepted by the patient.

This 1920s view of the way the forces are balanced derived from the psychoanalysis of adults, and led to a specific view about the analysis of children. Anna Freud asserted that the transference could not be used in this way with children. She argued that a child of three, say, was not yet out of the period of original love, on which transference would eventually be based. The child could not transfer this love, because it was not yet from the past. An analogy used at the time was that transference was a 'new edition' of an old love, so it could not be a new edition until the old was exhausted.

The child loves the current parents, and cannot bestow a childlike love upon the psychoanalyst in the way an adult patient does. So Anna Freud believed that child analysis had to rely on other methods for gaining the child's willingness to accept interpretations. She thought that the psychoanalyst had to do two things: first cultivate a sufficiently positive attitude in the child on a *realistic* (not transference) basis; and, second, actually to function *as* a parent, with educative and disciplinary qualities. Anna Freud recommended that this particular kind of relationship in a child analysis had to be won in a preparatory, or 'warming-up', phase before interpretations could be made. She vehemently criticized Klein, too, for making interpretations at the beginning of an analysis; her vehemence resulted from a considerable anxiety about making sexual interpretations to children. Their dispute has persisted to this day, even though a lot of the theory, on both sides, has changed, and the so-called 'warming-up' phase is no longer regarded as necessary.

The reaction to reading Melanie Klein's interpretations might be an aversion to talking to young children so explicitly about sexual and murderous phantasies. If we try to take the heat out of that reaction, however, and look at the evidence, we can see two women, Anna Freud and Melanie Klein, presenting their clinical evidence in support of one or other point of view. I shall restrict my account now to Klein's evidence, though the reader, in fairness and curiosity, might at some point want to consult the beautifully clear writings of Anna Freud (*Four Lectures on Child Analysis*, 1926). In any case, the arguments are now rather outdated, and my purpose is to continue to look at Klein's method in so far as its contributions have led to present-day themes.

At the time – 1926 – the debate, hinging on the necessity or otherwise of a preparatory phase, was conducted by giving supporting clinical material. Klein took as the crucial test children who were initially very difficult to relate to and who, instead of forming a positive relationship with the psychoanalyst, immediately formed an exactly opposite relationship: one of suspicion and antagonism. This is called the negative transference – hate, anger and fear. In the next example, we see Klein struggling to relate positively to a child who is set persistently against her. She used two methods to overcome this child's negativity: first she tried to coax and cultivate a friendly atmosphere, and to stimulate and entice her into play and conversation – that is to say, a 'warming-up' phase; later she tried deep interpretation. Her results astonished her. The case of Ruth was conducted in 1924.

Example: Anxious Ruth

Ruth was four years and three months old. She was ambivalent, and clung strongly to her mother and certain other women with an enormous dislike of others, especially strangers. She had anxiety attacks and was generally very apprehensive. Klein was very interested in how this child related to herself as a stranger whom she greatly disliked and shunned. The child had had difficulty in getting on with a new nursemaid, and could not relate at all easily to other children.

> In her first analytic session she absolutely refused to remain in the room with me alone. I therefore decided to ask her elder sister to be present during the analysis. My intention was to establish a positive transference to achieve the eventual possibility of working alone with her . . .

Here Klein is reporting her attempt at the approach advocated by Anna Freud: achieving a positive transference. However, she could not make contact with this child:

> . . . but all my attempts, such as simply playing with her, encouraging her to talk, etc., were in vain. In playing with her toys she would turn only to her sister (although the latter remained quite unresponsive) and would ignore me completely. The sister herself told me that my efforts were hopeless and that I had no chance of gaining the child's confidence even if I were to spend weeks on end with her instead of single hours.

They might have given up. There are various possibilities: perhaps this child is unanalysable; or one could wonder if the analyst is just too imposing for her. However, Klein persevered, this time with her own preference – to interpret directly and simply to the child:

> I therefore found myself forced to take other measures – measures which once more gave striking proof of the efficacy of interpretation in reducing the patient's anxiety and negative transference. One day while Ruth was once again devoting her attention exclusively to her sister, she drew a picture of a tumbler with some small round balls inside and a kind of lid on top. I asked her what the lid was for, but she would not answer me. On her sister repeating the question, she said it was 'to

prevent the balls from rolling out'. Before this she had gone through her sister's bag and then shut it tightly 'so that nothing should fall out of it'. She had done the same with the purse inside the bag so as to keep the coins safely shut up.

Here Klein is describing a repeated pattern of activity in the play: shutting things up inside something else which will keep them from falling out. She mentions that this pattern of activity had apparently been going on for some time:

> I now made a venture and told Ruth that the balls in the tumbler, the coins in the purse and the contents of the bag all meant children in her Mummy's inside, and that she wanted to keep them safely shut up so as not to have any more brothers and sisters. The effect of my interpretation was astonishing. For the first time Ruth turned her attention to me and began to play in a different, less constrained, way.

Klein obviously gives us this material because of the impact of her interpretation on this apparently intractable child. Put baldly the interpretation seems wild, but by touching on a frightening, unconscious phantasy, the child's demeanour changed completely. Ruth began to relate differently to the analyst who had understood her at that unconscious level: for the first time she allowed contact with Klein. The claim is that such a change of demeanour indicates that the interpretation *was* significant to the child; and that indeed it was the *only* significant contact that could make a change; coaxing and friendliness had not worked. We note again the significance of the sequence anxiety–interpretation–response. The 'astonishing' effectiveness of this interpretation is quite different from (and, Klein believed, more important than) the attempt to engage the child's positive affections directly. Looking back, in 1926, when she had to defend her method, it seems to me that this event in Ruth's analysis must have stood out sharply for her.

Now that the child was more positive and in contact, Klein enquired further into Ruth's jealousy: how was it that jealousy was connected with such an extreme degree of terror in this child? The answer gradually emerged. We are told of another session three weeks later, when Ruth's sister fell ill. With great difficulty the child managed to stay with Klein on her own. Klein began by again trying to soothe her in a motherly way, and entice her to play with her analyst, but she could do nothing with her. Then Klein played by herself, describing what she was doing to the terrified child:

I took as the subject of my game the material which she herself had produced the previous session. At the end of it she had played round the wash-basin and had fed her dolls and given them huge jugfuls of milk, etc. I now did the same kind of thing. I put a doll to sleep and told Ruth I was going to give it something to eat and asked her what it should be. She interrupted her screams to answer 'milk', and I noticed that she made a movement towards her mouth with her two fingers (which she had a habit of sucking before going to sleep) but quickly took them away. I asked her whether she wanted to suck them and she said: 'Yes, but properly.' I recognized that she wanted to reconstitute the situation as it happened at home every evening, so I laid her down on the sofa and, at her request, put a rug over her.

We see Klein continuing her struggle to relate to this child, with whom she had previously achieved some rapport, by playing the child's game. This did seem to mean something to Ruth, who did respond, yet minimally and fearfully. The analyst's appreciation that the child had been trying to convey something seemed to make Ruth feel that she had some sort of ally with whom she could communicate; then the analyst intuitively understood that the child wanted to go through the calming ritual that she was familiar with at bedtime, and she became 'visibly calmer and had stopped crying'. The analyst could now build on the flickering moments of contact that had fleetingly begun. At this moment this is not happy play, but a serious business of the child communicating distress:

As I was putting a wet sponge beside one of [the dolls], as she had done, she burst out crying again and screamed, 'No, she mustn't have the *big* sponge, that's not for children, that's for grown-ups!'

Here is the moment of terror again. Because it is in the play, the sequence that gives rise to the terror is under direct observation. Klein proceeded with an extremely explicit interpretation: the unconscious phantasy that the child hated her mother, who had incorporated father's penis, and that Ruth wanted to steal his penis and the children out of her mother's inside, and kill her mother. The terror concerning the sponge for grown-ups, then, was little Ruth's attempts to stop the phantasy and keep the sponge (penis) safely for (and in) her mother. Again, it may seem an extraordinarily explicit challenge to interpret to a child such a horrendous oedipal phantasy which, if true, must indeed seem terrifying to her. In response, however,

Ruth grew visibly quieter, opened her eyes and let me bring the table on which I was playing to the sofa and continue my game and my interpretations close beside her.

Once again, the change in the child's demeanour and the reduction in the level of anxiety and suspicion towards the psychoanalyst are striking. At the end of the session the nurse was also struck by the abrupt change in Ruth's mood:

... she [the nurse] was surprised to find her happy and cheerful and to see her say goodbye to me in a friendly and even affectionate way.

Klein's implicit question to the reader is: would this change in the child occur if the interpretations were not significant for her? Each reader, of course, will assess how convincing is her evidence for the 'correctness' of the interpretations. Whether it is 'correct' to interpret in this manner remains contentious within the psychoanalytic world. In purely technical terms, the deep interpretation enabled this child to relate, in a way that was impossible otherwise. It allowed the possibility of an analysis. Thus it was empirically effective: it achieved its ends. Of course this is not to say that it is morally acceptable, since ends do not necessarily justify means. The question of whether interpretations of sex, babies, envy, and so forth are acceptable seems to be an ethical rather than an empirical one. In any case, despite the clinical evidence, it did not resolve the issue between Anna Freud and Melanie Klein, who continued to disagree in fervent rivalry. Indeed, the Kleinian debate on practice has gone ahead through various phases supervening on this 'early analysis'. We will consider contemporary views on practice in Part III.

THEORETICAL DEVELOPMENTS

Klein's purpose in presenting her material had been to demonstrate the play technique and its effectiveness in helping children with their anxieties. Another test of her technique, however, was whether it replicated the results of other psychoanalytic methods. In other words, did her observations confirm the established psychoanalytic conclusions on the development of the child? Indeed, she did believe that the response to her explicit interpretations of phantasies of an oedipal kind, of parental coitus and the birth of siblings, confirmed those psychoanalytic theories, which had previously been rooted in evidence from adult psychoanalyses. Direct confirmation of children's sexual interests had come from Freud's report on Little Hans in 1909, though this was not a psychoanalytic treatment but an observation method conducted by the child's father. Since Klein confirmed these theoretical points using her own psychoanalytic method with children, she believed that her play technique was confirmed as a valid psychoanalytic method.

Having tested her technique against known theory, she began to realize that in certain minor respects her observations did more: they could refine the details of that theory. For instance, Freud had declared female development a 'grey and shadowy area', but Klein believed that the material she was interpreting in the cases of little girls like Ruth was important in showing the *content* of anxieties specific to girls. In the 1920s other psychoanalysts (Karen Horney and Helene Deutsch, for instance) were investigating early female psychological development. Klein considered that her observations

> . . . have led me to recognize the existence of an anxiety, or rather anxiety-situation, which is specific for girls and the equivalent of the castration anxiety felt by boys. This anxiety-situation culminates in the girl's idea that her mother will destroy her body, abolish its contents and take the children out of it and so on . . . It is based upon the child's impulses of aggression against her mother and her desires, springing from the early stages of her Oedipus complex, to kill her and steal from her. These impulses lead not only to anxiety or to a fear of being attacked by her mother, but to a fear that her mother will abandon her or die. (Klein, 1932, p. 31)

Klein made an original claim: there is a specific unconscious phantasy behind anxieties in the development of little girls: the girl's attacks upon her mother's inside, which contains unborn babies and father's penis in intercourse with mother, and then retaliatory retribution by mother. In fact this may have been an overambitious claim to further Freud's uncertain psychology of women. In fact, as Abraham's work had indicated, boys may also develop phantasies about an inside space which contains things – inside an object (mother) and inside and outside his own self – and the passage of good and bad objects in and out of that space.

This notion of an internal space was later understood to be a fundamental preoccupation in all people, irrespective of gender (see Chapter 6). At the time, however, it contrasted with Freud's standard theory that girls were merely boys who lacked something. On the whole he did not recognize that the girl's vagina, her *internal* genitals, played any part in her psychological development. Thus Klein, influenced by Horney, pointed to the little girl's awareness of her vagina, of her insides, and of the phantasies connected with them and mother's insides. She claimed that since her play technique provided evidence for new theories of this kind, this play technique was a powerful psychoanalytic instrument for investigating childhood. This, however, was a dangerous claim which could easily backfire: if her results with this technique modified theory too much, it could then be ruled out as an invalid technique which got the wrong results. And this, of course, some opponents did enthusiastically conclude.

I shall now mention briefly some theoretical results which challenged the standard theory so radically that opponents claimed that Klein's results were artifacts. Some still claim that her theories are due to vigorous and overintrusive interpretations. There are three specific developments of theory in her early work that will be noted in the remainder of this chapter: the pre-genital Oedipus complex; the early super-ego; and paranoid cycles.

The Pre-Genital Oedipus Complex

Klein's observations began to present her with far-reaching theoretical implications concerning the Oedipus complex and the origins of the super-ego. These conclusions no longer complemented Freud's ideas but contrasted with them. In particular she began to contest the timing of the Oedipus complex – Freud had dated this rivalrous phantasy to the fourth and fifth years of life. Klein found that it commenced much earlier, before the genital phase of development. She reported oral phantasies about feeding at the breast in which an obstacle, a third object (equivalent to father or his penis), prevents feeding. Often the couple (parents) are envisioned as permanently joined together in a mutual, and exclusive, activity. She termed this phantasy object the 'combined parent figure' (see the example *Attacked by worms*, p. 62). Klein also challenged the sequence to which Freud, Abraham and other classical psychoanalysts had adhered. The three phases – oral (feeding, sucking and biting), anal (related to dirt and cleanliness and control), and genital (recognizing relations, including sexual relations, between others) – were extensively collapsed together, with much overlapping.

Here is a brief example of a girl who conceived the parental activity as a feeding one. These sorts of phantasies are very reminiscent of Abraham's discoveries about oral incorporation (see Chapter 2), but they clearly occur in an oedipal or triangular setting.

Example: Erna's Oedipus complex

Klein's patient Erna was six. She

> . . . began her play by taking a small carriage which stood on the little table among the other toys and letting it run towards me. She declared that she had come to fetch me. But she put a toy woman in the carriage instead and added a toy man. The two loved and kissed one another and drove up and down all the time.

I chose this example because the child so clearly indicated the relationship between a couple – the analyst and her partner, mother and father – as a very loving but *oral* (kissing) relationship. There is obviously a great deal of loving in this child's perception of the (parental) relationship. However:

> Next a toy man in another carriage collided with them, ran over them and killed them, and then roasted and ate them up.

Into this rather idyllic, loving couple intrudes a third person. Being excluded (like the child herself), it attacks the couple. The aggression of the excluded figure in the Oedipus complex is, like the intercourse, orally conceived (roasting and eating). Another version of the phantasy:

> Another time the fight had a different ending and the attacking toy man was thrown down; but the woman helped him and comforted him. She got a divorce from her first husband and married the new one.

Erna's phantasies are varied, but always violent – and oral:

> [In another example] the original man and his wife were in a house which they were defending against a burglar; the third person was the burglar . . . Then again the third person was a brother who came on a

visit, but while embracing the woman he bit her nose off. This little
man, the third person, was Erna herself.

All these phantasies are aggressive and typical of the Oedipus
complex in which the parents have a loving but exclusive
relationship together. But they are persistently oral, both the loving
(kissing) and the aggression (biting). According to classical
psychoanalysis, at six years of age Erna should be engaged in genital
phantasy and activity. However, she was still restricted, at times,
to these oral phantasies of relations between others. They could be
traced back as early as the age of one, because her symptoms
(obsessional actions) originated at that time, when a difficult potty
training was completed unusually early. Thus the phantasy
problems that terrify the child from as early as one year old must
in this case be oedipal ones, but couched in pre-genital (feeding)
phantasies. This contrasts with Freud's view that the Oedipus
complex is specific to the genital phase, and to activities of the
genitals. Klein concluded that the three discrete phases – oral, anal
and genital – were not in fact separate and in sequence, but
overlapped considerably.

Klein went on to mention a series of games in which Erna wished
to oust her father from his position with her mother[8] – the reverse
Oedipus complex; and games that indicated Erna's direct oedipal
wish to get rid of her mother and win her father.

THE EARLY SUPER-EGO

Relations with parents can become extremely troubled and
frightening for the child through destructive and aggressive
phantasies connected with being excluded from *their* relationship
together. The child's anxiety states then arise from the fear of
aggression towards the loved parents. Klein recognized this
configuration of affects as that of the super-ego – the child
condemns him- or herself. Erna was anxious about her aggression,
and used obsessional symptoms and defences which had been
noticed since the age of one. Erna, and other very young children
too, reacted to their own aggression and to the damage it might do
in phantasy as if they suffered an internal conflict of a super-ego
(self-condemning) kind. In the next example Klein describes Rita,
a little girl aged two and three-quarters who had suffered night

terrors and complicated sleep-ceremonials from eighteen months of age.

Example: The little girl with the elephant

Rita had bedtime ceremonials which were plainly obsessional:

> . . . her doll was tucked up to go to sleep and an elephant was placed by the doll's bed. The idea was that the elephant should prevent the 'child' from getting up; otherwise the latter would steal into its parents' bedroom and either do them some harm or take something away from them. The elephant (a father-imago) was to act the part of a figure who *prevents.*

Klein had spotted that for Rita the elephant was a physically external presence, but one which must represent for her an internal preventer of the harm that could come from the aggressive impulses inside her. In other words, if the aggression is met by a preventer inside her, it could be regarded as a super-ego figure. This, however, was at a very early period in Rita's life:

> In Rita's mind her father, by introjection, had filled this role of 'preventer' ever since, at the time she was a year and a quarter to two years old, she had wished to usurp her mother's place with him, steal away the child with which her mother was pregnant and to injure and castrate both parents.

Little Rita's obsessional rituals can be seen as connected with the need to prevent a 'child' from doing something – damaging or robbing her parents. She tried to control her own aggressive impulses towards her parents, especially during her mother's new pregnancy. Her rituals consisted of this compulsive wish to prevent her aggression. They occurred early (at fifteen to twenty-four months) because the night terrors and sleep rituals originated then and remained continuous with those phantasies analysed later, when she was three. These excessive uprushes of anxiety (issuing from the self-condemnation over aggression) clearly indicate a sort of super-ego long before it is supposed to develop according to Freud's schema.

Klein's challenge was that early evidence of a super-ego meant that it could not be, as Freud had claimed, the 'heir to' the classical Oedipus complex (see Chapter 1). It would then have to arise *after* the Oedipus complex, and therefore not at about the age of five or six years, as Freud had said. Here it is much earlier, and involved *within* the Oedipus complex, long before the classical theory requires. In fact Klein found that the younger the child, the more powerful and damaging the aggression and the more intense the super-ego kind of anxiety (guilt). In consequence she was impelled towards the conclusion that there is likely to be very great aggression occurring at the outset of life. She was driven to severing her views from those of Freud in this respect: 'According to my observations, the formation of the super-ego begins at the same time as the child makes its earliest oral introjections' (Klein, 1933, p. 251).

PARANOID CYCLES

In the sequence of Erna's play (see *Erna's Oedipus complex* above) we can see recurrent states of aggression and anxiety. Children sometimes play out terrifying phantasies of spiralling aggression.

Example: The boy huntsman

Another child patient of Klein's, a boy, showed a similar endless cycle:

> George, who at the time was six years old, brought me for months on end a series of phantasies in which he, as the mighty leader of a band of savage huntsmen and wild animals, fought, conquered and cruelly put to death his enemies, who also had wild beasts to support them. The animals were then devoured.

Here is the same kind of aggression expressed characteristically in oral terms of killing or devouring. However, the battle was ceaseless: 'The battle never came to an end as new enemies always appeared.' Killing the enemies did not deal with the situation, because they came to life again and returned to wreak worse vengeance. Both Erna and George were preoccupied with aggressive phantasies which somehow could not be put to an end. These become spirals of aggression – every round of aggression, as the enemies cooked and ate each other, resulted in further retaliation towards them, which they feared. These are entrapped situations which Klein called 'paranoid cycles' where hostility breeds fear, which breeds further hostility. Another very clear example of this cycle is *Peter's naughtiness* (see p. 139). At times the child, she thought, lives in a more or less permanent relationship with bad objects; so, at the time, she called this the *paranoid position*. (Later she extended these observations and used the term 'paranoid-schizoid position' – see Chapter 7.) This kind of material represents Klein's understanding and discovery of the quantities of aggression and aggressive phantasies that can occur in children, and how much distress they cause.

Crises of fear and aggression are common enough in children, and they occur often enough in adults under stress. In some people, however, such occurrences in childhood are prolonged and become instituted as a way of life, as an established part of their personality. Such personalities regularly live out their habitual attitudes of brutish aggression, or their phobic fearfulness of others. Klein thought that the persistence of very extreme forms of this paranoia laid the basis for psychotic illness in later life. Conclusions of this kind were attainable through the use of the play technique because of her detailed observations of children at an earlier age than had hitherto been possible. Her play technique seemed to have proved its validity: because it resulted in palpable changes in her little patients; because it brought about a psychoanalytic co-operation in the most difficult cases; because it confirmed psychoanalytic theory; and because it could point to certain elaborations of such theory. Despite Klein's confidence in her technique and her conclusions, they remained under continuous debate, much of which was carried on between two camps – the British psychoanalysts and those on the Continent, especially in Vienna. In the next chapters we will consider more major contributions which Klein made from 1934 onwards, which led to an increasing dispute with classical psychoanalysts. By 1946, however, there was little further serious discussion between Klein and her followers on the one hand and, on the other, the classical psychoanalysts, many of whom had moved from the Continent to Britain (see King and Steiner, 1991) or the USA.

5   INTERNAL OBJECTS

What is the evidence for internal objects? This odd experience of objects felt to reside physically *inside* the self or inside the body is, as we have seen (Chapter 2), a very primitive experience deriving from mental functioning at a remote developmental period – that is to say, remote from the reality of the external world and, indeed, remote from consciousness. It seems like a contradiction – an experience which is unconscious; and it has been debated a good deal, from Freud onwards. In Chapter 3, however, we considered a similar contradiction – unconscious phantasy, a level of psychology that is so close to a bodily biological function that the distinction becomes blurred. I cannot go into the contradiction of 'unconscious experiencing', except to state how useful it actually is in psychoanalytic theory and practice, and that the emergence of a patient's insight into such experience is both possible and, ultimately, a healing influence. Internal objects are, on the whole, one such primitive experience that is not consciously known about. They are the stuff of unconscious phantasy.

Following Klein's description of the depressive position in 1934, the notion of internal objects beguiled and perplexed the British Psycho-Analytical Society for the next decade. Internal objects had, however, previously been described by Karl Abraham (see Chapter 2) in discussion of his psychotic patients, and then extended to 'normal' individuals. Abraham thought his patients conceived of an internal world, or space, into which objects can be taken or from which they may be expelled.

The examples in this chapter will show how internal objects are deeply involved in processes which may give identity, or create deep rifts within the personal identity of the individual. Identity is thus deeply bound up with the internalization of objects (introjection), with the degree of hostility towards them in the internalization phantasies and the resulting alienation from, or assimilation to, the internalized object. The term 'introjection' denotes a psychic process; but it is linked with – in fact it operates through – an unconscious phantasy in the patient's mind, the subjective experience of taking something in ('internalizing' or, sometimes, 'incorporating' it).

The first two case examples are adult patients with hypochondriacal symptoms. They express a (disordered) view of what is inside them, inside the body. Through psychoanalytic work the unconscious meaning – and phantasies underlying hypochondriasis – could be displayed.

First we may recall the dream of Abraham's bereaved patient (see *The bereaved analysand*, p. 25). Abraham understood the juxtaposed material – eating as butchering, and eating as restoring – as interconnected. You will remember how the different conceptions of the patient's dead wife – in the dissecting room, and in the butcher's shop – indicated two oral phantasies about killing or about restoring his wife through incorporating her inside himself. In our next example, physical complaints about manifold troubles alternated in the patient's free associations in the session with strong feelings of suspicion towards people in his environment. Such an alternation in the material is similarly suggestive evidence for an equivalence between the two. Physical and bodily troubles are linked at an unconscious level with paranoid fears about people outside him. We can therefore make a hypothesis that, to his mind, the threatening people in his external world are linked with objects inside him, his diseased organs.

Example: Little people inside

The following patient described by Klein suffered strong paranoid and depressive feelings, and hypochondriacal complaints. This patient, Y, began to change:

> . . . after hard analytic work, distrust and suspicion diminished . . . It became clear that, buried under the continuous paranoid accusations, complaints and criticisms of others, there existed a very profound love for his mother and concern for his parents as well as for other people.

> At the same time sorrow and severe depression came more and more
> to the fore. During this phase the hypochondriacal complaints
> altered . . . For instance, the patient complained about different
> physical troubles . . .

Notice the dual movement – suspicion towards people outside him
declined, while he developed a different experience of what was
inside him. At the same time his dominant feelings changed;
concern and responsibility increased:

> . . . and then went on to say what medicines he had taken – enumerating
> what he had done for his chest, his throat, his nose, his ears, his
> intestines, etc. It sounded rather as if he were nursing these parts of his
> body and his organs. He went on to speak about his concern for some
> young people under his care (he is a teacher) and then about the worry
> he was feeling for some members of his family.

As readers we are asked to note this attitude of concern – concern
for his inside objects (his organs) mirrored in his concerned
relations towards external objects (pupils and relatives) as well.
The implication is that he relates to those internal organs as he
would to actual people, except that they are inside him. These
internal objects, his organs, are merely his organs; but he seems to
experience them, in his unconscious phantasies, as actually like
people to take care of. These internal objects and external people
are linked by being adjacent in his associations; but they are also
strongly linked by the similar activity with them, and particularly
by the similarity of his feelings for them (concern):

> It became quite clear that the different organs he was trying to cure
> were identified with his internalized brothers and sisters, about whom
> he felt guilty and whom he had to be perpetually keeping alive.

The sense of 'otherness' (or rather, others who belong) of internal
objects is conveyed strongly through the link with similar external
objects whom he loves – his family. This correspondence – of
internal with external – is very concrete in this case. The internal
objects (organs and parts of his body), like little people inside him,
are looked after physically like ill members of his family. This
experience is not a conscious one, and in fact it remains remote
from consciousness. It is expressed only indirectly in the material
by alternating between internal organs and external people.
Repeated observations of this kind from Abraham's work onwards

have presented evidence of unconscious phantasies of an internal world populated by objects like little internal people.

In fact, having an experience of live objects inside the person may not always be so far from consciousness. In an everyday idiom we might talk of butterflies in the tummy to express a state of anxiety; but the anxiety is expressed as a relationship with objects inside – the butterflies, which are the interpretation of actual bodily sensations in the tummy. Going to a meeting with anxiety-provoking people in the outside world (say an examination or a job interview) forms an experience, but one that takes the form of bodily reactions conceptualized as real objects actually occupying the tummy. It is not uncommon for people to have some conscious concern and caring relationship with parts of their body that are actually diseased or damaged. One might say 'my poor foot' if it has been bruised and hurt, rather than 'poor me', although both phrases amount to a similar caring. Or someone may have a 'raging' toothache – to the point where they rage back at the tooth and demand that it be extracted from their mouth. These everyday examples are illustrative of the way a bodily state and an emotional state are linked through unconscious phantasy, as relations with an internal object.

In the next clinical example (that of patient X), internal objects, as alien beings, are explicitly represented in the conscious material of the patient's free associations. The patient believes that a live entity dwells inside him in the form of intestinal worms. He experiences his organs similarly in terms of medical conditions (hypochondriasis), but once again there is no actual physical disturbance. His belief is a dominant aspect of his view of himself. The patient described in the previous illustration (patient Y) loved his good internal objects; but for X the objects are mixed – some loved and good; some feared, hated and bad. In fact he had a medical disorder long ago in childhood. For some reason, his childhood anxieties about that disorder (intestinal worms) persisted into adulthood. This reason might have been stated by Klein as follows: the original physical problem matched an unconscious phantasy so closely that the problem was retained as a means of conscious expression of this phantasy, which could then pass, for the patient, as an actual reality.[9]

Example: Attacked by worms

With X, another hypochondriacal patient, Klein again demonstrated an elaborate interest in concrete internal objects:

> I may mention that this patient remembered during his analysis that at
> about ten years of age he had definitely felt that he had a little man inside
> his stomach who controlled him and gave him orders, which he, the
> patient, had to execute, although they were always perverse and wrong
> (he had had similar feelings about his real father's requests).

The child experienced having tapeworms – though, in fact, he
never saw them – and this experience seems to be linked up with
the childhood phantasy of the bad man in his stomach. In this case
the experience of an internal object was clearly expressed in his
memories of childhood. The worms seem to be an alternative form
of expression about something he felt was bad inside him; perhaps
we could call it an 'internal father', as he had felt the same about
his actual father. We are told that he reported phantasies of a
tapeworm eating its way through his body; in addition, it transpired
that whenever he had such phantasies he developed a strong fear
of cancer. Cancer, too, was experienced as a malevolent object
inside him, and this link – between the tapeworm and cancer as
attacking objects that were eating him away – indicates cancer as
X's third desperate form of expressing his experience of internal
objects. Such internal bad objects are engaged in an oral aggression
towards him (eating him away), and suggest a very early origin in
his life. How did the patient deal with this terrifying internal state
in which he felt his inside was occupied by malevolent objects
(represented as tapeworms, a little man or cancer)? Klein described
her patient's attempt to recruit the analyst's help with these
phantasies:

> The patient, who suffered from hypochondriacal and paranoid
> anxieties, was very suspicious of me, and, among other things,
> suspected me of being allied with people who were hostile towards
> him. At this time he dreamt that a detective was arresting a hostile and
> persecuting person and putting this person in prison. But then the
> detective proved unreliable and became the accomplice of the enemy.

We are told now how the analyst, an object external to the patient,
becomes linked or allied with those internal 'bad' objects (worms,
little man or cancer). Again there is the correspondence between

the external *person* and the internal objects, but we are also presented with this because of the despairing patient's anxiety about where to turn. There is an important link between the detective who (at first) wants to help with the bad people and the analyst who similarly wants to help. She, the psychoanalyst, is supposed to help with the dangerous internal criminals, as it were. But then it seems that she cannot be wholly trusted as a helper with his troubles, and can easily change into a 'bad' enemy with the others:

> The detective stood for myself and the whole anxiety was internalized and was also connected with the tapeworm phantasy. The prison in which the enemy was kept was his own inside – actually the special part of his inside where the persecutor was to be confined.

When the dream indicated that the criminals were put in prison, Klein believed that this was the patient's awareness of the internalization process – they were put *in* prison as a way of representing putting the situation *inside* himself in order to control it. It is a desperate attempt at some form of solution that goes wrong:

> It became clear that the dangerous tapeworm (one of his associations was that the tapeworm was bisexual) represented the two parents in a hostile alliance (actually in intercourse) against him.

This is important for reasons we discussed above concerning the Oedipus complex (see Chapter 4); despite the oral nature of the phantasies about his internal objects, this is an oral form of the Oedipus complex. And this added material gives some indication of why the patient is in difficulties. His parents have been internalized, but the intense aggression and danger of the oedipal situation remain; in this case the parents remain sexual – unlike the desexualized parents who are internalized as the super-ego in Freud's account. But internally, where they are supposed to be controlled, they remain a danger.

Father and mother, conjoined, exclude the patient – apparently he feels that this is so even when he has them inside him. The union into one object (represented as bisexual) demonstrates Klein's notion of the 'combined parent figure' (see below). It differs from the more mature idea of two separate parents in a relationship with each other. The combined parent figure is to be regarded as characteristic of the very early stages of the Oedipus complex (see Chapters 11 and 12), and in contrast to Freud's descriptions of its later and more mature form. Because it is an excluding and exclusive intercourse, the oedipal phantasy becomes frantic and is injected with violent imaginings; on this primitive level, as it is internalized it creates a desperate internal situation to be controlled:

> At the time when the tapeworm-phantasies were being analysed the patient developed diarrhoea which – as X wrongly thought – was mixed with blood. This frightened him very much; he felt it as a confirmation of dangerous processes going on inside him. This feeling was founded on phantasies in which he attacked his bad united parents in his insides with poisonous excreta.

The internal location of his diarrhoea, and the associations to those symptoms, show that the drama of his parents together, and his violent reaction to that, were relocated unconsciously to *inside* the patient.

INTERNALIZATION

In this patient, these childhood phantasies and fears had not been modified, as the usual process of development would require. Instead the aggression, the damaged objects, and the fearful situation were internalized, and remained unchanged as an *internal* situation (a similar solution to a terrifying relationship will be illustrated in the next example, *The man who assaulted his buttocks* – see p. 66).

The very violent drama is so bloody that he actually thinks he sees blood in his diarrhoea. But how strange to locate this whole frightening and dangerous drama inside himself; one finds oneself asking: why? My purpose is not really to answer such why-questions in general; it is more to describe what is there: to say, look, it happens, and this clinical material is illustrative evidence. It is true, however, that in the world of the patient introjection must make sense, has a reason. Although she is not very explicit about the reason in this case, Klein provides the material in order to show the patient trying to deal with criminals by locking them up. That is his phantasy; he can somehow control the violence, exclusion and fear if he can find a lockable prison somewhere; and perhaps for this patient the only lockable space he can find is in his own body. With a more contemporary eye, a psychoanalyst might now wonder if the patient, as a child, was prompted towards an emphasis on introjection by his father's quite demanding intrusiveness into him. A similar impulsion towards introjection might also be found in the intrusive father reported by *The man who assaulted his buttocks*.

THE COMBINED PARENT FIGURE

Hated and destructive composite figures like this form a very early phantasy in the Oedipus complex. Klein was very impressed and affected by the violence of these phantasies, which turned up frequently in the play of her child patients. The parents, supposedly locked together in mutual activity with their various orifices – such as the mouth (e.g. eating each other) – combine into one. Because they are combined and exclude the patient, the whole situation is suffused with aggression of the most terrifying kind. In consequence, the figures are equally hostile and threatening – to the subject, but also to each other, in a global disaster to which all three succumb. The terror is enhanced because, of course, the figures seem so large and so much more powerful than the infant's own self, or its abilities to control the big figures. These primitive phantasies occur in the early Oedipus complex; Klein had described them as an elaboration of Freud's description of the mature form of the Oedipus complex. These 'primitive' phantasies are remote from the reality of the parents and of their relationship, and display a raw hostility not mitigated by concern and care. This occurs when perceptions are not yet reliable, and the actual reality of the world and the people in it are constructed partly out of phantasy. The 'real' parents are not accurately perceived, though the infant can nevertheless feel left out of 'something'. Klein argued that these complex (yet primitive) phantasies demonstrate an elaborately rich life at the earliest stages of psychological development. They represent a complex interplay between what is believed to be happening both outside and inside. Their fine detail is idiosyncratic for each individual.

It is not only hypochondriacal patients who have direct experience of internal objects – schizophrenics, too, experience disastrous internal situations in which the patient desperately contends with persecuting internal objects which cause a disabling fragmentation – usually with very few helpful ones (see Chapter 7). As I have indicated, there is some kind of experience of internal objects in everyone that is expressible in socially acknowledged idioms. In fact, as we saw in Chapter 3, unconscious phantasies of relationships with objects constitute a bedrock component of the human mind. Now, we must add that this bedrock is unconscious phantasy of relationships with internal as well as external objects.

THE INTERNAL FATE OF THE OBJECT

Experiences of internal objects, therefore, survive beyond the infantile period, though as the person grows up the unconscious phantasies sink further beneath consciousness; they are more difficult to discover in the affairs of adult life, or in an adult patient's clinical material. They become more and more overlaid by sophisticated reality-based and rational thinking. Nevertheless, it is these underlying phantasies that give meaning and emotional charge to the coolly perceived objects of external reality; and clear evidence may be found in adult patients that internal objects are part of the underlying meanings of the later adult's evaluations of life, and his or her activities.

In the next example, reported by Paula Heimann, the internalization of an object leads to another very weird state of affairs. This case shows how a permanent hostile relation has become an ingrained part of the patient's personality – that is, actually *inside* him. This kind of phenomenon shows the dramatic extension of Abraham's ideas on introjection and projection that Klein's work generated. It illustrates the world inside the person as a whole dramatic complex interaction with and between objects that exhibit their own motivations.

Example: The man who assaulted his buttocks[10]

In this example the persecutory situation, originally one between the patient and his father, had been transferred to the internal arena – inside the patient – where it survived into the adult structure of his personality. The hostility was contained in a violent (and excited) aggression against his own buttocks. This formed the basis for a perverse, sexual acting-out as a concrete relationship with this part of his body.

> Superficially his anal-sadistic behaviour in the analysis was a repetition of experiences he had had with a mistress to whom he was alternately cruel and kind, exploiting and generous. In sexual situations with her he particularly enjoyed breaking wind while with her, and it was important for him that she disliked this but quietly tolerated it. He used to go to prostitutes as well, for beating and masturbation; he did not have sexual intercourse with them. These experiences were also enacted in the transference. By his complaints – the phrase 'letting off steam' is an apt description – he repeated the anal activities (breaking wind) in the presence of his sexual object, and when he moaned that he suffered at my hands and that my treatment was the cause of his pain and misery, he reproduced in the transference his beating experiences with the prostitutes.

We are shown a description of an exciting form of perverse cruelty and suffering, but Paula Heimann goes on to describe an ill-defined entanglement at its core – his own suffering is also actually a cruelty towards the complained-about analyst:

> The wish to be beaten was by no means altogether a wish to suffer pain. The obvious passive-masochistic aspect of his beating experiences is misleading, and loses much significance when the total situation is taken into account.

This patient's 'superficial' experience of himself is as a suffering masochistic victim. The 'total situation' has a deeper and unconscious level of meaning that includes more than his sadomasochistic impulses. In fact the confusion at the core of his sexual preferences is clarified by attending to the internal objects. When the internal aspects of this man's object relations are analysed, his sexual tastes disentangle in a particularly distinct way:

> Since the woman who beat him was employed and controlled by him, he could determine and regulate the amount of pain he wanted to experience. Besides this consciously accepted fact, . . . [unconsciously he] was strongly identified with the prostitute and in phantasy was taking her role. Such identification with the manifestly sadistic partner in masochistic relations has long been recognized by psycho-analysis.

But this unconscious identification with the prostitute was only part of the complexity of the identifications. He was also partly identified with his father:

> In this case it meant that, whilst the beating woman represented himself, he who was beaten represented his father.

How do we know about the identification with father?

> On many occasions the patient traced all his misery to his upbringing by his father, whom he described as a ruthless and cruel dictator. He asserted that his father had the power of thrusting himself into his victims, depriving them not only of their freedom, but of their personality. He felt that he carried this loathsome and cruel father within himself . . .

The patient has some conscious experience of a loathsome entity which is carried inside him – indeed, which thrust itself into him. Despite that internal location, the patient strongly repudiated it:

> . . . and this feeling was so strong that he attributed all the features of his appearance and the character-traits that he disliked to this internal father. Whenever he admitted anything bad in himself, it was not really part of himself, but it belonged to his internal father. It transpired that the blows in the beating practices were not directed at himself, but at the other whom he carried in his body.

We are shown that the repudiated entity carried internally has properties corresponding to the external object, his father. This correspondence resembles that of the man who looked after his internal organs with the same defining emotions as he felt for the external members of his family (see *Little people inside*, p. 59).

So the unconscious (perverse) muddling of the identity of who is suffering and who is being beaten becomes clear. It is an unconscious phantasy of hostile relations going on inside him, between his identification with a woman (the prostitute) and with his father. It is all wrapped up and disguised, much as the narrative of a dream is. It is a drama played in the internal arena, *inside* himself. And the sexual quality to the hostile activity indicates, with a rare clarity, the phantasy of an internal sexual couple.

This has a major effect on the patient's own sense of identity. His hostile father, internalized, is represented by a part of his body – his buttocks; and is beaten there. The introjection of his father is experienced as a form of intrusion into him and domination of him from inside. Indeed, the phantasy of being intruded upon may well have been compounded by some actual aspect of the father's personality (compare this with the introjection of a hostile drama in the example of *Attacked by worms*, p. 62). The internal object is experienced as intrusive (a) because it comes from the particular kind of hostile impulses expressed in his own phantasies (his intrusive farting and controlling, for instance); and (b) because the introjection produces an internal object that is hostile and cannot therefore be properly identified as really him – only an alien part of him. Normally, one might more affectionately say that he was a chip off the old block; but this kind of affectionate owning of his likeness to his father is not possible for this patient. Instead he felt intruded upon by something alien. The internalization of his loathsome father led to an alienated feeling about his own identity.

This loathsome father had become a loathsome part of himself; so it was identified with one part of him only – his buttocks, the part of him closely connected with loathsome and offensive faeces. This internalized object could not be properly identified with and persisted internally in an unassimilated state, as if it were an alien foreign body (see the later example in this chapter, *The woman with a devil inside* – p. 74 – for a similar 'unassimilated' object). This intricate tracery of identities involves one identification between a part of himself – his buttocks – and his father; and another between himself and an object outside him, the prostitute who did the beating. His sexual excitement could be greatly heightened by this enacted drama in which he was no longer excluded by the couple in violent intercourse – in fact, he included them.

INTERNAL OBJECTS AND PERSONAL DEVELOPMENT

Hostile relationships may be prolonged into adult life as part of the personality, creating severe personality disorders, often of a perverse kind. They have been an area of recent investigation and will be described below, especially in Chapter 14. The usual solution to the oedipal problems involves the assimilation of the object – because it is more loved than hated. In the less typical cases we have seen in this chapter, the internal object was identified with a *part* of the self, but then isolated there, disrupting the personal identity – because it was more hated than loved. This atypical line of development has been useful to us in understanding internal objects because they stand out more in their alienated and

unassimilated state. In the next example we will consider a more
usual internalization.

IDENTIFICATIONS

What is an identification? When a baby first begins to recognize its
mother, at whatever stage that may be, it is identifying her as its
own. The notion is that as this perception occurs, it actually has an
experience that mother is completely possessed by it. Children
identify with their parents (and others) in very concrete ways –
their mannerisms, sayings, accent, the way they dress, and of
course in mental features such as attitudes, religion, politics, and
so on. Doctors' children grow up to become doctors; actors'
children go on the stage. As adults, equally, we go on forming our
identity around objects/people who are significant to us; the
students of Kleinian analysts become Kleinian analysts! And in
dotage, husband and wife dress alike and grow more and more
'together'. In identification something of the other gets into the
subject, and forms him or her in its likeness.[11]

In these instances a good, loved, and helping object is
internalized. However, a great deal of importance hangs on
whether the subject identifies with a 'good' internal object or a
'bad' one; in effect, whether the balance of feeling at the time of
introjection is loving or hating (biting or kissing/sucking). With
strong loving and concerned impulses, an internal state of love
leads directly to a more or less stable sense of well-being and
self-confidence – 'I love my father and I am like him' – as the internal
object is assimilated into the sense of self. Then the internal object
is fully identified with, though the awareness of the coexistence of
the external object continues undistorted. The person comes to
feel, without thinking about it, that she or he is like the other
person. Often children are assisted by adults who say, 'And how
like your father you are, aren't you?' When there is an identification
with a bad (hated) object inside, a pathological development of the
personality occurs, as we saw in the last example. With phantasies
of internalization accompanied by strong hostile impulses, the
sense of owning is considerably limited. The freedom is restricted
by an unresolved conflict instituted within the self – between
separate parts of the self.

The identification with a 'good' internal object allows the infant another crucial psychological change of perspective. It can begin to accept the parental relationship as, at times, excluding; and can then bear to become a *witness* of a relationship, instead of always an intruding participant in it. This is a step towards respecting the truth of the situation (the parental relationship). On the other hand, the unusual line of development in, for example, the case we have just been examining is a failure to identify with a 'good' internal object and instead some concrete sort of identification with a 'bad' one, the hostile father. As a result, the reality (separateness and exclusion from the parental relationship) could not be achieved and experienced. The patient avoided his reality, and the result was a highly distorted personal identity. By sustaining a confusion of identity, the infant, and subsequently the child and the adult patient, could persist in a phantasy of continuing involvement *within* the parental intercourse, in which the patient achieved bizarre kinds of identification with both the prostitute/mother and the father/buttocks. This kind of multiple identification with both parents in intercourse was a feature of Freud's important case of the Wolf Man (Freud, 1918). Also Peter (in the example *Inhibited play*, p. 39) showed the same kind of identification with both parents (see also Chapters 11 and 12).

We will now look at the internalization of a 'good', loving object. Melanie Klein recorded all the sessions of her treatment of Richard, a text which was published just after her death and some twenty years after the treatment was conducted during the Second World War. It is, however, an important and fascinating document on the way Klein was working in 1940.

Example: Identifying with a 'good' object

In this example a growing internal sense of well-being follows an internalization of a good object. Richard was a ten-year-old child, timid and frightened of other children to the extent that he had not been able to go to school since the age of eight. This is the twenty-first session. The day before, the playroom had not been available and the session had taken place in Mrs K's house:

> Richard met Mrs K on the way to the playroom. He was delighted to find that she had the key to the house. It now appeared that yesterday's incident meant to him that the playroom might never again be available.

> He said with feeling, 'Good old room, I am fond of it and glad to see it again.' . . . He settled down contentedly to play with the fleet [of toy ships] and said that he was happy.

We are shown the connection: when the familiar object of affection (the playroom) was regained, his sense of well-being increased; he was content and happy.

> Mrs K interpreted his fear of losing the 'old playroom' as the fear of losing Mrs K through death.

As we have seen already, the objects to which the child refers can be interpreted as representing people:

> She referred to the time (Ninth session) when she and Richard had to fetch the key, after that he had told her his dreams about the black deserted car, and switched the electric fire on and off which, as Mrs K had pointed out, expressed his fear of Mrs K and Mummy dying. The fear of losing the *old* room also expressed his grief about the death of his granny.

Klein amplifies the interpretation, linking herself, mother and grandmother as those whom Richard feared losing:

> Regaining the room meant to him that Mrs K would remain alive and that Granny was revived.

The room, available or not, people coming and going, living and dying, looking after him or deserting him, the fire coming alight and dying: these the analyst saw as multiple expressions of his underlying unconscious phantasy that his good objects, which make him feel warm and safe, may be lost but can be recovered:

> Richard interrupted his play with the fleet and looked straight at Mrs K, saying quietly and with deep conviction, 'There is one thing I know and that is that you will be a lifelong friend of mine.'

Richard responded deeply to the interpretation. He was moved by Mrs K's interpretation about losing important people. Her understanding (about this distress) had got *into* him (the internal sense of well-being). It made him feel that he had got it as a part of him – it would become a lifelong friend.

> He added that Mrs K was very kind, that he liked her very much, and that he knew that what she was doing with him was good for him, though sometimes it was very unpleasant. He could not say how he knew it was doing him good but he felt it.

This testimonial to Mrs K as a kind person, towards whom he felt affectionate love, records the relief at his own changed state of mind.

> *Mrs K* interpreted that her explaining to him his fear of her death and his sorrow for his granny gave him the feeling that his granny was still alive in his mind – a lifelong friend of his – and that Mrs K, too, would remain alive for ever in this way, because he would contain her in his mind.

And his subsequent play was happier, lively and inventive.

Richard had gained support, hope and well-being; and could then address other fears which Klein went on to interpret in his play. The confident permanence about his hope and security conveys the sense that it is a part of him – hence an internal object. When the patient can internalize a good, helping, parental figure, there is a great relief and a flow of affection. Introjection then secures an internal sense of goodwill and security – that is the state of mind which derives from having an internalized a good object in a congenial relationship with the self, available to be assimilated and identified with. This example demonstrates the particularly helpful quality of the psychoanalyst as an object who understands the anxieties. In her account Klein emphasized that touching on very painful anxieties is particularly potent in establishing a secure internal object, and an internal well-being and sense of being alive: 'It is in fact striking that very painful interpretations . . . referring to death and dead internalized objects . . . could have the effect of reviving hope and making the patient feel more alive' (Klein, 1961, p. 100). The capacity to understand seems to function as a particularly potent 'good' object for internalization.

IDENTIFICATION WITH A 'BAD' INTERNAL OBJECT

As we have seen, however, internalization is not always like that. In the example from Paula Heimann's work (*The man who assaulted his buttocks*, p. 66), the patient did not internalize a good object which could help properly, and he hated his internal object so much that he failed to identify with it properly. It remained an alien and estranged part of his body. Instead of building an internal sense of well-being, it caused internal warfare. Another case presented by Heimann also demonstrates the internalization of a 'bad' object introjected in a state of anger. It resulted in a dominance over the self by this hated object inside the patient; it demanded a slavish allegiance and a highly restricted identity. The process of identification with that object – becoming it – is described; also the ensuing internal struggle with it because it was an enemy, not a loving good object. The creative part of the patient (she was an artist) had been taken over momentarily by an alien object that painted in a different way; thus the patient's personality came to resemble, for a moment, that introjected ('bad') object. It is a state which could be called mad; indeed, the patient had certainly been paranoid.

Example: The woman with a devil inside

The occurrence of the introjection could be observed, as it were, in slow motion in the report the patient gave during one of her psychoanalytic sessions, which repeated a lifelong repetitive sequence that continually resulted in the patient feeling taken over by something bad. In fact the patient had begun her psychoanalytic treatment with the experience of being full of devils inside her which demanded her obedience. In unconscious phantasy, the self had taken in and then come to be dominated by objects felt to be bad. The following description of the session shows this 'mad' internal state actually coming about:

> . . . she began the hour thus: 'I am fed up. My mouth is full of ulcers.' She then told me a story of what had happened to her car that day. She said: 'A fool of a man drove into it. Would you believe it? All the scratches on my car have been made by other people.'

We can pick out the passive complaint about damage to her car as a way of representing her persecuted state. But she was also *internally* scratched (the mouth ulcers were a handy way of expressing that internal state) – a damaged external object (her car) is linked with the sense of something damaged inside.

> She then proceeded to describe in a very emotional way another unpleasant experience she had had that morning. When she was going along in her car, after all her excitement and anger about the man driving into it, another car exceeding the speed limit drove up on her wrong side. 'Of course', she said, 'it was a woman driver.' In front there

was a lorry which gave a sign and turned to the right into a side turning. Immediately after that the woman on her left, without giving any sign, turned to the right also, passing in front of my patient's car, and in order to avoid a collision she herself quickly swerved her own car into the same right-hand turning.

More passivity and helplessness – being pushed into some acquiescence to an external object; again it is like the devils that demanded obedience inside her.

She was 'livid with anger' . . . and now took her revenge on the woman by getting in front of her and crawling along at five miles an hour and making it impossible for the woman behind to pass. Presently they came to red lights. The woman pulled up and now on the same level with my patient, who poked her head out of the window and said: 'that was the worst piece of road-hogging I have ever seen. Do you know that by cutting in front of me from the wrong side you forced me to turn to the right so as to avoid a collision, though I wanted to go straight on?' The woman, who had a red bᵣery face, gave a shrug and a laugh and said: 'What do I care?' My patᵢ ᵣt was furious and sat trying to think of a most scathing remark. Finally she found it: 'On second thoughts', she said, 'there is an excuse for you. I can see you are well beyond your prime. You should leave driving to women who are younger and more intelligent than yourself.' The woman gasped, but before she could reply the traffic lights changed and my patient drove off. She was very pleased with herself.

This describes a powerfully hostile relationship with an external 'bad' object that forced her into a new direction. So far it seems she has mastered that external object with her triumphant insult. However, the consequences of her aggression are considerable and fascinating:

. . . My patient now drove to her art school and started on a sketch to a given theme . . . but found that there was something wrong with her drawing, both while she was working on it and when she had finished and hung it up on the wall. She could not find out what it was, and she said to me: 'That was the most awful thing about it.'

The patient now turns to a dreadful quality of some *internal*, albeit unconscious, interference in her abilities:

When the artist who criticized the sketches came to hers, he said in surprise: 'Good God, what has happened to you? This looks like a drawing from a Victorian family album.' My patient now realized what it was she felt to be wrong with it. She said: 'it looked like a drawing that had been done fifty years ago.'

Something had literally got into her that turned her off from her own apparent intention and diverted her into following a style of someone fifty years ago – that is, a much older woman. The explanation offered is that the older woman in the car who had turned her off the road she had wanted to go along had actually got into her – an introjection, and then a dominance, by the 'bad' object:

She felt so awful about this that she had to go and have three sherries. Later she noticed the ulcers in her mouth.

The identification with the 'beery-faced', drunken woman had become extremely concrete and internal as she drank her sherry. The scathing attack she made on the woman with her mouth was experienced by the patient as a corresponding attack upon part of herself, her own mouth, of which the ulcers were serendipitously noticed evidence for this:

. . . She had carried out her impulse to hurt the woman and was consciously pleased with her success. But unconsciously – as the woman stood for me and her mother, towards whom she had love impulses as well as hostile ones – she could not bear the injuries she had inflicted on her nor could she remain at a distance from her. She had immediately internalized this mother-figure and she had internalized her in the injured condition for which she felt responsible and guilty, namely as a worn-out, fifty-year old . . .

Because the object had been internalized in hatred, it was related to internally in a particular way. It was hated, so that the internal world was dominated in a hostile, confused way until the patient did not know properly who she was. The patient felt taken over by the alien object, like devils controlling her, and felt a depletion of her own life, of her own direction and intentions. She then performed as if she were that woman fifty years older – the old style of drawing, the alcoholic drinking. Capture by this internalized object replicated the hostile aggressive relationship in which the external object had made her helpless. Internally it disturbed her sense of self and identity by diverting her into another direction, the Victorian-style painting.

The object, once internalized, is the focus of deeply important dramas. We have considered the manner of internalization – in hate or in love – which has profound implications for the sense of personal identity. But not only that – it also affects the fate of the object inside. In the next chapter we will follow further the anxious concerns about the fate of the good internal object.

6 THE DEPRESSIVE POSITION

Melanie Klein formulated the depressive position in 1934–5. The infant takes a major step forward in its development from the paranoid cycles and states during the first six months of its life. This idea is central to all later developments in Kleinian psychoanalysis.

Children are anxious at the scale of their own aggression, and this anxiety had previously been seen as a function of the super-ego, in line with classical psychoanalysis (see Chapter 4). However, Klein now began to describe guilt in terms of object relations: aggression means attacks on objects, which are damaged or die; and concern is felt for the object's state. This contrasts with the self-orientated anxiety of the paranoid cycles – a fear for oneself at the hands of persecutors. Klein began to use the term 'paranoid position' for these states to make the contrast with the depressive position. She described that contrast between the two positions in her comments on one of the cases discussed in the last chapter (*Attacked by worms*, p. 62).

> While the paranoid anxieties predominated and the anxiety of his bad united parents prevailed, X felt only hypochondriacal anxieties for his own body. When depression and sorrow had set in, the love and concern for the good object came to the fore and the anxiety-contents as well as the whole feelings and defences altered. (Klein,1935, p. 274)

Here she is pointing to a move from fear to concern. That crucial step is the entry into the depressive position. We must look in detail at how 'love and concern [come] to the fore'.

Crucially, objects are no longer purely good or bad – threatening or protecting – as in the paranoid states. For instance, in the example *Attacked by worms*, the patient had a dream of a detective who was a helper against enemies at one moment, and at the next was in alliance with those enemies. That black-and-white division between helpers and enemies is characteristic of the paranoid position. It is termed splitting of the object – either the object is felt to have all good aspects, and none of the bad; or it has all bad aspects, and no good ones.

In the depressive position these sets of qualities and functions move towards a more realistic mixture. Therefore, *mixed* feelings towards them arise – like anger plus remorse, which we have already seen in so many of the worried children and adult patients in our examples. Klein argued that the success of this step into concern and mixed feelings depends entirely upon the process of internalizing a good loving object, producing an internal state of well-being. If the good internal object is felt to be possessed for all time, as in the example *Identifying with a 'good' object* (p. 71), it gives strong support and confidence when the subject is under stress.

The specific new anxieties, feelings, object relations and defences develop as the infant begins to feel *for* the object, and becomes less egocentric. Typically the *anxiety* that is felt is a fear of damaging a loved one. The *feelings* are characteristically ambivalent; hate being transformed by the infant's own love into remorse. *Objects* become threatened, or damaged, and that brings out concern for their suffering. *Relationships* with objects then begin to allow more separateness; less control (omnipotence) is demanded. And *defences* (typically the manic defence) which operate against anxiety and remorse are different from the primitive and violent ones previously described against the paranoid fear of being persecuted.

Sadness is a profoundly painful human emotion. It is important to distinguish sadness (a feeling central to the depressive position) from clinical depression. Often Klein is criticized for confusing the two states by using the term 'depressive position' for sadness and concern. All this work has descended as a continuous stream from Abraham and Freud, and their work on manic-depressive illness. Freud particularly distinguished mourning from melancholia. Klein's view of this distinction was that sadness related to feelings about the damaged loved object, both the external object and the internal one; whereas depression is a more complex and paranoid state. Clinical depression protects against the poignancy of sadness and concern; the subject identifies with the damaged object and then protests at the suffering state the subject is now in. All attention is focused on the state of the self, and away from that of the object that might otherwise evoke concern, guilt and remorse. Thus the anxiety of the depressive position is abolished by reversion to paranoid states – this is one form of paranoid defence against depressive anxiety (see below).

THE INTERNAL DRAMA OF THE DEPRESSIVE POSITION

We have met the next patient before (see *Attacked by worms*, p. 62). His unconscious phantasies expressed through his actual medical history when young – having worms – had resulted in considerable paranoid anxiety that something bad was harming him, eating him up inside. These worms were intensely evil, and even corrupted his helpers (remember the dream of the analyst/detective). Klein then described the progress of the analysis as the patient was emerging from his paranoid and hypochondriacal states. In the example below we will concentrate on the anxiety and feelings associated with the depressive position.

Example: Concern and depressive feelings

The analysis of this patient, X, progressed, and his distrust of the analyst – who, he felt, had fallen under the influence of the bad objects (worms) inside him – began to diminish:

> . . . the patient became very much concerned about me. X had always worried about his mother's health; but he had not been able to develop real love for her, though he did his best to please her. Now, together with the concern for me, strong feelings of love and gratitude came to the fore, together with feelings of unworthiness, sorrow and depression.

Note the significant link in the patient's progress: new feelings of anxious concern came together with real love and gratitude.

> . . . In his analysis he went through phases of deep depression with all the symptoms characteristic of this state of mind. At the same time the feelings and phantasies connected with his hypochondriacal pains

changed. For instance, the patient felt anxiety that the cancer would make its way through the lining of his stomach; but now it appeared that, while he feared for his stomach, he really wanted to protect 'me' inside him – actually the internalized mother – who he felt was being attacked.

We must remark once again on how the change in his feelings for others – mother and analyst – coincides with a change in his relations to something inside him. His concern for his mother was matched by his concern for something he called his stomach, which was being damaged by cancer. The new anxiety – a fear for his helping object – was felt both for the external object and also for one inside him, his stomach. Inside, it is attacked by a hostile internal object, the cancer (or worms). Here internal objects are described as in conflict with each other. One internal object, his stomach connected through his associations with the mother/analyst, needs protection from another – a cancer, or worms. And with that comes the crucial change from paranoia to concern. This new crucial anxiety focuses on the preservation of the endangered and loved object.

If a person's aggressive impulses are strong, unconscious phantasies are experiences of attacks upon objects, parents, and so on, who are thereby damaged. When they are mingled with hatred, love seems weaker and threatened, and so do the loved objects. However, because they are also loved, it gives the characteristic agonized position in which the person fears for those who are under attack. We have seen examples where conflicted and paranoid states are internalized in hatred – that is, with biting and damage; then the internal state is very troubled, because it now contains an object that may be hostile (as in the paranoid states of the example of *The man who assaulted his buttocks* and *The woman with a devil inside* – pp. 66, 74). If, instead, love is mixed in, then the object may be experienced as damaged, insecure and no longer capable of giving protection and well-being. It is this *damaged internal object* which gives the characteristic mixed feelings of the depressive position. We will look at this in the next example.

These internal dramas (unconscious phantasies) have profound internal consequences – one is that the sense of an internal and permanent well-being (see *Identifying with a 'good' object*, p. 71) is never properly secure.[12] In the next example we follow Richard, the boy in the example *Identifying with a 'good' object*; but now his good internal object becomes shaken. It is shortly before the end of his psychoanalysis, and this prospect arouses considerable anger and anxiety in Richard. The evidence in his play is that he attacks his psychoanalyst, but what actually happens is that he feels pain inside him as attacks and potential loss of the external good object result in a loss of the security and well-being provided by the corresponding internal good object. The internal one, too, must have been attacked.

Example: The insecure internal object

Here is part of another session with Richard, the ten-year-old boy, who figured in *Identifying with a 'good' object*. This is the 92nd session, just before the psychoanalysis finished at the 93rd:

> He made angry sounds representing the trains whenever they came near to each other. The play centred on avoiding collisions between the trains. They were often quite near to colliding, but Richard always prevented the disaster at the last moment, this conflict visibly giving rise to great mental strain in him.

By this point in the analysis, the collisions of the trains were understood by both analyst and patient as collisions between people. We can therefore see Richard anxiously at pains to avoid any such collision. Does the play represent the psychoanalytic situation itself? We could begin to wonder if Richard is bothered about a 'collision' between himself and his analyst, who will be departing the next day. Is poor Richard intent on preventing himself from having a violent quarrel with her?

> During this play Richard repeatedly made suggestions about changes of times, choosing particularly times at which he knew quite well that Mrs K saw other patients.

Clearly he is preoccupied with continuing to see her, but he tries to do so in a way which the analyst cannot help but deny him. In his requests for different times, Richard is seemingly provoking a deliberate clash. You can see at one and the same time how he contrives near-collisions in his play, and also contrives clashes in his request to the analyst:

> *Mrs K* said she could not arrange the times he asked for but offered alternatives. Richard, at one moment when both trains were standing in the station, suddenly said he felt unwell and had a pain in his tummy. He looked pale.

The dangerous relationship expressed in the play, and then in the relationship with the analyst, is now superseded by a pain inside him. Suddenly he is occupied by an internal situation, inside his tummy.

> *Mrs K* interpreted the station as Richard's inside. He expected all the time a collision inside him between the electric train, containing Mrs K and the good Mummy, and the hostile goods train, standing for all the angry patients and children from whom Richard wanted to take Mrs K away and run with her to his home town.

When Mrs K refused his requests, his protective concern seemed to become inadequate and the stressful clash was immediately internalized as an actual internal pain.

The internal situation, expressed in the toy station, contained a potential violence between the analyst (felt as his mother) and angry children who felt they were going to lose 'Mrs K'. This is slightly complex. Richard's anger at losing 'Mrs K' was represented as the anger of rival patients, while he, in phantasy, fulfilled his wish to run away with her (to internalize her). The complexity here is that the anger, and his wish for her, remain unmixed – the anger is attributed to his rivals. We will have many opportunities in later chapters to become familiar with this form of attribution to others (projective identification). Here it represents a way of avoiding the full intensity of his fear for 'Mrs K' which is causing him such mental strain:

> The collision between the good objects and what he felt to be bad ones (because he had attacked them and wanted to deprive them) was also a conflict between one part of himself felt to be good and allied with the good object and the hostile part of himself allied with the objects felt to be bad. (Klein, 1961, p. 461)

In a sense Klein, in this later quote, is modifying the interpretation she gave at the time. However, the original interpretation of the conflict in the toy station, in the consulting room and inside Richard's tummy was sufficiently accurate, it seems, since it brought the following response:

Richard said, looking at Mrs K in surprise, 'The pain has now gone –
why?' The colour had come back into his face.

This example shows once again the internalization of objects; a
conflict between those objects inside, and thus an endangering
conflict – one which leads to a pained internal state. The internal
sense of well-being gained in the previous example, *Identifying
with a 'good' object* (p. 71), is lost and becomes a pain instead, as
the good object comes under threat. The threatened external
object (actual loss of 'Mrs K') leads, through the hostility, to a
similar condition of the internal one, together with a pained sense
of responsibility for the violence which had to be disowned.

Phantasies in the depressive position are preoccupied with damage
to objects, with responsibility, regret and guilt, and with a new
impulse – the wish to repair the objects. The shakiness of the
internal object provokes an attempt to make good that damage, and
to effect a repair. At times, however, the prospect may seem
hopelessly vast, arousing great stress and distress.

REPARATION

Reparation, to which we will now turn, is both an important
impulse and a crucial outcome of the depressive position. The pain
of guilt, loss and concern is turned into constructive effort of an
altruistic kind. In the phantasies of the depressive position, the
complex of damage and concern brings remorse, the form that love
takes for an object when it has been damaged. This remorse, in
turn, contains within itself the wish to repair the damage. It is often
said that Klein was pessimistic in tracing the root of remorse,
concern and altruism to aggression; but it is really just as much a
result of love – of the *interaction* of love with hate, aggression and
fear. Of course there are many other forms of love: gratitude,
appreciation, joy, are some of them. All these are generous attitudes
towards the object. They are not simply the love of personal
satisfaction or security, though that does also continue on from the
earlier positions of the infant, but the forms of love now become
various mixtures. The depressive position is a moment in which a
major differentiation of these forms of love begins to flower from
its interaction with anger and aggression.

In the next example the patient (an adult) was driven, from hate at his experience of his parents as a sexual couple (the Oedipus complex), to attack them and their relationship. His concern, remorse and subsequent efforts to look after them came immediately to the fore.

Example: Damaged parents

This man had a dream of his parents, and Klein goes through the associations to the dream in great detail. In the dream:

> The patient felt that he was 'managing the whole thing', taking care of the parents, who were much older and more in need of his care than in reality. The parents were lying in bed, not side by side, as they usually did, but with the ends of the beds joined together. The patient found it difficult to keep them warm.

The dreamer's protective worry – he wanted to keep his parents warm – seems to be connected with having disturbed them; that is, he damaged their relationship by separating the beds – splitting up their intercourse – and is now concerned and fearful for them:

> Then the patient urinated, while his parents were watching him, into a basin in the middle of which there was a cylindrical object. The urination seemed complicated, since he had to take special care not to urinate into the cylindrical part. He felt this would not have mattered had he been able to aim exactly into the cylinder and not to splash anything about. When he had finished urinating he noticed that the basin was overflowing and felt this as unsatisfactory. While urinating he noticed that his penis was very large and he had an uncomfortable feeling about this – as if his father ought not to see it, since he would feel beaten by him and he did not want to humiliate his father.

One striking feature of the dream is the rivalry – between the patient's penis and his father's. The dream can be said to stand for a wish to be bigger than father, but he also regretted that wish and sought to prevent it.

> At the same time he felt that by urinating he was sparing his father the trouble of getting out of bed and urinating himself. Here the patient stopped, and then said that he really felt as if his parents were a part of himself.

The rivalry with the father is clear in the comparison of penises, in the danger to which the 'cylindrical part' was exposed, and in the humiliation (pissing on) that he feared father and the parental couple were subjected to. The poor damaged father was beaten in the rivalry, and father's relationship with mother was disturbed (by changing the beds to an end-to-end position). The tension of the situation is created by the patient's regret at the condition of his parents; he feels responsible and wants to protect them. We notice again, at that point of stress, the *internal* quality to the situation; he had internalized it and then experienced, partially consciously, that these parents were a part of him.

Anxieties about the damage done to the parents continued. More associations emerged about harmed objects (the parents) and his regret and concern:

> In the dream the basin with the cylinder was supposed to be a Chinese vase, but it was not right, because the stem was not underneath the basin, as it should have been, it was 'in the wrong place', since it was above the basin – really inside it

The cylinder in the wrong place could be linked to the parents in bed together; he felt that they were in the 'wrong' place because he wanted to separate his parents (keep the cylinder out of the bowl, put their beds end to end instead of together). These anxieties continued:

> The patient then associated the basin to a glass bowl, as used for gas-burners in his grandmother's house, and the cylindrical part reminded him of a gas-mantle. He then thought of a dark passage, at the end of which there was a low-burning gas-light, and said that this picture evoked in him sad feelings. It made him think of poor and dilapidated houses, where there seemed to be nothing alive but this low-burning gas-light.

Listen to the concern and sadness; they are very poignant here – the darkness and low level of light and life are fairly clear metaphors, symbolizing his sense that his loved objects – parents, his home, and so on – are becoming faded and dilapidated. After the aggressive rivalry we then hear about this sadness at the sorry state of his objects.

The narrative (unconscious phantasy) emerging from the dream comprises his rivalry with his father, which led to 'managing' the situation by separating the parents and 'pissing on' them, with the subsequent remorse and responsibility, mixed with poignant sadness and concern *for* them, which finally led to the re-creation of an *internal* state of debilitated life within himself. His further associations indicate something of the fears that keep this situation going:

> It is true, one only had to pull the string and the light would burn fully. This reminded him that he had always been frightened of gas and that the flames of a gas-ring made him feel that they were jumping out at him, as if they were a lion's head. Another thing that frightened him about gas was the 'pop' noise it made, when it was put out.

I think the patient's dilemma is that he could bring the whole situation back to life again, but if he does so, out pops a lively set of parents who will be back together again and frighten and endanger him – the jumping-out lion's head and the 'pop' noise. It seems that his dilemma is that he cannot bear his parents in a lively union together, but if he separates them he suffers an equally painful remorse, sadness and concern. This range of feelings, which unfolds as a narrative drama, is felt to be so real as actually to move the patient emotionally, both in the dream and in the thinking about it in the analytic session.

Klein then made an interpretation:

> After my interpretation that the cylindrical part in the basin and the gas-mantle were the same thing and that he was afraid to urinate into it because he did not want for some reason to put the flame out, he replied that of course one cannot extinguish a gas-flame in this way, as then poison remains behind – it is not like a candle which one can simply blow out.

This is an interesting response. The patient's association – an extinguished flame leaves 'poison' behind – takes up the interpretation in a very concrete way, as if seriously considering the chemistry of burning gas. It seems likely, however, that within his understanding of gas there is embedded, as in dream symbols, an unconscious pursuit of the meanings that derive from his anguished unconscious phantasies: the damage he has done (in extinguishing father) will leave an *emotional* poison of despair and guilty concern.

There was a further response, a dream the next night which the patient reported in the next session. The concern, active in the first dream, and the interpretation continued to preoccupy the patient in an agonizing way:

> The night after this the patient had the following dream: he heard the frizzling sound of something which was frying in an oven. He could not see what it was, but he thought of something brown, probably a kidney which was frying in the pan. The noise he heard was like the squeaking or crying of a tiny voice and his feeling was that a live creature was being fried. His mother was there and he tried to draw her attention to this, and to make her understand that to fry something alive was much the worst thing to do, worse than boiling or cooking. It was more torturing since the hot fat prevented it from burning altogether and kept it alive while skinning it.

The patient conveys an agonizing cruelty carried out in the inside situation (in the oven). He had many associations of unpleasant torturing, but the final one was that he had a cold. I think we can see that the patient's sense of an internal disorder, his cold, represents the suffering of his internal objects: he internalized the damaged parents whom he had originally wanted to keep warm, and their 'cold' state has come to be represented as his state.

Klein reviewed the complex associations. In summary, the kidney frying in the pan represented father inside mother, like the cylinder in the basin – that is to say, the inflaming oedipal situation which leads to the torturing aggression (again oral: frying the kidneys). The new dream goes over the same problem again. In addition there is a plea to a mother (the psychoanalyst, we might wonder?) to attend to and help him with the problem which he cannot manage on his own. It is as if an unconscious message to the analyst appeals to her further understanding of this kind of concern for the dreadfully damaged loved objects. The representation of these issues is another kind of confirmation of the work on the dream the day before.

The achievement of the depressive position is to sustain the feelings of concern without always reverting to paranoid fears. With that successful step the patient then mobilizes the new set of feelings known as 'reparation' – the wish to put right, reinstate or repair the object that has been damaged or destroyed:

> . . . his main way of overcoming the depressive position is reparation. In the dream he devotes himself entirely to his parents in order to keep them alive and comfortable.

We can see the attempts in this example to keep the parents warm, to protect his father from humilation, and so on. Reparation is made more possible when he can check on the state of his external objects – that his actual parents are in fact well. While they are phantasies, and while he is concerned with the phantasies of internal parents, he is prone to being overwhelmed by his feelings. But when he can begin to distinguish between the phantasies and the reality of his objects, he can begin to internalize a more stable object and a sense of permanence.

GUILT

One way of describing the remorseful situation is in terms of guilt. The complex of feelings in the depressive position is a form of guilt – the sense of having done something wrong, and of the demands imposed upon oneself to put it right. These demands may be of a total kind – 'devoting oneself entirely' – so that there is no sense of freedom. Then the guilt is extremely burdensome or tormenting. To some extent the punitive quality of the guilt reflects the severity of the torturing damage done. It is this quality of a punishment to fit the crime that is the quality of the early super-ego in the infant, operating on the talion law – an eye for an eye.

Guilt may be so severe that the concern has to be avoided. This is not uncommon; it is frequently possible to observe people evading guilt through a convinced blaming of others. However, the avoidance may be so persistent as seriously to hamper the progress into and through the depressive position. Commenting on her case of X, who believed he had tapeworm (*Attacked by worms*, p. 62), Klein described how the patient felt forced to concentrate on keeping his brothers and sisters, and his internal organs, alive:

> It became quite clear that the different organs he was trying to cure were identified with his brothers and sisters, about whom he felt guilty and whom he had perpetually to keep alive. It was his *over-anxiousness* to put them right, because he had damaged them in phantasy, and his *excessive* sorrow and despair about it which led to such an increase in paranoid anxieties and defences that love and concern for people and identification with them became buried under hate. (Klein, 1935, p. 275)

When the pain of concern and guilt reaches quite intolerable proportions (as the depressive position approaches) the sense of a helping object is critically important. We saw this in the internalization of a 'good' object in the last chapter. The infant needs to feel that a mother is there to help give realistic proportions to the unconscious phantasies: to help with recognizing the reality of the actual external objects and the reality of the world of objects and feelings inside. If an object which can help to test reality is forthcoming through an external object, the experience enhances the internal good object, through internalization of the external helper – as we saw in Richard's case in Chapter 5 (*Identifying with a 'good' object*, p. 71). Then the internal sense of well-being is further buttressed against the floods of guilt.

With a secure good object, the actual *reality* of any damage to real people becomes more accessible to the infant's perception. In the last example, the patient could experience his mother, in the second dream, as a helper for him. The experience of mother surviving as a helper – not just engaged in the hated intercourse with father – enabled this patient to struggle on with the awful and agonizing experiences of his dream. But this complex situation may go wrong. The helping internal object is also at risk of being damaged – then the subject needs the reassurance of the external object. If there is no reassurance that adequate help has survived, a bleak and hopeless internal world develops. Sometimes the outside world (mother or carer) may indeed be a depriving environment and fail the subject; or that person may have their own difficulties in introjecting the helping object. Either way, despair and lack of resources emerge; and, probably, a persecuting guilt that goads towards a permanent servitude of caring for damaged objects. The internal world is then believed to be populated with 'bad' and harming objects (such as those in the examples *The man who assaulted his buttocks* and *The woman with a devil inside*, pp. 66, 74) and devoid of helping ones. The experience then is of an internal domination over the self by a harsh super-ego from which emanates a punitive guilt.

DEFENCES IN THE DEPRESSIVE POSITION

In the course of successful development, a different outcome is achieved. Instead of remaining persecuting, guilt is modified. This, however, depends on one condition: whether one's sense of one's own goodness is sufficient. Goodness needs to survive the uprushes of jealousy, rivalry, hatred and impulses felt to be bad. The infant depends on having a relatively benign external world to introject; and also on a capacity to mobilize loving feelings in the course of introjecting helping objects.

If things have gone wrong for the infant – either because of a deficient environment or because of special difficulties in introjecting (we will come to those later) – then the pain may be so strong that the guilt and the capacity to repair (reparation) become too burdensome and punishing. Then the infant needs defensive measures, psychological mechanisms to ensure that the experience of guilt is not felt consciously. There are two broad means for defensive avoidance of excessive pain arising from concern and guilt: the paranoid defence against depressive anxiety; and the manic defences.

THE PARANOID DEFENCE

When the sense of guilt is very extreme, it is intensely persecuting. We have briefly noted the way in which clinical depression is a move from concern for the object to wretched ruminations on the self. But more frankly paranoid situations can supervene; an example of this will be given below (*Peter's naughtiness*, p. 139), where the patient Peter gets into an ever-increasing spiral of violent punishment in relation to his super-ego. His concern about his naughtiness towards his parents results in violent persecutory phantasies about roasting and eating them, or being eaten. Then the route back out of the depressive position is into paranoid cycles which re-create a paranoid position. Guilty concern for the object is transformed into a fear for the self at the hands of a harsh punishing agent. So far as X, Melanie Klein's patient, (*Attacked by worms*, p. 62; and mentioned again above) was concerned:

> buried under the continuous paranoid accusations, complaints and criticisms of others, there existed a very profound love for his mother and concern for his parents as well as for other people. (Klein, 1935, p. 275)

The concern was buried (defended against) by paranoid fears and by the claim that he was being attacked by tapeworms (or cancer inside). In the last example (*Damaged parents*, p. 85), as the man felt more despair about his ability to protect his parents, he felt more persecutory fear – the explosive gas mantle like an attacking lion-head which made him fear for himself instead of for his objects. This is a reversion to a *paranoid* mode of experiencing the situation. With this reversion there is a renewed splitting of the object – for instance, when a helper oscillates between being an enemy and an analyst (see *Attacked by worms*).

MANIC DEFENCES

The other main method of turning away the pain of concern is recourse to the *manic defences*. Then, characteristically, the patient rules that the loved person is not important at all; their condition, damaged or sound, does not matter. So, since it is no longer important, the object's fate can be ignored; the subject cultivates imaginary states of superiority, triumph, and control over the object; and a feeling of omnipotent supremacy over the insignificant object is sustained through asserting phantasy relations with it. That manic superiority is supported by specific defences: a *denial* of the true qualities of the object; a sense of *triumph* over the object, which becomes insignificant; and a *control* over the object, making it dependent instead on the subject.

The next example is a case in which the internal situation suddenly becomes shaky again as a result of a bereavement in the external world. An internal shakiness resulting from an external loss was detailed in Abraham's material (Chapter 2) as well as the case of Richard (*The insecure internal object*, p. 82). In elaborating this work, Klein pinpointed the specific defences employed against the depressive anxiety, guilt and remorse.

Example: The death of a son

We will consider a case of an actual bereavement. The patient Klein described was mourning the death of her son.[13] At first she did not cry very much,

> and tears did not bring the relief which they did later on. She felt numbed and closed up, and physically broken.

Note again the comment on the bodily experience of being damaged, 'broken', as an internal consequence of the actual external loss. Bereavement of her son sparked off this woman's unconscious phantasies of attacks upon an *internal* loved object as well as the actual external one, her dead son:

At this stage Mrs A, who usually dreamed every night, had entirely stopped dreaming because of her deep unconscious denial of the actual loss. At the end of the [first] week she had the following dream:

She saw two people, a mother and son. The mother was wearing a black dress. The dreamer knew that this boy had died, or was going to die. No sorrow entered into her feelings, but there was a trace of hostility towards the two people.

The dream explicitly denies sadness, though other feelings (a trace of hostility) can still exist. In her associations Mrs A remembered with strong feelings that her brother was tutored by a schoolfellow, 'B', of the same age. B's mother had been patronizing, and her own mother was dejected. This brought up an important memory; Mrs A

herself felt that fearful disgrace had fallen upon her very much admired and beloved brother and the whole family. This brother, a few years older than herself, seemed to her full of knowledge, skill and strength – a paragon of all the virtues, and her ideal was shattered when his deficiencies at school came to light. The strength of her feelings about this incident as being an irreparable misfortune, which persisted in her memory, was, however, due to unconscious feelings of guilt.

It seems that the preoccupying event in Mrs A's life – her bereavement of her son – has come to be represented in the dream in a disguised way as the disgrace of her brother; he had fallen from an elevated position, an irreparable misfortune. The sense of an irreparable damage linked three things: her brother's humiliation; her son's death; and her broken internal state:

In the dream, the two people whom Mrs A saw were B and his mother, and the fact that the boy was dead expressed Mrs A's early death wishes against him.

Klein is now telling us that the dream is dealing not just with sadness and grief, but also with hostility – a hostility directed towards a figure from the past, B, who deserves it because he humiliated her brother and mother:

One dream-thought, therefore, ran: 'A mother's son has died, or will die. It is this unpleasant woman's son, who hurt my mother and brother, who should die.'

We can see here the way phantasies move the loss progressively away to other figures, who were much less important to her: from her son to her brother to her brother's colleague, B. Despite this diminished importance of the objects in the dream, Klein nevertheless thought there was a link with the grief at the son's death:

> She had carried over some of her feelings for her brother into her relation to her son. In her son, she also loved her brother; but at the same time, some of the ambivalence towards her brother, though modified through her strong motherly feelings, was also transferred on to her son.

We are drawn steadily to the awful conclusion that the bereaved mother harboured some hostility to her son as well, and that his death had made that real in a particularly final way. The guilt she felt in the midst of her sadness rendered it unconscious. Thus she largely suffered unconscious guilt.

Despite her admiration and love for her brother, she had also been jealous of his greater knowledge, and his mental and physical superiority. In her dream, she had reduced both sets of feelings to insignificance because of the guilt and remorse which had to be rendered unconscious. The way this was done revealed some of the typical defences used in this position; the components of the manic defence: denial, triumph and control of the internal objects.

Denial: The denial of guilt was evaded when she avoided all feelings, in the first week after her loss:

> Let us consider the interplay of defences as they appeared in this material. When the loss occurred, the manic position became reinforced, and denial in particular came especially into play. Unconsciously, Mrs A strongly rejected the fact that her son had died.

This is especially a denial of the internal reality, her feelings, as well as the denial of the actual loss.

Triumph: However, she also reorganized the significance:

> When she could no longer carry on this denial so strongly – but was not yet able to face the pain and sorrow – triumph, one of the other elements of the manic position, became reinforced. 'It is not at all painful', the thought seemed to run, as the associations showed, 'if *a* boy dies. It is even satisfactory. Now I get my revenge.'

The triumphant relegation of the significance of the death is a way of dealing with the fact of dependency; the boy B who is disposed of is actually the needed source of knowledge. The attempt is to create a view that no one is needed; there is no dependency. It is a pained, albeit disguised, attempt to include her son among the unimportant ones.

Control: Her reckless self-sufficiency reduced important people, in phantasy, to a supposed unimportance. They became mere things to be controlled within her internal broken state:

> But this triumph was associated with control of the *internalized* mother and brother, and triumph over them.

The mother's broken state was dealt with within the first week by an initial denial, but this was followed by phantasies, revealed in the dream, in which the dead and grieving figures were rearranged:

> . . . at this stage the *control* over her internal objects was reinforced, the misfortune and grief were displaced from herself onto her internalized mother. Here denial came into play – denial of the psychical reality that she and her internal mother were one and suffered together.

The rearrangement is an internal one in which she no longer identifies with a mother, or with a mother's feelings. This is an omnipotent control of the broken internal situation. The emotional loss has then been dealt with. The whole internal world of feelings, and the sense of internal contents, is emphatically controlled.

POSITIONS

At the time (in the 1930s) Klein termed this sort of constellation of anxieties, feelings, object relations and defences a 'position' – 'depressive position'; she had also used 'paranoid position', and even 'manic position'. She sought to distinguish it from the notion of a developmental phase; Freud had used the idea of a phase – oral, anal, and so on – to denote simply the character of instinctual impulses, fundamental bodily satisfactions such as feeding, sexuality and so forth. A constant to-and-fro into the depressive position and out again means that there is no clear-cut phasic sequence. External and internal worlds interact and create anxieties, and continually move the subject from fear to concern and back again. The subject continually takes up characteristic positions vis-à-vis his objects. These involve satisfactions from them, their assistance for the characteristic psychological defences, and feelings *for* those objects as people. This to-and-fro movement is much more fluid than Freud's notion of phases and regression.

In 1935, when Klein first introduced the depressive position, she contrasted it with the paranoid position – a position much as described in the previous chapters. Further development of her theories, however, resulted in a modification of the 'paranoid position', which she came to call the 'paranoid-schizoid position'; to this we will now turn.

7 THE PARANOID-SCHIZOID POSITION

An infant's ability to sustain the new feelings of the depressive position depends on its internal security – that is, a sufficiently stable internal good object. But what makes internal security sufficient – or insufficient? The answer lies in the states of aggression and paranoia which Klein had found so prominent in children. These states, arising very early in infancy, set the scene for the development of the internal world. If objects are internalized in a process that is angry and hostile – that is, with phantasies of aggressive biting and tearing to pieces, and so on – then the state of the internal world is persecutory and dominated by hostile internal objects (see Chapter 5).

In the 1940s Klein began to rethink the nature of this 'paranoid' position, and how the internal world forms. Previously she had focused her attention on the fear of being attacked by bad hostile objects; this she contrasted with the depressive position, where the anxiety concerns fear of damage to or death of the loved object, especially the internal good object. In 1946 she took a new step by postulating certain phantasies in which the person's own mind was in danger *from itself* – a phantasy of self-directed aggression leading to a fear of falling to pieces. She thought this was the infant's earliest fear – the fear of attack from within the self. She and her students began to note experiences, particularly in their more disturbed adult patients, in which the mind seemed to lack a wholeness, or could not operate in an integrated, coherent way: parts of the mind seemed to go missing. Although this state was observed largely in adult patients, Klein thought that it represented the recurrence of experiences and phantasies that could operate from the very beginning of life. The paranoid phase seemed to be augmented by states in which the mind and the self were themselves split up and therefore damaged. She took over the term 'schizoid' in the sense of it used by Scottish psychoanalyst, Ronald Fairbairn, and combined it with hers to coin a new term: the 'paranoid-schizoid' position.

Very early in development, certain personalities evade their intolerable fears by attacking those parts of the mind that are aware of their experiences. Most infants alternate between states of bliss and terror, gradually evolving towards the mixed states of the depressive position. Schizoid patients, in contrast, retain and exploit self-directed attacks against the self with the purpose of keeping those 'good' and 'bad' states from becoming mixed. Thus confrontation with the mixed feelings of the depressive position is strictly limited. In consequence, however, the subject persistently fears an impending fragmentation of him- or herself.

Splitting the Self

Before this new idea, the structure of the ego had been thought of in terms of a core good object around which the internal world stabilized, but now Klein described the stability of the person and their identity as radically affected by attacks upon the self. It is not just that the good object is attacked (as in the ambivalence of the depressive position), nor that the object is introjected in hostility and remains unassimilated from the ego; she now explored how parts and functions of the ego may themselves become split apart:

> As we know, under pressure of ambivalence, conflict and guilt, the patient often splits the figure of the analyst; then the analyst may at certain moments be loved, at other moments hated. Or the analyst may be split in such a way that he remains the good (or bad) figure while someone else becomes the opposite figure. But this was not the kind of splitting that occurred in this instance. The patient split off those parts of himself, i.e. of his ego, which he felt to be dangerous and hostile to the analyst. He turned his destructive impulses from his object *towards his ego*. (Klein, 1946, p. 19)

In this chapter I have collected various examples of fragmenting attacks on the ego itself. Associated with this specific splitting of the self is another process which Klein labelled 'projective identification'; this will be discussed in Chapter 8.

Many of the examples of splitting illustrate very strange mental processes. Once again we have to return to the very strange minds of seriously mentally ill patients. As we go on with these examples, it will require a deliberate act of suspending ordinary thought if we are to contemplate the kinds of experiences that emerge. For the reader coming to this for the first time, it may confound all common sense. But that is the nature of madness, and the nearer we come to it the more we need to suspend ordinary thought. If you are reading this for the first time, it may be better to allow the incomprehensible to remain so, and press on – returning only later, if you find your fascination growing.

Example: The man who lost his feelings

Klein described a curious problem: the patient did not feel things which he, and others, might have expected him to feel. Instead he felt, and seemed, flat and empty. The patient actually felt that one part of himself had been lost or annihilated. He had told the analyst that he felt anxious, but he did not know why:

> He then made comparisons with people more successful and fortunate than himself. These remarks also had a reference to me. Very strong feelings of frustration, envy and grievance came to the fore.

We enter the story at the point in the course of his psychoanalysis when he was at last beginning to have strong and painful feelings – feelings connected (albeit indirectly) with the psychoanalyst herself. But notice what happens:

> When I interpreted . . . that these feelings were directed against the analyst and that he wanted to destroy me, his mood changed abruptly. His tone of voice became flat, he spoke in a slow expressionless way, and he said that he felt detached from the whole situation. He added that my interpretation seemed correct, but that it did not matter. In fact he no longer had any wishes, and nothing was worth bothering about.

Klein offers us a dramatic moment: the moment at which this patient's feelings literally went missing. The interpretation confronted him with certain immediate feelings – towards his supposedly successful psychoanalyst. At that moment he lost them – something, quite specifically, had disappeared. That experience was conveyed in the *actual* change in him, the flatness that came into his tone of voice, as well as in his words ('it did not matter'). This response to the interpretation is interesting. It is certainly a striking response, but not with the sort of relief expected. Instead, making him aware of the immediate (here-and-now) focus for his pain brought out an emotionally debilitating effect. Klein explained it as a strong and destructive defence:

> The patient split off those parts of himself, i.e. of his ego, which he felt to be dangerous and hostile towards the analyst. He turned his destructive impulses from his object *towards his ego*, with the result that parts of his ego temporarily went out of existence. In unconscious phantasy this amounted to annihilation of part of his personality. The particular mechanism of turning the destructive impulse against one part of his personality, and the ensuing dispersal of emotions, kept his anxiety in a latent state.

The destructiveness that he felt towards the analyst at first was too intense, or too immediate, or both. His frustration, envy and grievance turned away. But the crucial point is: they did not just disappear, as if they had never happened; rather, they left a debilitated person. He could no longer emotionally connect – 'he felt detached from the whole situation'. He experienced something as *not* mattering. Klein then attributed his feeling of a lack to an attack on his capacity to have his own feelings. And in particular she tells a specific story: if the attacks on the psychoanalyst – frustration, envy and grievance – disappear, they re-emerge, but in a quite different mode, as the attack on the self, a cause of the ego losing one of its functions.

This is the characteristic anxiety felt in these states: the fear for one's own integrity. Klein argued from such clinical material that the patient's unconscious phantasy is that he has annihilated a part of himself. It is not exactly the feeling that is obliterated so much as the capacity to have that feeling – he felt emotionally 'detached'. It is therefore, she argued, an attack upon the mind itself. This fear of annihilation from within is different from the paranoid fear of persecution by a bad object.[14] Potentially it could become a very terrifying experience, and Klein believed that when it reached a certain intensity it became the core terror driving schizophrenic psychosis.

We need further evidence to show that these states of something missing can in fact be conceived as an attack on the mind. We will need to distinguish such attacks from, for instance, repression. Repression renders parts of the mental contents unconscious; they are excluded from consciousness. In contrast, splitting in the paranoid-schizoid position removes a faculty of mind (part of the ego). An example of the way splitting and repression are contrasted in clinical material may be seen in the example of *The man who split off his aggression* (p. 125). In the next example we can see the deep splitting in the patient's personality which obliterates the capacity for self-awareness and therefore, in this instance, the capacity to make judgements.

Example: The woman who lost her capacity to need

In this example a dream actually pictures the self as having lost its capacity to know certain emotionally important things (represented as blindness). This woman patient was a manic-depressive who had greatly improved during the psychoanalysis. Klein reported that her mood cycles stopped as the psychoanalysis progressed, and her personality and object relations changed:

> Productivity on various lines developed, as well as actual feelings of happiness (not of a manic type). Then, partly owing to external circumstances, another phase set in. During this last phase, which continued for several months, the patient co-operated in the analysis in a particular way. She came regularly to the analytic sessions, associated fairly freely, reported dreams and provided material for analysis. There was, however, no emotional response to my interpretations and a good deal of contempt for them.

We must note the missing emotional responses, resembling the previous patient's transient states. This patient, too, had an awareness of her disability in these states, and called it her 'hide'. Instead of having her feelings, there was a characteristic aggression (contempt) towards the analyst for referring (in interpretations) to them. The emotional responses might, of course, be absent because the interpretations were simply wrong. However, the conscious contempt suggests that something was being done to the interpretations, which were not, therefore, insignificant:

> During this stage she decided to bring the analysis to an end. External circumstances contributed strongly to this decision and she fixed a date for the last session.

The conscious decision – to end the psychoanalysis – is in accord with the patient's conscious rejection of the importance of the analytic work. The reasons for terminating are apparently impeccably practical; it is possible, however, that other unconscious attitudes may lie concealed, and unconscious, behind the practical issue. For instance, could rejection of interpretations, and the apparent indifference to terminating, indicate a self-directed aggression that has obliterated her awareness of her emotional responses to the analysis? (That would correspond to the defences we examined in the previous patient.) In fact the contempt could represent that attack against her interpreted feelings. Can we check all this? In other words, has an unconscious reaction been obliterated, leaving only the conscious dismissal of her psychoanalysis? In fact a dream, reported on the day of the last session, illuminated this question:

> . . . there was a blind man who was very worried about being blind; but he seemed to comfort himself by touching the patient's dress and finding out how it was fastened. The dress in the dream reminded her of one of her frocks which was buttoned high up to the throat. The patient gave two further associations to this dream. She said, with some resistance, that the blind man was herself . . .

We can see that one of the figures in the dream seems to be a part of the patient herself, but it is clearly at this point an *estranged* part, since it figures in the dream as another person, the blind man:

> . . . and when referring to the dress fastened up to the throat, she remarked that she had again gone into her 'hide'.

This association connects her state of 'hide' with being buttoned-up, her emotionally shut-off state. However, the dream seems to convey that she was actually interested in this buttoned-up state – the blind man touched the fastening of the frock; that is to say, she was in fact very worried about it. Yet that worried awareness was quite missing from her conscious interests – blinded, as it were; and we could argue that it is the dream's way of representing the obliteration of a whole area of reactions:

> I suggested to the patient that she unconsciously expressed in the dream that she was blind to her own difficulties, and that the decisions with regard to the analysis as well as to various circumstances in her life were not in accordance with her unconscious knowledge. This was also shown by her admitting that she had gone into her 'hide', meaning by it that she was shutting herself off, an attitude well known to her from

previous stages in her analysis. Thus the unconscious insight, and even some co-operation on the conscious level (recognition that *she* was the blind man and that she had gone into her 'hide'), derived from isolated parts of her personality, only.

The dream seems to demonstrate how the structure of the patient's personality has divided: one part of her is blind to her need for her analysis, and is therefore terminating it; another part, which worries about and is aware of her 'hide' and shut-offness, and conscious of being worried, is relegated to a state of blindness, and out of touch with the rest of herself or with the analyst: 'It was not only that parts of her personality did not co-operate with me; they did not seem to co-operate with each other.' Her worries and her complacent decision to terminate analysis do seem to represent a genuine splitting of herself. They are too cut off from each other to form an ordinary mental conflict, since one seemed to be an entirely obliterated awareness – blind. Her capacity to see herself (i.e. her analysis) had been attacked, split off from useful contact with the rest of the personality, and to all intents and purposes annihilated; she became blind to the psychoanalytic investigation of her buttoning-up. Thus the patient, in effect, split off her capacity to remain aware of the internal reality of her feelings.

The quality of aggression involved in this process is also illustrated in the next example. A patient beset by extreme states of murderous aggression eventually resorts to violent phantasies revealed in a dream which 'kills' a 'child' part of her personality. A later example (*The man who was broadened out*, p. 105) describes these similar self-destructive mechanisms carried out to a more extreme degree at the root of the complete psychotic breakdown of the mind. The later understanding of these highly destructive relations with the self is conveyed in the example of *Perverse internal relations* (p. 199).

Example: The wicked child

Another briefly reported example of Klein's clearly shows how aggression is turned against a part of the self, killing or annihilating it. The split occurred within the self between a child part of the patient and the part that attempted to control the child:

> . . . a woman patient had dreamed that she had to deal with a wicked girl child who was determined to murder somebody. The patient tried to influence or control the child and to extort a confession from her

which would have been to the child's benefit; but she was unsuccessful. I also entered into the dream and the patient felt that I might help her in dealing with the child.

In the dream the child has to confess to somebody, and the patient came to her analyst; these two similar accounts suggest that it is two versions of the same person who confesses. Although in this instance Klein left out the associations to the dream, she concluded:

> The child, of course, stood also for various figures in the past, but in this context she mainly represented one part of the patient's self.

That wicked murderous child part of the patient must be controlled; it must also be confessed – that is to say, it must be brought to the analytic sessions for help. The psychoanalyst is needed to help in the patient's struggle with herself. The dream goes on with an increasing desperation:

> Then the patient strung up the child on a tree in order to frighten her and also prevent her from doing harm.

The progress of the dream threatens a violent solution to dealing with (killing off) the murderous impulses. It is a part of the self which is now threatened:

> When the patient was about to pull the rope and kill the child, she woke. During this part of the dream the analyst was also present but remained inactive.

Because the psychoanalyst seems inactive in the dream (it may represent the psychoanalyst being unavailable during the night) the patient felt, I think, that she was without help, and had therefore to resort to more violent attempts to control the child, that is, to kill it – in fact, to kill (obliterate) that part of her own personality. The dream therefore represented increasing despair about controlling herself; and as the situation became more desperate, the aggression became first more violent and primitive (from controlling to killing) and then, in the process, the patient turned away from murdering someone to the murder of a part of the self. The aggression was turned against *a part of the patient's own ego* – against the child part that was felt to be so 'bad'. Thus a severe attempt by the super-ego to repress the infantile aggression failed, and a primitive defence came into play: a splitting, obliterating attack upon that part of her.

That extreme defence of attacking the self was a measure of last resort against the states of intolerable aggression which the patient felt desperately unable to control. For the next patient, however – a schizophrenic – the deployment of self-destroying attacks on his own mind is no longer really a last-resort defence; it has become habitual. The schizophrenic is characterized by a fragmented mind, and his or her own fears about it.

Herbert Rosenfeld, one of Melanie Klein's students, analysed this schizophrenic patient in hospital. He found a splitting of the ego or self, but one that was not the rather clear split we have seen in the last few examples; instead, this was a shattering or fragmentation. Such multiple splitting seriously hampers mental functioning, to the point of becoming madness. It is typical of the schizophrenic personality that it is so damaged by these internal attacks on the self that a major degree of apathy and inertia results. The patient loses appropriate feelings as well as the capacity to think properly. This is different in degree from the kinds of patients reported above, in whom certain discrete, and defined, aspects of the ego were missing (no proper emotional response: *The man who lost his feelings*, p. 99; or the motivation for analysis appears to have been lost: *The woman who lost her capacity to need*, p. 101). The capacity for awareness has been so eroded by so many aspects being split off that the patient seems to lack any capacity to experience meaning in life at all. Typically, schizophrenics exist for long periods in states of apathy, emerging only with bizarre, and sometimes violent, manifestations when they are emotionally intruded upon.

Example: The man who was broadened out

In this example the patient appeared to make little contact with the psychoanalyst. He was a chronic schizophrenic whose mind was severely damaged in its capacity to sustain thought and communicate meaning. Before the session that follows, he had recently assaulted one of the nursing staff: he had attacked the Sister suddenly while he was having tea with her and his father, hitting her hard on the temple. She had been affectionately putting her arms around his shoulders at the time. The attack occurred on Saturday:

> I found him silent and defensive on Monday and Tuesday. On Wednesday he talked a little more. He said that he had destroyed the

whole world and later on he said, 'Afraid.' He added 'Eli' (God) several times.

Here we see the typical communication of a chronic schizophrenic – apathetic, disjointed and fragmented. It expresses the state he believes his mind is in. In a sense he has literally destroyed his world of meaning:

> When he spoke he looked very dejected and his head drooped on his chest. I interpreted that when he attacked Sister X he felt he had destroyed the whole world and he felt only Eli could put right what he had done.

It seems that meaning could in fact be restored to the fragmented words once it could be realized that recent events had affected the patient in an extreme (and apocalyptic) way. But should we agree with Rosenfeld? Did he find the right meaning:

> He remained silent.

That response does not immediately move us to accept the interpretation as valid. So Rosenfeld continued:

> After continuing my interpretation by saying that he felt not only guilty but afraid of being attacked inside and outside, he became a little more communicative. He said 'I can't stand it anymore.'

Rosenfeld revised his interpretation. He included feelings of the paranoid-schizoid position (fear) in addition to those of the depressive position (guilt). There seemed, then, to be a more direct moment of contact, a direct reply – 'I can't stand it anymore'. This was a strikingly emotional response, despairing. It now seemed, for the first time in this session, more appropriate. But the patient then returned to his disabling form of communication:

> Then he stared at the table and said, 'It's all broadened out, what are all the men going to feel?' I said that he could no longer stand the guilt and anxiety inside himself and had put his depression, anxiety and feelings, and also himself, into the outer world. As a result of this he felt broadened out, split up into many men, and he wondered what all the different parts of himself were going to feel.

This is an extraordinarily detailed interpretation derived from few or no associations. Perhaps it is the result of the analyst's intuition, or his prior knowledge of this pattern in the patient's experiences. It is a highly inventive interpretation, and depends for its inspiration partly upon the understanding of the manner in which splitting and projection occur in schizophrenic patients. Before checking it against the response, let me summarize the meaning that the interpretation attempted to restore. Rosenfeld elaborated the patient's communication into a coherent, albeit weird, phantasy: the persecuting situation with the nurse (for whatever reason) could be dealt with, *in extremis*, by turning a fragmenting aggression against the self; and then the resulting fragments of the self are spread out into many other objects. This phantasy is what he told the patient.

This phantasy, in which parts of the patient's self are projected, and located actually in an external object, is termed 'projective identification', and we will consider many more examples of this weird process in Chapter 8. It is a remarkably concrete phantasy that becomes a reality; the spreading of the patient's mind abroad does deplete him, makes him actually helpless, and renders his world of meaning fragmented and dispersed. The correctness of this surprising interpretation can be judged by the patient's ensuing response:

> He then looked at a finger of his which is bent and said, 'I can't do anymore, I can't do it all.'

Again we have a sudden communication of his heavy despair. It is direct and clear, filled with feeling; and it makes contact with the analyst and with us:

> After that he pointed to one of my fingers which is also slightly bent and said, 'I am afraid of this finger.'

A kind of identification has occurred; a part of the patient (his bent finger) is linked to a part of the analyst (who also has a bent finger). Rosenfeld took this as confirmation of his interpretation that something of the patient is discovered in an external object, *in* the analyst in this moment – that is, in his bent finger. But what part of the patient has he projected? What does the patient's finger represent?

> His own bent finger had often stood for his illness, and had become the representative of his own damaged self . . . I interpreted to him that he put himself and the problems he could not deal with inside me, and feared that he had changed me into himself, and also was now afraid of what I would give back to him.

The coincidence of the two bent fingers offers a peculiar, but effective, method of communicating. The patient felt that his mind was damaged, and his finger was an adequate way of representing that damaged part of him. The analyst's damaged finger also represented to the patient how he must indeed have evacuated his own damaged mind into the analyst. The bent finger had a kind of communicational function, and became actual concrete evidence for the patient of his projection into the analyst. That projection into the analyst's mind is as real for the patient as the blow he gave to Sister X's head. The schizophrenic assumes that it is his own damaged mind which, through projection, now occupies the analyst.[15]

The illness and helplessness now located in the psychoanalyst made the patient believe the psychoanalyst was disturbed as well – 'what is *this* man going to feel?'. Therefore Rosenfeld understood that the patient was frightened that his psychoanalyst was disturbed at that moment, and that he no longer had a helpful analyst. The patient also felt responsible for this debilitation of the psychoanalyst's help – now an object that had been damaged by his 'broadening out' (projection) into external objects:

> He replied with a remark which showed his anxiety that I might stop treatment and he added explicitly that he wished that I should continue seeing him.

It is evident that the patient remained in a communicative state of mind (conveying his worries explicitly). The remarkable change in the form of communication, and the evident increase in contact between patient and analyst, suggest that the interpretations were, on the whole, touching something important in the patient. The psychoanalyst was succeeding in restoring the patient's meaning, and thus his sense of having a mind and feelings; in addition, his capacity to communicate began to be restored. There is a clear process in which the interpretations elicit from the patient more material which enabled more meaning to be interpreted. We might summarize this:

> *Association*: his uncommunicative, dejected manner and frag-
>   mented words.
> *Interpretation*: the patient's attack had destroyed the world.
> *Association*: he was broadened out, and so on.
> *Interpretation*: the patient has projected parts of himself,
>   because of the fear following his attacks.
> *Association*: he points out his bent finger, and the analyst's.

Interpretation: the projection of damage and illness into the analyst.

Association: fear of damage to, and the loss of, the analyst.

Putting the patient's meaning back together into a coherent verbal communication allows the patient to make better efforts to understand himself and to communicate with the psychoanalyst.

One important feature of this kind of material is the striking employment of projection in contrast to the emphasis on introjection in the examples previous chapters. From the 1950s onwards, in fact, Kleinian psychoanalysis changed steadily towards understanding the importance and prevalence of disabling projective processes.

SCHIZOPHRENIC PROCESSES

Wilfred Bion continued Klein's and Rosenfeld's psychoanalytic investigations into schizophrenic patients. He emphasized that the subject (or ego) attacks a specific part of the self – the *capacity to perceive reality*.

Example: The man who lost his sight

Bion described a patient's struggle to convey, despite all the hampering of his mind due to the mutilating attacks upon his own capacities, what had happened to his perception:

> On this morning he arrived a quarter of an hour late and lay on the couch. He spent some time turning from one side to another, ostensibly making himself comfortable. At length he said: 'I don't suppose I shall do anything today. I ought to have rung up my mother.' He paused and then said: 'No; I thought it would be like this.' A more prolonged pause followed; then, 'Nothing but filthy things and smells', he said. 'I think I've lost my sight.' Some twenty-five minutes of our time had passed.

This fragmented communication of the schizophrenic patient may now be familiar. His capacity to communicate is almost lost. However, he did achieve a communication of helplessness, and also the self-attacking criticism. But particularly he reported the loss of his sight. Bion eventually made an interpretation, but not until after some considerable discussion of the material and past sessions, some of which I have transferred to an Appendix to this chapter. Eventually, the analyst tells us:

> I told him that these filthy things and smells were what he felt he had made me do, and that he felt he had compelled me to defecate them out, including the sight he had put into me.

This interpretation, unsupported here by the evidence from associations which I have excluded, describes the psychotic process: the disintegration of the ego under attack, and the removal into the analyst of a part of the patient's mind – his sight. This resembles Klein's patients (*The man who lost his feelings* and *The woman who lost her capacity to need*, pp. 99, 101) and the way Rosenfeld's patient in the last example put the damaged parts of his mind into the analyst – the 'broadening out' signified by the analyst's bent finger. In this patient's view, the analyst dealt with the projections into him by discharging these disturbing things out again as faeces or farts. That was the analyst's interpretation; in response,

> The patient jerked convulsively and I saw him cautiously scanning what seemed to be the air around him.

The patient certainly responded – as if the interpretation had physically impinged on him. This wariness led Bion to continue the interpretation:

> I accordingly said that he felt surrounded by bad and smelly bits of himself including his eyes which he felt he had expelled from his anus. He replied: 'I can't see.' I then told him he felt he had lost his sight and his ability to talk to his mother, or to me, when he got rid of these abilities so as to avoid pain.

In his original account Bion proceeded to describe material that gave an indication of what the patient 'sees' when he has dismantled his own sight. Instead of having a mind which is capable of seeing – capable of insight, and of making and containing meaning – this patient, like other schizophrenics, had a mind dedicated to 'evacuating' experiences. How Bion came to such conclusions is a complex process of psychoanalytic deduction, and may be best passed over on first reading of this chapter. An abbreviated account of it is, however, set out in the Appendix, though a reading of the original account by Bion might serve better. The following interpretations give us further views of the way the patient uses his mind to evacuate its contents or the damaged parts of himself. Let us follow the patient's response to Bion's interpretation that his sight had been split off, fragmented and expelled:

Patient. My head is splitting; may be my dark glasses.

Bion interposes that he himself had worn dark glasses on one occasion some months previously.

Analyst. Your sight has come back into you but splits your head; you feel it is very bad sight because of what you have done to it.

The patient has had to resume the pain of seeing, for which reason he had expelled it. The glasses – which, the patient implies, were responsible for his regaining his sight – can also represent the analyst, or at least the analyst's function of putting the meaning back into his experiences. The glasses thus represent a sight which he feels is bad (indicated as dark, to convey a bad, angry or retaliatory part of him which hurts him – darkened as faecal remains).

Patient (moving in pain as if protecting his back passage). Nothing.
Analyst. It seemed to be your back passage.
Patient. Moral strictures.
I told him that his sight, the dark glasses, were felt as a conscience that punished him, partly for getting rid of them to avoid pain, partly because he had used them to spy on me, and on his parents.

Like Rosenfeld's interpretations, these are inventive reconstructions of the processes disrupting the patient's mind. These are 'psychotic problems' and contrast with the more ordinary problems which act as pained stimuli to the psychotic. In fact Bion gave the next association as an indication of just such a problem – the prospect, for the patient, of enduring the thought of separation over the coming weekend. The patient continued:

The week-end; I don't know if I can last it.

As with Rosenfeld's patient, *The man who was broadened out* (p. 105), the patient can return to a much more ordinary contact:

This is an instance of the way in which the patient felt he had repaired his capacity for contact and could therefore tell me what was going on around him.

The analyst has effected some return of the parts of the patient's mind. Bion continues, in his account, to demonstrate how much it hurt the patient to have this contact again. The analyst's function of returning parts of the patient's mind in this way will be examined in detail in the next chapter.

ATTACKS ON LINKING

Bion later reconceptualized the attack on the self as one specifically directed at the capacity to make links – links within the mind, such as in 'putting two and two together'; or links between one mind and another; or links with reality through the perceptual apparatus. Difficulties in sustaining proper links within the internal states, and communicating them, in another of Bion's patients are described in the next example.

Example: The man who stammered

Bion's short account demonstrates the 'attacks on the links' the mind most frequently uses – between words:

> I had reason to give the patient an interpretation making explicit his feelings of affection and his expression of them to his mother for her ability to cope with a refractory child. The patient attempted to express his agreement with me, but although he needed to say only a few words his expression of them was interrupted by a very pronounced stammer which had the effect of spreading out his remark over a period of as much as a minute and a half.

We can see how Bion is viewing the stammer as a process in which the patient attacks and disrupts his own words. The patient has dismembered something – his initial agreement. This is somewhat similar to the fragmentary words of the chronic schizophrenic patient. The stammer separates the words, and the sounds, from one another. It is an extended occurrence of a self-directed aggression. He has attacked his own capacity to link words, and attacked words themselves as the links between his mind and someone else's (his analyst); and this seems to be brought out by making the patient aware of his grateful link with his mother. Bion considered these occurrences a manifestation of an attack on – and a near-annihilation of – a part of the patient's mind that could have perceived the meaning in the interpretation, and thus his capacity to communicate in response. Bion continues his report of this case with evidence that such an attack on the self is truly murderous, and that it raises a fear of death (in this case, drowning):

> The actual sounds emitted bore resemblance to gasping for breath; the gaspings were interspersed with gurgling sounds as if he were immersed in water. I drew his attention to these sounds and he agreed that they were peculiar and himself suggested the descriptions I have just given.

The deathly quality of suffocating and drowning is clear in the images that he and the patient produced. The utterance of these products (the stammer) is then an evacuation of the remains of words after their links have been murderously severed. In a way a communication does remain, but a communication of the desperate state the patient's mind is in, rather than its erstwhile contents.

Much of this splitting and fragmentation is associated, as we have seen in the examples in this chapter, with the processes of projection. The defensive processes in the paranoid-schizoid position – notably splitting and projection – create abnormal forms of identification; and, in turn, an internal state in which the personality is weakened by self-inflicted damage. This hampers the patient's attempt to establish the good internal object securely, and jeopardizes the stable core of well-being. It also renders the person weaker in facing the pained concern and guilt of the depressive position. These projective processes are the most important source of problems for the satisfactory introjection upon which a stable personality can develop. The formation of an identity upon an enduring sense of self and confidence is not available as a base from which the depressive position can later be approached.

So the major step to a more realistic relating to objects may not really get going, or a weak point is left to which the person reverts extremely quickly and intensely from the depressive-position feelings. Then the paranoid anxieties, object relations and defences of the paranoid-schizoid position become paramount once more. The person retains a propensity for serious disturbance, often psychotic. On the other hand, when the paranoid-schizoid position goes well, internal objects and the self are spared too much damage; the subject then has a foundation from which to advance with greater strength into the depressive position.

The kind of material reported by these psychoanalysts, typical of schizophrenic thought, is remarkable for the way the patients remained, in one non-psychotic part of their mind, partly aware (a damaged awareness) of what was happening. And that part, remaining capable of communicating, does continue to try to convey the state of those remnants of awareness. The patient's despair about reconstructing their mind needs a psychoanalyst capable of understanding and restoring the meaning and communication that have been destroyed. As the means of communication are profoundly hampered by the damage to the mind, the patient resorts typically to the abnormal, concrete form of symbolization that Bion calls the ideogram (see the Appendix to this chapter).

Rosenfeld's work and Bion's later elaborations contrast with Freud's earlier view that schizophrenics do not form a relationship with the analyst. They do; but it is a very peculiar relationship. Bion described its double quality: while one part of the patient (the psychotic part) destroys their world of meaning and seeks to reconstruct it in line with mad delusions, another part (which remains non-psychotic) seeks a link with the psychoanalyst despite the fragmenting, disjointing and hampering attacks. Later in his life Freud did predict something of this kind of splitting:

> Even in a state so far removed from the reality of the external world as one of hallucinatory confusion, one learns from patients after their recovery that at the time in some corner of their mind (as they put it) there was a normal person hidden, who, like a detached spectator, watched the hubbub of illness go past him. (Freud, 1940, pp. 201–2)

In the cases we have examined here, one part of the patient remains struggling to link up with the analyst and use him or her as a depository for aspects of the patient's mind which are felt to be hopelessly damaged or destroyed – the illness represented as the bent finger in Rosenfeld's example, the damaged sight in Bion's. This form of relating, in which the patient puts damaged aspects of the self *into* the psychoanalyst, is an important discovery which tipped Kleinian research towards concentrating, in latter years, on projective processes.

Bion's work also profoundly affected the way Kleinian analysts approach the patient's communications. Different patients – and different parts of the same patient – communicate in different ways: 'The non-psychotic personality was concerned with a neurotic problem, that is to say a problem that centred on the resolution of the conflict of ideas and emotions to which the operation of the ego had given rise. But the psychotic personality was concerned with the problem of repair of the ego . . . ' (Bion, 1957, p. 56). Kleinian practice was changed for ever by the realization that the patient is communicating more than a disguised message – he or she is communicating a plea for help with a mind that is no longer capable of the important messages, disguised or otherwise.

In the next chapter we will consider more of this research on the disruption of the integrity of the mind (of the ego, or the self).

APPENDIX: THE MIND AS AN APPARATUS FOR EVACUATION

Bion has interpreted to his patient, *The man who lost his sight* (p. 109), that 'he felt he had lost his sight and his ability to talk to his mother, or to me, when he got rid of these abilities so as to avoid pain'. He had made the patient jerk physically when he had put together the patient's evacuation of his sight through the anus into the analyst, who then also evacuated it.

The background to Bion's interpretations to this patient derived from previous psychoanalytic sessions, which he explained to the reader. In those sessions, Bion had been concentrating on the patient's movements on the couch, which were characteristic all through the psychoanalysis. In an earlier session Bion had recalled that many years before, the movements were connected with a hernia the patient had; but more recently responses to queries about the movements had generally elicited the comment: 'Nothing' – meaning 'Mind your own business'. Bion noticed, however, that he had recently remarked 'Nothing' about a dream he had just reported, and connected it with the 'nothing' he knew about the movements. To this the patient had agreed, and when Bion pushed him further, reminding him that he had once known that the movements were to do with a hernia, he had added, 'That's nothing'. This kind of thinking, using words in a more literal, concrete way, is confusing. This idiosyncratic use of the word 'nothing' resembles Peter's use of the phrase 'No, that's not nice' in the example *Inhibited play* (p. 39) – though Peter's was a rather less bizarre way of expressing himself.

'That's nothing' indicates that there is something that is equivalent or reduced to nothing. In the case in point, the patient refers to the hernia that the analyst had just mentioned. So Bion completed the deduction – 'Nothing is really a hernia'. The patient replied, 'No idea, only a hernia'. Bion is explaining that the 'nothing' or 'no idea' which keeps being introduced into the associations has a special meaning. The word 'nothing' is being used in place of the word 'hernia', which itself connects with some idea of expulsion of anal refuse. Thus the 'nothing' and 'no idea' are the end result of evacuating something, or an idea, through his hernia (anus). In Bion's view this is particularly characteristic of schizophrenics. He called these condensed uses 'ideograms' rather than words.

As, in fact, the patient himself says, it is not, strictly speaking, an idea – that is, 'no idea'; and he was not intending to use his mind to contain and think about things. However, the patient went on trying to convey what his hernia, and his movements, meant, in the form of a very concrete picture. Similarly, Rosenfeld's patient had used the bent finger as a very idiosyncratic attempt to indicate madness and damage he had done. Such a picture, an ideogram, is not visual so much as one which is more *felt* by the analyst – in Bion's case it was a sense of going flat, emptying of meaning. When the patient said 'That's nothing' in response to the link he mentioned between the movement and the hernia, he obliterated the meaningfulness of the insight. But in addition, the ideogram conveyed something more; in fact it could also be made to convey the patient's own despair about his analyst. It communicated his expectation that the analyst would merely produce some filthy dirty (faecal) remnants of something which the patient had lodged into the analyst.

The patient's 'nothing' and 'no idea' comments represented the gaps, the emptiness, the absences of some ego-functions (like sight or meaning) which had been removed (split off), annihilated through anal expulsion like damaged faecal contents of the bowel (hernia). There is a direct correspondence between Bion's description of faecal expulsion and the kind of material Abraham reported from his manic-depressive patients, who equated the use of the anus with the mental expulsion of loved ones.

Bion elaborated a theory of two divergent routes for the development of the human mind. One was to develop as an 'apparatus' for having or containing thoughts; the other was to develop as an apparatus for evacuating them. The latter is the psychotic's predicament. The psychotic patient has lost so much of the mind through the evacuation of parts of it with his or her disposed-of experiences that she or he is almost incapable of continued mental activity. This process severely hampers the process of recovery itself. Another of Bion's examples of this ideogrammatic form of communication was his patient who said:

'I don't know what I mean', [Bion assumed he was] talking articulate English. It took me a long time to realize that he was not, but when, after six months, I did, the experience was instantaneous. *He* was an ideogram. *He* was something that ought to have reminded me of a person lying on the couch. The person had a meaning and I could say to him, 'You do not know what you mean; but you expect *me* to know that when I see someone lying on a couch, two people have been having sexual intercourse'. What the patient 'meant' was that his parents, or two people, had been having sexual intercourse. (Bion, 1974, p.13)

The willingness to suspend judgement on the apparent meaning, the willingness not to allow oneself to 'know' what the patient meant in the ordinary sense, produced a new knowledge from the 'ideogrammatic' communication. Bion translated the 'I' as indicating the patient's very existence, his body lying on the couch. His existence means something: it means that sexual intercourse has happened (between his parents). It is that intercourse which the patient is then intent on *not* knowing. His capacity for destroying his knowing is indicated in the ideogram – 'I don't know . . . ', and so on – but it is also indicated in his inability to use words in the ordinary sense, and their subsequent employment in the 'meaninglessness' of ideogrammatic communication. The meaning is, as it were, 'there is no meaning'. It is the end result of a destruction of the capacity to generate meaning.

8 PROJECTIVE IDENTIFICATION

In 1946, Klein reflected on the crises of anger and hatred that she had witnessed in children and infants. These crises had many forms, but one

> line of attack derives from the anal and urethral impulses and implies expelling dangerous substances (excrements) out of the self and into the mother. Together with these harmful excrements, expelled in hatred, split-off parts of the ego are also projected onto the mother or, as I would rather call it, *into* the mother. These excrements and bad parts of the self are meant not only to injure but also to control and to take possession of the object. (Klein, 1946, p. 8)

Klein called this phenomenon 'projective identification'. The schizoid and psychotic patients in the last chapter supplied many examples. In the example of *The man who was broadened out* (p. 105), for instance, the patient felt his personality, or self, to be 'broadened out' across a number of external objects which came to represent separated parts of himself. In that process his mind had been attacked, damaged or split, then the parts had been dealt with, in phantasy, by projection.

Klein described this as the prototype of the earliest aggressive relationship. But: 'In so far as the mother comes to contain the bad parts of the self, she is not felt to be a separate individual but is felt to be *the* bad self' (Klein, 1946, p. 8). These phantasies of relocated parts of the self are connected with anal impulses, the evacuation of faeces. But for the infant, they are narratives, unconscious phantasies that are real. The infant believes in them completely. Part of the infant actually is in some other object that is outside the ego boundaries – that is to say, *inside* an external object. There is then a peculiar identity. The infant *is*, in a way, the external object. That object (say, its mother) *is* the infant, rather than merely the infant's.

These beliefs become decisive. The subject believes either that the part is lost – then she or he actually comes to feel depleted, as in the examples of *The man who lost his feelings* and *The woman who lost her capacity to need* (pp. 99, 101) – or that the external object is experienced as part of the self and annexed to the self (*The man who was broadened out*). Phantasies which are believed in so strongly as to affect the real state of relationships are called 'omnipotent'. These phantasies are the counterpart of the equally 'omnipotent' ones in which an external object is felt to be physically installed as an internal object (see Chapter 5). These phantasy processes often occur with the expenditure of a great deal of aggression, but the strength of belief ensures that the object is feared as if it were actually such an embodiment, in reality, of the aggression.

The problem is to capture what this sort of experience amounts to: what does it feel like? Klein was quite pessimistic about grasping, verbalizing and communicating these experiences, because 'description of such primitive processes suffers from a great handicap, for these phantasies arise at a time when the infant has not yet begun to think in words' (Klein, 1946, p. 8, footnote). Nevertheless, our purpose is to take a stab at giving some idea of these experiences; or at least to depict how psychoanalysts come upon them. The next patient's material conveys something of the experience (conscious or unconscious) of expelling.

Example: The object as lavatory

Herbert Rosenfeld described a psychotic patient, a paranoid man who had elated periods of intense homosexual activity:

> . . . there is a memory of excitedly riding on his father's knee combined with a fantasy of defecating in his own knickers on these occasions, without his father knowing this. Before this memory appeared he frequently felt very anxious and depressed about certain thoughts and feelings which he had in his mind.

I have selected this example for the clear evidence of anal function, defecation; father's lap is related to as if it were a lavatory:

It was sufficient for him to tell me what he had in his mind to feel relieved and elated.

The connection is provocative – between the relief of expressing himself in words, to the analyst, and his childhood expulsion of faeces into his father's lap. There seems to be a relieving phantasy that part of him (mentally part of his mind; or bodily what is in his rectum) could actually be relocated:

It seemed that he relieved himself of his depression by the process of expelling it into me (projection) as if he had defecated into me. He himself related this transference process to anal processes.

He seemed to react – with the same emotional state – as if part of his mind (one that is anxious and depressed) could be evacuated as concretely as defecating in the lavatory. The patient's talking serves a similar excited function to relieving himself on the lavatory:

We realized also that, apart from the obvious anal projection mechanism, in addition he had sexual fantasies of forcing his penis into me during these periods of elation.

We have to appreciate that this man's phantasy of forcible entry has various modes – the forcing of faeces into father/lavatory; the talking to, and putting words into, the psychoanalyst; and the excited homosexual phantasy of entering the analyst's anus with his penis. These variants on a basic phantasy recur in various imaginative forms for this man:

After each such occasion where he seemed to expel some material in the way I described, he first felt elated, but afterwards the persecution by his voices increased . . . It was found that he was terrified after he had expelled his thought material and that therefore he detached himself completely from any interpretation which I tried to make, as if he feared that something awful was being forced back into him by me.

The aggressive quality of these entering phantasies (projective identification) frightened him and made him fear that the analyst would *actually* retaliate in kind – by forcing something faecal, aggressive and excited into him; and he could not distinguish an interpretation from that aggressive intrusion. This becomes a cycle of fear, familiar to us as the paranoid cycles in Klein's descriptions of her child patients (Chapter 4); this patient's own active forcing something of himself into people – there to dominate, use and empty them – recurred as a fear of being subjected to the same treatment from the person to whom he had done it.

Rosenfeld reported another schizophrenic patient who believed she could dispose of unwanted aspects of her personality into other people. At first the analyst describes the projection of her sexual feelings, but later more radical and disastrous phantasies of this kind occur.

Example: Occupying the object

Rosenfeld's patient was feeling very insecure at this time, and often other people seemed to represent parts of herself:

> To give a short example of this process: Denis, the husband of her best friend, had a nervous breakdown while he was separated from his wife, who was expecting her second child. He tried his best to seduce my patient. At first she had great difficulty in controlling him. The wish to take him away from his wife soon came up as a conscious impulse, but it did not seem that she had any difficulty in coping with this wish directly. Her whole anxiety turned on whether she could control *his* wishes and arguments. She repeated some of his arguments to me, and it was clear that Denis stood for her own greedy sexual wishes which she had difficulty in dealing with and which she therefore projected on to him.

By comparing the nature of the arguments, Rosenfeld could see how Denis's sexual advances represented the patient's own, yet she believed that they actually were his. Certain states of mind (insistent sexual feelings) were difficult for this patient. It seemed that as a result of locating them in Denis, she could more effectively cope with them at this distance, and if necessary avoid them altogether through evading him.

At times this patient showed another – and remarkable – form of projective identification. As we have just seen, she could experience part of herself split off and located in an external object; but in the next material it is more than that: at times she could locate the whole of herself there. It was bizarre and perplexing for the analyst to try to understand. Rosenfeld described it through the patient's account of her experiences:

> . . . another symptom reappeared which she had mentioned only once before at the height of the psychotic state. She felt that she was swelling up like a balloon twelve times her own size. At the same time she felt she was only a tiny self inside this balloon. My patient described this state as most unpleasant and the only clue she gave me was that

expectancy had something to do with it. If she expected something from another person or from herself, or someone wanted something from her, this symptom greatly increased.

Rosenfeld added that he found himself reminded of a period in this psychoanalysis when the patient had an acute paranoid fear about the analyst; whenever he spoke to her or expected her to speak, she believed he would force himself into her. It seems that being needy (as in the instance of sexual neediness) had extreme, and literally mind-blowing, results. Neediness – the experience of expecting something which has not yet arrived – is one of those experiences that cannot be contained by this woman. Instead it has for her quite other – and bizarre – connotations of intruding and being intruded upon. However, at this point in the session she was also capable of knowing more consciously how she bound herself to her fiancé:

> . . . she now realized that she did not want her fiancé to go abroad. The frustration connected with his going had stirred up her greedy aggressive wishes. They had taken the form of fantasies in which she forced her way into him to compel him to do what she wanted and at the same time she felt she was emptying him of all that was good in him. The result of this greedy aggressive attack was that she felt herself to be inside him.

We are asked to envisage a rather extraordinary experience: not just that she projected parts of her mind into his, but that she seemed to have located the whole of herself forcibly inside her fiancé in order to commandeer the whole of him for herself:

> The sensation of the big balloon was connected with the fact that the object she had forced herself into was dead, emptied through her oral demands and full of air through her anal controlling attacks. She felt dead through her projective identification with the object.

Rosenfeld describes these as real 'facts' for the patient, however phantastical they may appear to us. Once she had entered and taken over the object, she actually became the object's identity as far as she was concerned. And in this case it was an alarming identity, as her fiancé seemed to her to have been rendered dead by the aggressive phantasy of greedily devouring him. She is inside him; he is dead.

These phantastical beliefs are not conscious, though the end results – like terror, or feeling dead – may indeed appear as conscious feelings while the phantasies from which they arise remain hidden and unconscious. Let us seek confirmation of Rosenfeld's powerful interpretation of these weird phantasies in her reaction to it:

> ... she went into a long silence and then I wondered whether she could cope with what I had pointed out. At last she could speak again and said that she had felt immediately that my interpretations were right, but, with that realization, she had become so tired that she had lost consciousness for a few minutes; nevertheless had managed to get out of the state again by herself. We understood that this reaction was a confirmation of my interpretation and that this state of unconsciousness and complete loss of herself was connected with a fear of going completely into me and losing herself there.

The analyst feels confident that his interpretation of how the whole of the patients's self disappears was confirmed by the occurrence actually in the session – disappearing into the analyst this time. Having disappeared into the object, she lost consciousness – meaning, we understand, that she had lost her identity:

> It struck me then that her present fear of losing her feelings and the depersonalization were only quantitatively different from the complete loss of herself in the schizoid state of disintegration. If in her greedy desires she felt that she completely entered into another object, she either went to sleep or felt severely split up. If smaller parts underwent the same process she still retained the awareness of herself and was only aware of loss of feelings.

From Rosenfeld's patient we have learned something important: projective identification varies in degree – losing part of herself or losing all of her. This realization of various kinds of projective identification has been immensely important in the more recent development of Kleinian practice.

Another variation in projective identification occurs in one of Klein's cases. In this next example there is a variation in the distance to which the lost part is sent. In this case the degree of distortion of the personal identity is proportional to the degree of violence in the underlying phantasy.

Example: The man who split off his aggression

Klein's patient moderated the degree of projective identification during the course of a dream:

> . . . [he] reported the following dream, which shows the fluctuations in the process of integration caused by the pain of depressive anxieties. He was in an upstairs flat and 'X', a friend of a friend of his, was calling him from the street suggesting a walk together.

You may be familiar with the 'friend of a friend' as a common representation of the dreamer himself, and thus of a part of the patient's personality – a part that has been split off, disowned and located outside his own boundaries (in the street). We can then see that the invitation to walk together was an attempt at integration of the two parts:

> The patient did not join 'X', because a black dog in the flat might get out and be run over. He stroked the dog. When he looked out of the window, he found that 'X' had receded.

If you have conceded the symbolic meanings I suggested, then the integration attempted in the dream was not successful. One part of the patient, X, removed itself to a greater distance – the projection increased. What are these parts of the personality which are split apart in this way, and why do they grow further apart in the dream ('X' receding)? Klein reported associations that linked the dog, and also a cat, to the psychoanalyst. She continued:

> . . . the danger to the dog-cat – the analyst – was that she would be run over (that is to say, injured) by 'X' . . . The patient's concern with the safety of the dog-cat expressed the wish to protect the analyst against his own hostile and greedy tendencies, represented by 'X', and led to a temporary widening of the split that had already been partly healed.

Klein deduced that X represented the patient's aggression, notably towards the analyst. Then, to protect the psychoanalyst (and it is the psychoanalyst he carries inside him – *in* the flat), he employs his affectionate feelings – stroking the dog – and to do that he has to make a bigger split from his aggression (X receding into the distance).

The removal of the 'aggression' to a distance indicates increasing mental disturbance even though the patient may be less aggressive in his behaviour. The splitting is itself harmful to the mind, though from the patient's point of view it may seem that losing aggressive impulses is very beneficial. The patient fears his aggression as the really overwhelming thing from which he may not recover; or rather, his object may not survive it. Sending it away in this manner may be protective of the object, and also protective of the patient. However, because of the violent splitting of the mind that is entailed, it is destructive of the person's own integrity. To summarize the elements of this process in the example: the patient deals with his destructiveness by splitting it off (calling it 'X' instead of himself); and he has projected it outside himself (outside the flat); when he glimpsed it (X's invitation to a walk) he was frightened by his destructiveness, and that he might injure the analyst (run over the analyst); so he reassured himself that he loved her (stroked the dog); and to protect her and his loving feelings he projected his own destructiveness further away ('X' receded).

Projective identification is a method that varies; it is a whole set of unconscious phantasies, and it is associated with various degrees of splitting, of violence and of omnipotence; and with various intentions. An approach towards a greater respect for the awareness of the internal world implies a lessening of the degree of violence in the process. When the splitting is less, there is more realization of the identity of 'X', the friend of a friend. The projective identification in this example is less aggressive. It contrasts strikingly with the much more violent obliteration that is evident in previous examples we have discussed. Nevertheless, the location of the part of the patient as *outside* the place of the self, clearly described in the dream, still crucially stamps this as a splitting and projective identification. At the beginning of the dream, 'X' approaches the subject, and the invitation to walk suggests the beginnings of integration of the personality; it indicates a movement towards an arrangement more like re-pression, in which the parts may begin to live together. In Klein's terms, as personal development takes place, the nature of the projective identification changes. The understanding that violent forms of projective identification may be modified, and how that is connected with a movement towards the depressive position, has been one of the major developments in recent Kleinian psychoanalysis.

Correlated with this change in the degree and in the violence of the phantasy, there are a multitude of motives for a projective identification. A complete catalogue has yet to be compiled, but we have seen some of the broad categories: evacuation of intolerable experiences; disposal of unwanted, intolerable functions of the mind, especially those presenting reality; a defence against separation from an object – or against acknowledging a difference from it – so that the object is invaded and occupied instead; retaining the experience of omnipotence through sustaining the control over others' minds. Others include the projection of good parts of the self into an object where they may be kept safer; and finally the circumstances that have given a special thrust to recent Kleinian research and practice, a form of projective identification as *communication* which gives the experience of being 'contained'.

PROJECTIVE IDENTIFICATION AND COMMUNICATION

During the 1950s, several Kleinian analysts had begun to describe a form of projective identification that seemed to be not so closely linked with obliteration and aggression. It had different aims from the earlier examples in this chapter.

Example: The mother who could not understand

Bion summarized some material that gave a vivid reconstruction:

> The analytic situation built up in my mind a sense of witnessing an extremely early scene. I felt that the patient had witnessed in infancy a mother who dutifully responded to the infant's emotional displays. The dutiful response had in it the element of impatient 'I don't know what's the matter with the child.'

We are invited to imagine a mother who is at a loss to understand her baby's state, but we must particularly consider the baby's experience of that mother.

> My deduction was that in order to understand what the child wanted the mother should have treated the infant's cry as more than a demand for her presence. From the infant's point of view she should have taken into her, and thus experienced, the fear that the child was dying.

From this we gather that mother is a person who is needed by the baby to introject, and know about, the baby's projected part:

> It was this fear that the child could not contain for himself. He strove to split it off together with the part of the personality in which it lay and project it into mother. An understanding mother is able to experience the feeling of dread that this baby was striving to deal with by projective identification, and yet retain a balanced outlook.

The patient demands a particular role for projective identification – as a form of *communication*. It is not merely for expelling. Projective identification can retain meaning of a kind, and mother is supposed to pick up that meaning. Despite the retained meaning, projective identification nevertheless performs some evacuative function. Mother is confronted with this difficulty: she must receive a projective identification of something the baby cannot tolerate and has needed to evacuate; but without being overwhelmed by it. As in this case, however, she cannot always do it:

> This patient has had to deal with a mother who could not tolerate experiencing such feelings and reacted either by denying them ingress, or alternatively by becoming a prey to the anxiety which resulted from introjection of the infant's feelings.

We can recognize that something similar is also sought in psychoanalysis. A psychoanalyst also needs to 'contain' what the patient cannot tolerate in order to begin to understand it. The patient strives for an experience of an object that does cope with the projected part of him- or herself. This goes beyond a mere expulsive projection, an evacuation. The patient's phantasy of mother (and psychoanalyst) struggling with their anxieties in this way, and longing for mother/analyst to perform a particular activity upon them, is quite different from the uninhibited aggression of forcing destroyed parts of the mind upon a hated external object (for example *The man who lost his sight* and *The object as lavatory*, pp. 109, 120).

Projective identification often does cause some impact on the other person. When a baby cries, for instance, its mother is instantly alerted. Alarmed, she assesses what the meaning of the cry is, and then endeavours to meet whatever need or mood the cry represents. It is not too exaggerated to say that mother does often feel that it is a panic in her infant; then she has to face that, with rising panic in herself. Indeed, how mothers can be so attuned to a baby in this way is a mystery; there may be something inherently biological in the response to a baby's cry. We see the way in which people in a bus queue or in a shop, for instance, do get anxious when a crying child is present.

Of course, as with the forms of evacuation we saw in Chapter 7, there is still a splitting of the patient's mind (or the infant's) when it projects into mother or analyst for these purposes. It still entails a turning of the aggression against the ego, splitting off a part of it and projecting it into an external object. Also, as we shall see in the next example from Bion, the force of this kind of projection may also be very violent. The last example, however, seems to be a primitive method of generating meaning, or at least of recruiting the assistance of a maternal mind to help to make meanings. It involves a potential to think, and to generate that capacity. A psychoanalysis involves the restoration of that capacity to communicate, to raise it to a symbolic level in creating vivid images together. At times this capacity has to be preserved by the psychoanalyst's own mind, and can be given back to the patient (the psychoanalyst reprojects it; the patient reintrojects it). Such a process has come to be known as *containing*, and its form in the psychoanalytic setting will be investigated in Chapter 10. Bion's idea of containing is one elaboration of his notion of linking (see Chapter 7). The link between container and contained is an event in which one thing is inserted inside another – with various kinds of emotional colour, and consequences. Containing includes the link between mother and child, or analyst and patient; it is also clearly associated with the activity between a woman and a man.

CONTAINING

The patient's intention is to project parts of their mind into the analyst's mind, and 'if they were allowed to repose there long enough they would undergo modification by my psyche and could then be safely introjected' (Bion, 1959, p. 103). This is quite an extended phantasy. It includes an external object; one that has a mind to receive; one which can modify experiences; and then the experiences, once modified, can be reintrojected. So two different groups of phantasies are involved in the two different kinds of projective identification. In the violent expulsive form the part of the mind expelled is meaningless and completely rejected; the state of the object is not considered. In the communicative form, on the other hand, there are specific qualities: a willingness to relax omnipotence and, to some degree, a willingness to grant a dependency upon an object that can perform certain functions.

Bion became aware of the communicative kind of phantasy from occasions when it failed (as in the last example) – the object did not always allow the part of the patient to repose long enough inside. The patient is acutely aware that the object (psychoanalyst) may or may not allow the use of this mechanism to contain anxiety and to modify it for the patient.

Example: The cheated patient

Bion's patient whom we met in the previous example was notable for his use of projective identification, which he practised

> ... with a persistence suggesting it was a mechanism of which he had never been able sufficiently to avail himself; the analysis afforded him the opportunity for the exercise of a mechanism of which he had been cheated. I did not have to rely on this impression alone.
>
> When the patient strove to rid himself of fears of death which were felt to be too powerful for his personality to contain he split off his fears and put them into me, the idea apparently being that if they were allowed to repose there long enough they would undergo modification by my psyche and could then be safely reintrojected. On the occasion I have in mind the patient had felt . . . that I evacuated them so quickly that the feelings were not modified but had become more painful.

If the object – analyst or mother – does not allow and tolerate being used like this, a disastrous sequence ensues:

> Consequently he strove to force them into me with increased desperation and violence. His behaviour, isolated from the context of analysis, might have appeared to be an expression of primary aggression. The more violent his phantasies of projective identification, the more frightened he became of me. There were sessions in which such behaviour expressed unprovoked aggression . . .

The appearance of this projective identification was simply aggressive, but it was not as it seemed; the need was for an understanding object:

> ... but I quote this series because it shows the patient in a different light, his violence a reaction to what he felt was my hostile defensiveness.

The failure of the container is an important instance for understanding the kinds of things that can go wrong with the development of the mind. It may be one source of aggression, flaring in the face of an impenetrable object. The psychoanalyst must carefully distinguish this frustrated aggression – his or her own failure to take in the patient's projection – from the aggression that seeks to attack links.

Example: The patient's failed container

In the next example Bion describes another patient's sensitivity to whether parts of himself are being contained for him:

> The session . . . began with three or four statements of fact such as that it was hot, that his train was crowded, and that it was Wednesday; this occupied thirty minutes. An impression that he was trying to retain contact with reality was confirmed when he followed up by saying that he feared a breakdown.

There is a desultory kind of communication, though it is clear that it is not as meaningless as the schizophrenic's. However, the patient is actually preoccupied with his fears about breaking down. His despair mounted:

> A little later he said I would not understand him. I interpreted that he felt I was bad and would not take in what he wanted to put into me.

Bion added, as an aside in his account, that this interpretation was guided by material in the previous session, when the patient had felt that the interpretations were an attempt to eject feelings that he wished to deposit in the psychoanalyst:

> I interpreted in these terms deliberately because he had shown in the previous session that he felt that my interpretations were an attempt to eject feelings that he wished to deposit in me. His response to my interpretation was to say that there were two probability clouds in the room.

We could wonder at this point whether or not the response

confirms the interpretation. Clearly the analyst thought that the probability clouds represented just what he had pictured – fragmented remnants of the patient's uncertainty (probability) about the analyst which had been evacuated into the air around the patient. Consequently, the psychoanalyst attempted to reconstruct this meaning (the patient's uncertainty):

> I interpreted that he was trying to get rid of the feeling that my badness was a fact. I said it meant that he needed to know whether I was really bad or whether I was some bad thing which had come from inside him. . . . I thought the patient was attempting to decide whether he was hallucinated or not.

The psychoanalyst has succeeded in reconstructing sufficient meaning in the sequence of utterances – I could summarize it as: the patient feared a breakdown; because he could not bear the uncertainty of his fear, he fragmented it, as well as the object he was uncertain about; he then evacuated it and the part of his mind that could have appreciated uncertainty (probability); then he further experienced a breaking down, this time of the object he needed inside him to hold him together (contain and understand him):

> This recurrent anxiety in his analysis was associated with his fear that envy and hatred of a capacity for understanding was leading him to take in a good, understanding object to destroy and eject it.

This kind of material from a session suggests that the good internal object on which security and mental stability rest (see *Identifying with a 'good' object*, p. 71) has a specific function – to contain emotional states, as the external mother or analyst does – and it is built up from them by introjecting them as internal objects. In this case destructive phantasies, deriving from envy, damaged the containing object that had been internalized, leading to the anxiety of going to pieces. It is a different aggression from the frustration of not gaining access. When, however, the patient projected his damaged internal object (internal container), he could not tell if the external container actually failed, or if he was just expressing his projection of the state of his internal container. The actual interpretation given now concerned the patient's doubts about the analyst himself. This difficulty was understood and carried – contained – by the psychoanalyst in the interpretation.

NAMELESS DREAD

The rejection of a projective identification is a serious disturbance for the patient who is already beyond the limits of what can be tolerated:

> If the projection is not accepted by the mother the infant feels that its feeling that it is dying is stripped of such meaning as it has. It therefore reintrojects, not a fear of dying made tolerable, but a nameless dread. (Bion, 1962a, p. 116)

In this process Bion is describing a particularly persecuting object – a 'bizarre object' which appears to strip meaning away rather than add or restore it.

Projective identification, an intrapsychic process, seems to be a central and crucial element in making emotional contact with other beings who also sustain an intrapsychic world. In this sense it functions as a form of communication, a non-symbolic one – not just preverbal, but pre-symbolic. Despite its extremely early occurrence in infants, it seems to depend on the infant already having an assumption that the object has a mind too. It may indicate that once mental life starts, it has an entirely mentalistic base – everything is a mind. A concrete, physical reality develops only as a later awareness. This confounds more usual notions of the development of mind: from an earlier stage of physical perceptions towards a sensitivity to other minds at a much later, more mature level. (Of course it may be wiser at this stage to retain an agnostic stance on the actual nature of the newborn infant's mind!)

If projective identification varies from expulsion to communication, then at the very furthest point on the benign end of the scale is a form of projective identification underlying empathy, or 'putting oneself in another's shoes'. Empathy occurs without serious distortions to the identity of either the subject or the object. In this case the violence of the primitive forms has been so attenuated that it has been brought under the control of impulses of love and concern. It is true, of course, that empathic enquiry can on occasions – or for certain people – be felt as intrusive, and may even become intentionally so if the object of enquiry is uncooperative.

Thus a process of maturation in the forms of projective identification can be plotted on a continuum:

-the violent 'prototype of the aggressive relationship'
-a more benign form intending to communicate with another
mind
-empathy, or a non-violating entering into someone else's mind
for the purpose of understanding them.

This continuum demonstrates how close this journey is to the
parallel movment in the attainment of the depressive position, and
its capacity for concern; both transitions are, of course, connected.

In the next chapter I shall turn to Klein's last important
discovery, which involved very early aspects of the aggression that
has permeated so many of the examples so far; and the processes
by which aggression gradually becomes changed by, and suffused
in, loving impulses.

9 THE DEATH INSTINCT AND ENVY

We have seen that the intensity of destructive impulses was among Klein's most important early discoveries. These impulses troubled children because, in their play, aggression might outbalance the loving, sexual and positive affects and impulses (libido). Because of this emphasis on the aggression found in the material of young children and schizophrenics, Klein and her followers took Freud's theory of the death instinct (Freud, 1920) seriously: *The death instinct is the hatred of life*. Freud's view of a fundamental and inherent clash between the life and death instincts meant that every individual has to struggle with a wish for life against a deathly wish to return to a state of disintegration, the silence of the grave. Hanna Segal (Segal, 1993) drew attention to a passage at the end of Jack London's *Martin Eden*. The main character, Martin, committed suicide by drowning, and as he did so he automatically tried to swim. The novel described how 'It was the automatic instinct to live. He ceased swimming, but the moment he felt water rising above his mouth, his hands struck out sharply with a lifting movement. "This is the will to live" he thought and the thought was accompanied by a sneer' (quoted in Segal, 1993, p. 55). The sneer, vividly captured by London, dramatically points to the hatred of life, the disdain and contempt the character felt for that wish to go on living: '"The will to live" he thought disdainfully.' As the character, Martin, drowned, the author described a tearing pain in the chest: '"The hurt was not death" was the thought that oscillated through his reeling consciousness. It was life – the pangs of life – this awful suffocating feeling. It was the last blow life could deal him.' In Freud's view, that struggle formed the bedrock challenge upon which all individual development is founded. The death instinct is a drive towards death itself, and attacks the life of the subject and the wish to live it. The death instinct is the primordial self-directed form of destructiveness. It is a factor to be considered in all self-destructive and self-harming attitudes. Causing pain and harm to the self has been encountered before, in Chapter 7, with the material from disturbed and schizophrenic patients.

From the first immediate moments of life, the death instinct becomes modified. Klein believed that one of the infant's first moves is from the

> . . . fear of an internal instinctual danger . . . it would appear that he reacts to his fear of instinctual dangers by shifting the full impact of the instinctual dangers on to his object, thus transforming internal dangers into external ones. (Klein, 1932, pp. 127–8)

She quotes Freud as describing this 'deflection' of the death instinct outwards. Instead of a self-directed destructiveness, the infant experiences an object that is intent on destroying the subject. Later, however, Klein elaborated this by describing another early state, in which the aggression directed against the life of the subject is directed against an object that is intent on keeping the subject alive. This she called 'envy', an attack on anything that is the source, or support, of life. One way or another, the infant is immediately concerned with its relations to objects.

REPETITION-COMPULSION

Freud postulated the death instinct after a consideration of the curious repetitions that occur in mental life: in the compulsion to repeat in children's play; in the re-enactments to be observed in the transference; and in the recurrent dreams and obsessive recollecting after the traumas that bring on war neuroses. He believed that as well as interpreting the *content* of these repetitions, the act of repeating unpleasant experiences has itself to be understood. At the time he was impressed by war neurosis in which the sufferer continues to go over the trauma, consciously and in night dreams. There is a constant worrying away at the wound. Such pain and unpleasantness could not result from the pleasure principle driven by the libido and the wish for life. Something exists 'beyond the pleasure principle', something that keeps going over these unpleasant memories. He termed it the 'death instinct'. The compulsion to repeat is buried in the very existence of clinical material – the fact of the transference, for instance – and Freud regarded it as evidence of the death instinct – an impulse to return to a previous condition, 'ashes to ashes'.

Example: The baby and the cotton-reel

Freud reported some simple observations from a very primitive, early stage of development in a boy of eighteen months:

> This good little boy, however, had an occasional disturbing habit of taking any small objects he could get hold of and throwing them away from him into a corner, under the bed, and so on, so that hunting for his toys and picking them up was often quite a business. As he did this he gave vent to a loud long-drawn-out 'o-o-o-o', accompanied by an expression of interest and satisfaction. His mother and the writer of the present account were agreed in thinking that this was not a mere interjection but represented the German word '*fort*' [gone]. I eventually recognized that it was a game and that the only use he made of any of his toys was to play 'gone' with them.

Freud noted that the activity was not just a game; there was a powerful emotional task behind it:

> It was related to the child's great cultural achievement – the instinctual renunciation (that is, the renunciation of instinctual satisfaction) which he had made in allowing his mother to go away without protesting.

He comes to the point about this repetition of a painful experience:

> The child cannot possibly have felt his mother's departure as something agreeable or even indifferent. How then does his repetition of this distressing experience as a game fit in with the pleasure principle?

After much to-and-fro debate, Freud eventually sides with the view 'that there really does exist in the mind a compulsion to repeat which overrides the pleasure principle' (Freud, 1920, p. 22). The child is preoccupied with painful loss – an odd preoccupation.[16] He regarded this odd occurrence, outside the pleasure principle, as an entirely new addition to his view of human drives, the so-called 'death instinct'.

He had considered one other possibility: that the repetition was an attempt at mastery of the painful experience; taking over control of a situation which the subject had passively suffered without control. He discarded this hypothesis on the grounds that clinical data and everyday life are replete with examples of the repetition of *passive* experiences. However, his conclusions have failed to be fully convincing, and the debate over the existence of the death instinct never properly closed. The psychoanalytic community remains divided over Freud's hypothesis. Freud himself felt that there was little direct clinical evidence for the death instinct.

Care must be taken in elucidating the nature of self-destructive attitudes and acts. It is all too easy, and glib, to jump on the death instinct as the explanation of aggression of all kinds. As Bion has pointed out (see *The cheated patient*, p. 130), what may look like 'primary aggression' may be something else – in that case a very primitive state of frustration. Indeed, a self-directed aggression such as suicide may also have various possible motives: to kill pain or suffering; to deny dependency; even to protect others from 'bad' parts of the self. The death instinct is so embedded in these activities, and so obscured beneath aspects of the pleasure principle, that Freud regarded it as clinically silent. This did not, however, stop him returning from time to time, in speculative and theoretical papers, to the idea of impulses deriving from the death instinct (for instance, masochism). However, its 'silence' – that is, its lack of symbolic expression – in the analytic consulting room made him regard it as remote to the researches of analysts. Instead he thought it was embedded in the *process* of the repetition itself (the transference). Nowadays, perhaps, the analysis of process is taken as routine, but in 1920 psychoanalysis was conducted mainly on the symbolic content of the free associations and dreams.

CLINICAL MANIFESTATIONS

Melanie Klein, however, came to different conclusions. For her the extreme primitiveness of the early form of the super-ego was a particularly good example of self-directed aggression (see Chapter 4). This, again, is well exemplified in Peter's play. We met

Klein's patient Peter in an early example (*Inhibited play*, p. 39). The following piece of Peter's material comes from another of Klein's papers; it demonstrates the violence that can supervene in the relationship with the parents.

Example: Peter's naughtiness

Peter, you may remember, was three years and nine months old, inhibited in play and difficult to manage:

> . . . he once played, representing himself and his little brother by two tiny dolls, that they were expecting punishment for their naughtiness to the mother; she comes, finds them dirty, punishes them and goes away.

This play is about punishment for 'naughtiness', and expresses Peter's view of himself as dirty and guilty, deserving punishment:

> The two children repeat their dirty acts again, are again punished, and so on. At last the dread of punishment becomes so strong that the two children determine to kill the mother, and he executes a little doll. They then cut and eat the body.

By now the narrative of this play, the unconscious phantasy, will be easier for the reader to elucidate. Although the punishment happens, it does not seem to stop the children, who go on with their 'dirty acts'. The cycle of fear and punishment is so persecuting that Peter resorts to counter-aggression against the punishing figures. In the end he and his brother destroy the punishing agent, the mother. This is a desperate attempt to deal with the child's fearful anxiety. We can note, too, that the aggression is still couched in oral phantasies of eating; this indicates an origin of this punishing super-ego in early oral phantasies:

> But the father appears to help the mother, and is killed too in a very cruel manner and also cut up and eaten. Now the two children seem to be happy, they can do what they like.

This attempt to destroy the punishing parent seems, at this point, to have solved the endless cycle of punishment and 'dirty acts'. However:

> But after a very short time great anxiety sets in, and it appears that the killed parents are alive again and come back. When the anxiety started the little boy had hidden the two dolls under the sofa, so that the parents

should not find them . . . The father and mother find the two dolls, the father cuts *his* head off, the mother that of his brother, and then they, too, get cooked and eaten.

Here is a crescendo of aggression and paranoid anxieties which conforms to the 'paranoid cycles' we discussed in Chapter 4. Klein had frequently described these cycles in her child patients, but it seemed to her that they became more violent the further back she went through the child's development. Reaching back, therefore, to earliest infancy entails, it would seem, an encounter with a phenomenal aggression. In Klein's view that represented, clinically, the efforts to externalize the self-directed aggression of the death instinct, and thus to deal with it via an external object.

The death instinct, clinically silent according to Freud, was noisy in Klein's view. It had very observable clinical derivatives. The primary aggression at the very beginning of life amounted to clinical evidence for the death instinct. The super-ego is manifested as a self-directed aggressive force – or, to put it the other way, the origins of the super-ego are in the first projection of the self-directed aggression into an object which then becomes the danger towards the self. Part of a recent impetus to investigate the death instinct *clinically* came from Klein's assertion, in 1957, that envy was close to the primary impulses towards death. Other evidence of the early origin of a self-directed aggression comes from the clinical evidence we have seen in the psychoanalysis of schizophrenics (Chapters 7 and 8). It has amounted to a whole new field of clinical observation and psychoanalytic work, which will form a great proportion of the ideas and developments referred to in Part III.

ENVY

In 1957 Klein postulated her concept of 'envy' as a manifestation of innate aggressiveness. If the death instinct is the impulse to hate the life of the subject, one manoeuvre is a hatred of an external object which gives or supports the subject's life. This contrasts with the other manoeuvre in which the hatred is attributed to an external object which hates the subject to live. Envious object relations form on the basis of hating objects which support or represent life. There is thus a spoiling of good things, apparently for the sake of it.

Let us now consider a patient who presented a dream of a very graphic struggle which resembled the kind of fight (noted by Segal – see p. 135) that Jack London's character, Martin, was caught in as he drowned. The case illustrates how the death instinct is related to envy and other impulses to hate.

Example: The struggle with death

One of Klein's patients reported the following dream, which indicates how the death instinct and its close relative, envy, can be discerned, and how they relate together:

> . . . a woman patient whom I would describe as fairly normal. She had in the course of time become more and more aware of envy experienced both towards an older sister and towards her mother . . . The patient reported a dream in which she was alone in a railway carriage with a woman, of whom she could only see the back, who was leaning towards the door of the compartment in great danger of falling out. The patient held her strongly, grasping her by the belt with one hand; with the other hand she wrote a notice to the effect that a doctor was engaged with a patient in this compartment and should not be disturbed, and she put up this notice on the window.

There is a desperate fear that the help, the psychoanalysis, should not be interrupted, as if there were a great danger that it will be (the deathly falling out of the carriage). But who are the figures in the dream? Klein offers us the patient's associations:

> From the associations to the dream I select the following: the patient had a strong feeling that the figure on whom she kept a tight grip was a part of her self, and a mad one. In the dream she had a conviction that she should not let her fall out of the door but should keep her in the compartment and deal with her. The analysis of the dream revealed that the compartment stood for herself.

We can see that internal to the patient (inside the carriage) there was a struggle between figures who probably represent separate parts of the dreamer. One part had the impulse to fall from the carriage and die, rather like a suicidal impulse – a self-directed aggression against her wish to live. This is felt to be mad, yet dangerously strong. The other part strove to keep her alive, to keep a grip on her self-destructive part. In this sense the dream gives an uncommonly clear picture of the struggle within the personality between a force for death and one for life. However, the dream represents more. Further associations reveal a different layer:

> The associations to the hair, which was only seen from behind, were to the older sister. Further associations led to recognition of rivalry and envy in relation to her, going back to the time when the patient was still a child, while her sister was already being courted. She then spoke of a dress which her mother wore and which as a child the patient had both admired and coveted.

The internal situation (in the compartment) is complex, since the figure who represents part of herself is also identified with her sister (hair) and with her mother (dress):

> This dress had very clearly shown the shape of the breasts, and it became more evident than ever before, though none of this was entirely new, that what she originally envied and spoiled in her phantasy was the mother's breasts.

The association to mother's dress points to her identification with the source of life (mother's breasts), which she would also throw out of the window. The dream struggle is therefore occasioned also by an attack on a life-giving object. The impulse to fall from the train, an impulse to death, is turned outwards and against a life-giving object (mother or her life-giving, feeding breasts). And that is envy, the destruction of the source of life. The dream illustrates the confluence of both an impulse against the patient's own life, and a very primitive attack on the external source of life. Condensed in this dream is the death instinct and its reorganization as a 'deflection' into an envy of the good in others.

JEALOUSY

The move from a primary self-destructiveness (death instinct) towards the hatred of the source of life in others (envy) is one step on a longer road. A further move can also take place: the destruction is displaced to rivals, rather than to the source of life. In the dream the destructiveness turns up as a jealous rivalry of the sister who was being courted for her beauty. There is thus a step on from envy of mother towards jealousy of the beautiful and courted sister: 'If envy is not excessive, jealousy . . . becomes a means of working it through . . . jealousy to some extent supersedes envy' (Klein, 1957, p. 198). Jealousy is distinct from envy; it is a form of aggression that does allow an acknowledgement that the rival possesses a good mother, life and beauty. To attain this step the acknowledgement of good has to survive sufficiently for it to be jealously wished for. The sister's beauty has to be tolerated and recognized as something good; envy, in contrast, spoils the 'good' itself and cannot allow it proper recognition. Thus jealousy, however painful, is a progression towards a state of mind in which appreciation (if not yet love) begins to show itself and grows stronger within the mixture of feelings. This positive regard, buried in jealousy, is a step towards mitigating the aggression, and shows the strengthening of loving feelings.

This movement from primitive self-destructiveness (death instinct) to a hatred of external sources of life (envy) to an eventual jealousy has yet another step: in good circumstances there is a further progress towards a 'healthy' competitiveness. In this progression, loving impulses advance to mitigate further and gradually to dominate the aggressive ones. This step-by-step process is complementary to the progress of a projective identification that is modified from violent expulsion to become an interpersonal form of communication, and eventually a benign empathy. However, the development of the personality along the steps of this route may fail. Another route is then chosen.

Much recent Kleinian work has concerned the way in which the personality may fail in its progress of mitigating the death instinct impulses. Some personalities have developed odd ways of dealing with these enormously powerful internal sources of self-destructiveness: in particular, to rigidify in a structure that is in effect an internal dance of death, like the dream struggle at the door of the railway carriage. These personalities become organized around relations between their omnipotent and their highly destructive sides. More detailed discoveries of these pathological organizations have been made possible by the recent study of countertransference (Chapters 10 and 14). Before moving on to that, there is one important developmental parameter which I want to summarize from the clinical discussions in these chapters. I shall do this in the form of an Epilogue to Part II. It may be skipped if, as a theoretical interlude, it seems to interrupt the clinical story.

EPILOGUE TO PART II:
OMNIPOTENCE OR REALITY

In this Epilogue I shall pause to draw together, in a systematic way, the set of important discoveries which are fundamental to Kleinian thinking so far. These had all occurred before Klein's death in 1960, and had all been instigated by her. In this interlude, I will not draw on more clinical material. These discoveries form a set because they all concern a particular discrimination, one which can be viewed from a number of angles. Generally, it is the transition from the paranoid-schizoid position to the depressive position.

Projective identification Let us start with the discrimination that was emphasized by Bion (see Chapter 8). Projective identification was explicitly described by Klein as a means of evacuating bad parts of the self together with bad objects. It featured a high degree of violence which greatly disturbed the sense of identity and reality. At the other end of the spectrum Bion described how projective identification may be used, with less forceful impact, to communicate. At this least aggressive end there is no confusion over the identity of the self and object (putting oneself in another's shoes without forgetting who you or they are). The dimension is from violent intrusion to empathy.

Omnipotent phantasy When a person evacuates parts of the self in phantasy, they feel a sense of loss or depletion, as if these parts of the self had in actual fact gone, disappeared. The effect of this kind of primitive phantasy is that the individual feels as if the phantasy actually had a reality to it. There is a sense of the internal world as a reality too; if something is believed in, it is as good as having happened. If the person believes strongly enough that they are less of a person, the sense of the self will be affected in such a way that it will actually feel smaller, emptier, more depleted; this in turn will result in attitudes, feelings and behaviour based upon that sense of smallness, hollowness or emptiness. This is covered by a phrase coined by Freud, 'the omnipotence of fantasy'. It is to be contrasted with the kinds of phantasy where there remains some awareness that it is 'simply' a phantasy. The discrimination is between phantasy that is so strong that it becomes determining of identity, attitudes, emotions and relationships; and phantasy enjoyed 'as a phantasy', and employed as imagination and the source of personal meaning. The first category of phantasies, called 'omnipotent' because they have an actual effect of some kind, can be said to be concrete; in the example of projective identification, it is as if some concrete lump of the person and their mind has actually been removed and placed in physical space elsewhere, into someone else. The omnipotence and concreteness, because of their 'real' effects, are more than just phantasies; they can also be regarded as real processes. There is an objective quality to their consequences as well as the subjective experience of them in phantasy. This is the *second* distinction: omnipotence contrasted with non-omnipotence.

Primitive defence mechanisms Freud hinted that the defence mechanisms of the very young infant may have a different quality from those of the neurotic defences. He hinted, too, that one of the differences may be the extra degree of hostility in the operation of those defences. Klein's results confirmed this: she described the primitive defence mechanisms of projection, splitting, identification, introjection and so on. These are in fact characterized both by aggression and also by operating as defences against the very early forms of aggressive impulses in the infant. Consequently, they are suffused with a very violent aggression. Klein contrasted them with the neurotic defences – the paradigm being repression – in the older child and adult. The primitive defence mechanisms, as we have seen (Chapter 2), have a subjective level of phantasy but also become psychological processes that determine basic aspects of the development of the early personality, especially in forming the sense of identity and of the self. They are modified in development – for instance, splitting of the personality with no contact between the parts becomes repression, where the split is between the conscious and unconscious parts of the mind which do interact (e.g. the dream in the example of *The man who split off his aggression*, p. 125). This distinction between primitive and neurotic defences is the *third* dimension.

Narcissism   The formation of the sense of self and identity coheres, as we have seen, around the experience of a good object installed reasonably securely inside the person. This, in the early stages of development (and with varying degrees all through life), may entail an exaggeration of the goodness of the self, achieved through persistent evacuation of the parts of the self that are felt to be bad and the continual incorporation of good things from outside. Thus states of massive and unrealistic redistribution of good things and bad things between the self and others occur at times in infancy (and also at times of stress in later life); and they depend totally upon the operation of omnipotent phantasies, the primitive defence mechanisms of splitting, projection, introjection and identification. These states are called narcissistic, and the redistribution of the parts of the self is believed in intensely; but because they involve aspects of other people who may not go along with the redistribution of worth, these states are usually unstable and threaten the person with breakdown. This *fourth* distinction exists between, on the one hand, narcissistic object relations and, on the other, the recognition of the separate reality of others and oneself, who are all more realistic mixed entities, both good and bad.

Symbolization   Later (in Chapter 11) we will see how symbols can be constructed in two ways. A symbol may represent what it symbolizes (its meaning) or it may actually be believed to *be* the thing it is supposed to represent. Although it will be described later, this *fifth* distinction, between two kinds of symbolization, is closely related to the distinction between omnipotent projective identification and empathy described above.

Identification   The need to give up the omnipotence of phantasy and to address the reality of oneself and others is part of the process of maturation. The particular site of this struggle for greater acceptance of reality is the early stages of the Oedipus complex. An infant has to make a movement across a kind of mental space – from experiencing itself as part of a couple, mother/infant, to witnessing a couple, mother and father, from which the infant itself is excluded. This is a particularly difficult transition because of the intensity of the passions, both loving and murderous, which are involved, and the Oedipus complex is particularly prominent in this developmental step. It is, however, a step which relates to the distinction I have been addressing between omnipotent phantasy and acceptance of reality. When Freud treated the Wolf Man, he discovered what he thought was an early trauma at maybe eighteen months of age, when the child had witnessed the parents in intercourse. Freud pointed out how the Wolf Man did not succeed in making that necessary psychological movement, but became preoccupied unconsciously with the parental intercourse by continually identifying himself with one or other of the partners. Because of the omnipotence of phantasy, he remained inserted into the parental intercourse through one identification or another. This seriously hampered his development. A more profitable development occurs in Freud's description of the little boy who accepts that he is *like* Daddy, and could do what Daddy does, *but not yet*. Freud thought that this act of delayed gratification was an important developmental step, but it is also a developmental step in the sense that I am talking about: there can be a recognition of being like Father, but without having any longer to believe one *is* Father – a similarity, yet a separateness. Identifying oneself as being like someone and identifying oneself as being equated with that person are two different forms of identification, corresponding to the two kinds of symbols. They are separate, and form the *sixth* discrimination between the early stages of the Oedipus complex and its mature form. Being someone, as a schizophrenic may believe he is the King of France, has the quality of omnipotence; being like someone has a different quality that comes from having given up the omnipotence and recognizing the separateness of the person one is like.

The death instinct We have just noted the final distinction in the last chapter: between envy and the more mature forms of aggression, jealousy and competitiveness. In the latter the capacity for appreciation of goodness and life survives; whereas in the former, envy, the attacks upon goodness, beauty and life are dominant, and remove all those good characteristics. This is the *seventh* and final distinction.

Summary The different aspects of this dimension may be set out in the form of a table:

	Paranoid-schizoid	Depressive
Projective identification	Evacuation	Empathy
Phantasy	Omnipotent	Realistic
Defences	Primitive	Neurotic
Object relations	Narcissistic	Differentiated and reality-tested identity
Symbols	Symbolic-equation	Symbols proper
Identification	Within the parental couple	Witnessing the couple
Death instinct	Envy	Jealousy, competitiveness

This multivalent set of discriminations are all part and parcel of the same developmental step. It is a wavering step and everyone, whatever their stage and age of adult maturity, will tend to oscillate from time to time from one side to the other. Mostly there is a general trend throughout life towards the right-hand side of the table; and this represents growing maturity with age. But some people become seriously held up in these movements, a stasis which is examined further in Part III, where recent developments will be discussed which concentrate on further detailed aspects of the bundle of distinctions summarized here, and derive from new aspects of technique that have built on the discoveries covered in Part II. In Part III we will examine these recent developments by Klein's contemporaries and students.

PART III

EMOTIONAL CONTACT AND THE 'K'-LINK

10 COUNTERTRANSFERENCE

The progressive development of Kleinian ideas has resulted in new views of the therapeutic process; thence modifications in technique have occurred and, in turn, further theoretical advances. The discoveries and developments that formed the body of Part II rested largely on investigations of the aggressive component of human life and relationships which flowered from the new play technique for children. The further development of Kleinian practice which will be discussed in Part III has clustered loosely around investigations of the human desire for knowledge (the epistemophilic instinct) deriving from work with schizophrenic patients; the practice of self-knowledge that is the core of psychoanalysis; the structure of the personality elaborating the internal struggle with the death instinct; and the detailed examination of the psychoanalytic process between two people. Broadly speaking, we are moving on to the progress that has been made since Klein's death in 1960; though influences spread freely across that particular threshold year, in particular the Kleinian reaction to new ways of looking at the transference and countertransference.

Around 1949–50, 'countertransference' suddenly came to be conceived differently across the whole of the international psychoanalytic community. Previously, the orthodox view was that of Freud (1910), though he wrote very little about it. He regarded countertransference merely as an emotional reaction to overcome – the psychoanalyst's own complexes and internal resistances evoked by the patient's transference. In meeting the intensity of a patient's transference, the psychoanalyst may become emotionally involved with the patient. The psychoanalyst may fall in love with a patient who falls in love with him, and so on; or he may find that he hates the patient who expresses hate towards him. In order to protect himself from the effects of the patient's transference, Freud recommended a neutral stance, comparing it with the surgeon who has to cut and mutilate without flinching; or with a mirror whose only feature is a reflected image of the patient. This tended to make psychoanalysts believe that the proper attitude to their feelings was to abolish them. From about 1920 onwards, every newly trained psychoanalyst was required to have their own therapeutic psychoanalysis to help dissolve complexes and resistances from their work. At the time, in fact, it was called a 'control analysis'. The ideal analyst was likened to a blank screen on which the patient will discover a transferred object.

By the late 1940s, despite these control analyses, there must have been many well-analysed psychoanalysts who still had their feelings about patients. The 'blank screen' did not seem to exist. A reaction set in. Psychoanalysts in several countries argued against the mechanical 'blank screen' concept of the analyst's technique (Winnicott, 1947; Racker, 1949; Berman, 1949; Heimann, 1950; Annie Reich 1951; Little, 1951; Gitelson, 1952). This was a critical thrust against the recommendation of a contrived, cool detachment.

To some extent psychoanalysts were attracted to the new ideas about countertransference because they added depth to the bare form of symbol interpretation which had become standard since Freud's *Interpretation of Dreams*. Simple interpretations of the form 'This is a phallic object', or 'I am your father-figure' sounded increasingly banal as patients arriving for treatment were drawn more and more from backgrounds where they gained a sophisticated knowledge of psychoanalytic ideas. That knowingness, I think, must have been one factor that led psychoanalysts to look again at the nature of countertransference, and at the nature of the process they were engaged upon with their patients.

The *relationship* between analyst and patient is 'not the presence of feelings in one partner and their absence in the other, the analyst' (Heimann, 1960, p. 152). With this realization, a more human understanding of the encounter suddenly erupted. The psychoanalyst's response can never actually be neutral. Nor is it useless:

My thesis is that the analyst's emotional response to his patient within the analytic situation represents one of the most important tools for his work. The analyst's countertransference is an instrument of research into the patient's unconscious. (Heimann, 1950, p. 74)

The point of the relationship between the analyst and the patient is

the *degree* of feeling the analyst experiences and the *use* he makes of his feelings . . . The aim of the analyst's own analysis is not to turn him into a mechanical brain which can produce interpretations on the basis of a purely intellectual procedure, but to enable him to *sustain* his feelings as opposed to discharging them like the patient. (Heimann, 1960, p. 152)

At the time, this was a radically new injunction: if the analyst can sustain feelings, they are positively useful, whereas discharging them could be damaging and certainly clouds the issue. For instance, the analyst may feel angry with the patient. He could then discharge feelings, perhaps, by having a go at the patient – giving the patient 'a piece of his mind', we might say. Or the analyst may feel overly positive, even erotic, towards the patient, and might then freeze up and perform the legendary emotionless blank screen. Alternatively, however, the analyst could hang on to those feelings, acknowledge whose they are, but understand how they have come about. This will inevitably tell something about the patient to whom the psychoanalyst is reacting. Of course it must also tell something about the analyst as well – provided the analyst is prepared to consider his feeling (rather than discharging it). But whatever the reaction in the analyst, there is something of the patient to which he reacts – and, as we shall see, whatever the patient's experience, there is very often something of the analyst to react to. It is the patient's contribution, however, that both need to attend to for the progress of a psychoanalysis. It is the analyst's contribution which can give clues about the patient's contribution, provided he can rely on his self-understanding. Such provisos, of course, can be only partially met by even the most insightful psychoanalysts; and later we will see moments when even the analyst's lapses may be turned to benefit an understanding of what is going on.

In this chapter, I want to examine how this new understanding of countertransference has been developed by Kleinians. It has come to be seen as a dialogue between two unconscious minds, with the conscious exchanges mediating the unconscious ones. In the first example, below, Heimann shows in a tiny detail from the end of a session how the new notion of countertransference can be a tool for understanding the transference relationship. We met this strange patient in the example of *The man who assaulted his buttocks* (p. 66). In the next example a sudden emotional impact on the analyst as the session ended revealed an important feature of how he related to his objects. It was not very easy for the analyst. Mostly, in ordinary social life, such impacts would be dismissed out of a kindly tolerance, without much thought; or responded to by keeping more of a distance from that person in the future. We can see, however, that by hanging on to the response without discharging it through a dismissal or an avoidance, an analyst can come to know something more about the patient.

Example: The introjection of the analyst

This patient, described by Heimann, often conveyed his love and admiration for his mother because of her kindness, and particularly her forbearance. For instance, he remembered

> how he once took her into his car and drove off with her, and how, when they had gone a good distance from home, he unburdened himself by accusing her of the many wrongs he felt she had done him. She had listened patiently and with her characteristic kindness.

The analyst is emphasizing to us the patient's story of how he takes his mother (like his father, described in *The man who assaulted his buttocks*) inside him (into his car) and then makes her suffer there as an internal object. Heimann then described one particular session which began as the usual report of his miseries – in his life and in his psychoanalysis. It then flowed on to a current life problem, though he seemed unwilling to subject this to the process of psychoanalysis:

> He demanded that analysis, which in his view had utterly failed to improve his condition, should now be put aside, that I should give him advice about the 'real' problem which was so pressing, and intervene directly in his external situation. I did not comply with his demand, but proceeded in the ordinary way; and he became less anxious and less persecuted and also gained more understanding.

We are shown the patient trying to take the psychoanalyst outside the analysis, to demonstrate how (in the transference) the patient re-enacts his relations with his mother, whom he took away in his car to unburden himself of the wrongs he has suffered. The analyst, like the mother, continued patiently:

> His attacks on the analysis and on me, and his pleasure in insulting and accusing me, seemed rather stronger, perhaps, than usual; and on leaving, though much relieved and with more insight about his actual problem, he stated that I had not helped him at all and that he would be as much tormented after the hour as he had been before it.

His claims against the psychoanalyst seemed invalid to her, as he had in fact been relieved and gained more insight. So what does it mean to the patient to deny that he has had a good experience? Heimann focuses on his manner of stating his complaints:

> The way, however, in which he made this statement did not accord with an anticipation of misery. It was with relish that he flung this parting shot at me. The effect accompanying his remark was triumphant and menacing.

Let me emphasize the impression we are now offered: it seems that the patient was more intent on *having an effect* on his object, the psychoanalyst, than on communicating with her in the content of his words:

> Manifestly his words contained two statements, one about my failure to help him and the other about the condition of torment he foresaw for himself. The hostile triumph in his attitude clearly related to the first statement – my failure as an analyst – and was in line with the many scornful remarks he had so often made; but in connection with the second part of his remark another message emerges. There was also an unmistakable threat in his attitude, which, if put into words, would run like this: 'I shall torment *you* after the hour exactly as I have done here. You cannot escape from me!'

The patient was indeed successful in having an effect on the analyst. She picked up, intuitively, an emotional moment. I think this conveys how the analyst is beginning to understand her own reaction as the patient's *intention*. He sought to threaten her, and to send her away from the session to continue *her* suffering – as a failed analyst:

> The unconscious meaning of the patient's parting words was that *I* was going to suffer. What he had said about himself unconsciously related

to his object, which he could triumphantly control and torment because he had *introjected* it.

He predicted his own suffering; and he was correct, but only in the specific *internal* sense – he would continue the masochistic kind of beating described in the earlier account of this patient. However, some aspect of himself had became identified with the psychoanalyst who will be made to suffer inside him:

> It takes much longer to describe than to perceive a process which takes place in a moment. It seemed to me that I could actually witness in operation the process of the patient's introjection of myself.

The analyst has constructed a narrative in which this man introjected his object and then subjected it to some sort of torture inside, as an internal object. She became aware of the patient's effect on her, and could hold on to it and think about it. She could then piece together two things: first, the content of the explicit story about taking mother for a ride; second, the momentary emotional impact on her (the countertransference). It is the psychoanalyst's work to set these two things beside each other: the content of the patient's material; and the countertransference experience and feelings. Each can support the other; in this case the picture of what happened in the car could be mapped onto the experience within the psychoanalytic session.

At this stage I am not making any point about the greater acuity of the analyst's sight of this immediate process; we will come on to that later. Nor do I want to comment on the analyst's contribution to her reaction, since that is not conveyed in the material Paula Heimann gave. However, we will begin to see how the internal worlds of both psychoanalyst and patient meet and reverberate together when we come on to the next example, *The abusing patient* (p. 160). Before that, however, I will make some general comments about this developing form of practice.

When the psychoanalyst does not bring the two elements – content and countertransference – into conjunction, there is the danger of rather wild interpretation. Heimann worried about this later, and felt that her original recommendations (1950) were at times taken up in a misleading and unhelpful way. She argued (in 1960) that some psychoanalysts based their interpretations on their feelings. They said in reply to any query 'my countertransference', and seemed disinclined to check their interpretations against the actual data in the analytic session. (Heimann, 1960, p. 153)

Banal interpretations on the basis 'because it felt right' could become as mechanical as the 'this is a phallic symbol' interpretation. Countertransference feelings alone are not the basis for an interpretation – just as interpretation of symbolic content can no longer stand alone either. Both have to be interwoven together to support each other. The countertransference deepens the symbol interpretation; the symbolic content steadies and directs the understanding of the countertransference. This mutuality between content and transference/countertransference is important.

Because of the risk of the wild use of the countertransference, Heimann's original paper in 1950 was not graced with Klein's approval. It seems to have led to the break between Heimann and Klein, despite Heimann's later warnings of these risks.

CYCLES OF PROJECTION AND INTROJECTION

Many Kleinians, however, did become interested in the countertransference as an aspect of the analytic relationship. They retained an *intrapsychic* view of what happens within the patient's psychic life, based on cycles of alternating introjection and projection. This is then linked with an *intrapsychic* view of what happens in the psychoanalyst's psyche too.

In what Roger Money-Kyrle (1956) called 'normal counter-transference', cycles of projection and introjection go around smoothly in both psychoanalyst and patient without undue delay. The patient comes to the analytic session with something on his or her mind, and *conveys the experience*. This is more than passing information over to the analyst *about* various happenings, or *about* a state of mind; such reports invariably convey to the analyst in a more direct way what the experience actually feels like. What is on the subject's mind is, in effect, projected into the analyst's to create an impact there. The analyst then has an experience, which consequently comes to be 'on his mind' too.

Consider a patient bringing particularly good or particularly bad news; say, the birth of a new baby or a death in the family. Whilst such an event may raise complex issues requiring careful analysis, in the first

> instance the patient may not want an interpretation, but a response; the sharing of pleasure or grief. And this may be what the analyst intuitively wishes for too. (Brenman Pick, 1985, p. 39–40)

The analyst does not simply listen to the news of the birth of a baby as a mere news report. The analyst has an experience with the patient; intrapsychically, we would describe it as follows: the analyst introjects what the patient has projected. It is not necessarily a violent, omnipotent form of projection as described above with the psychotic patients. Indeed, this process of gently giving another person an experience which they can savour is a normal part of conversation in general and, among other things, is what makes social contact enjoyable.

When the analyst has grasped the experience, he or she is in a position to say, 'I know how you feel', though an analyst does not say it exactly like that. The analyst puts into words an understanding of what the patient is feeling, especially the patient's unconscious experiences and phantasies. In those cases where the projection is of a more desperate nature, the analyst may have a much greater difficulty in recognizing what experience has been projected. Nevertheless, in those cases the analyst still plays the part of disentangling what she or he has received. If this disentangling is successful, the patient's original experience is thus modified – Money-Kyrle (1956) called it 'metabolized', to make the analogy with a physical process of taking in and digesting. The analyst's understanding gives the patient's experience a new shape, a more communicable shape. What can be conveyed only implicitly or vaguely by the patient through projection is changed or focused by the psychoanalyst's mind. The psychoanalyst must then find a way of announcing this to the patient. A verbal formulation of the original experience is put back to the patient, but now modified by transmission through the analyst's mind. Putting it back to the patient in words attempts to achieve a gentler form of projection by the analyst into the patient; it is in fact likely, and intended, to have an impact on the patient. The term 'reprojection' suggests itself, to cover the return of something to the patient that had previously been projected into the analyst. The patient may (or may not) *introject* that conscious understanding. Thus the 'reprojection' is not simply passing information back to the patient – it adds an increment from the analyst's own experience and understanding on to the patient's. The fact that the analyst's mind could work on the experience confirms for the patient that the particular experience does not necessarily clog up the mind; such experiences could then be recognized as thinkable, not merely for discharge. They can, though they are often disturbing, be reflected upon without causing a breakdown. If the patient can accept this, it adds to the stock of self-understanding and mental stability. The 'reprojection' by the analyst then becomes an addition to the patient which can be called an 'introjection' by the patient.

This kind of account describes the *intra*psychic occurrences of *both* patient and psychoanalyst. From the patient's point of view his or her intrapsychic world interacts with the world outside; but that world outside is the intrapsychic world of someone else. This focus on the *intrapsychic* qualities of interpersonal interactions often leads to criticism that Kleinian psychoanalysts neglect reality. In a sense they do, since external 'reality' for one person is the internal world of others. This approach has a disturbingly fluid quality that disrupts any sense of reality being a constant. In this view the interpersonal world is not like the physical world of inanimate matter. This is a complicated issue that has far-reaching implications well outside psychoanalysis. A limited discussion of it will be found in my *Dictionary of Kleinian Thought* under the heading 'Subjectivity'; and to some extent in my 'Reflections' at the end of this book.

In summary: from an 'intrapsychic' viewpoint the analyst can be said to introject the patient's projection; then to project (or reproject) it back to the patient in a form that bears the marks of the analyst's own mental work on it; the patient introjects the now-modified (metabolized) experience, together with an added capacity to 'understand himself', and thus to 'stand himself'.

WHEN COUNTERTRANSFERENCE GOES WRONG

We touched on the complicated process when the analyst/mother fails to take in (contain) in Bion's descriptions of it (*The mother who could not understand*, p. 127; *The cheated patient*, p. 130; and *The patient's failed container*, p. 131). There are a number of accounts of these cyclical processes. Here we will follow Roger Money-Kyrle's (1956). His invented fiction the 'normal countertransference' was intended to clarify the variations and deviations from that 'normal' process summarized in the preceding section. The analyst can go wrong if the emotional material touches on specific difficulties of his or her own; then she or he may get stuck in the cycle: either in the first phase, when he or she is projected into and so becomes full of, and bothered about, the patient's experience; or in the second, when reprojecting may discharge so much of the analyst's mind that he or she feels depleted.

If the first phase goes wrong, the patient projects and the analyst is burdened with an internal object that is then inadequately held on to and thought about:

> the analyst gets unduly worried, both on his own and his patient's behalf, about a session that has gone badly. He may feel as if he has regained some of his old troubles and become almost physically burdened with his patient's as well. (Money-Kyrle, 1956, pp. 25–6)

Or, secondly, when interpreting, the analyst excessively reprojects back into the patient:

> . . . for a little time after he has finished his week's work, the analyst may be consciously preoccupied with some unsolved problem of his patient's. Then he forgets them; but the period of conscious concern is followed by a period of listlessness in which he is depleted of the private interests that usually occupy his leisure. I suggest this because, in phantasy, he has projected parts of himself together with his patients and must wait, as it were, till these return to him. (Money-Kyrle, 1956, p. 26)

The two phases in which the analyst might get stuck – either introjectively burdened with the patient or depleted through excessive projection into the patient – both lead, Money-Kyrle pointed out, to a triple task: it is necessary to discern (a) the analyst's disturbance; (b) what the patient has contributed to it; and (c) how the analyst's stuckness has then affected the patient. To illustrate, Money-Kyrle described a neurotic patient who disturbed the psychoanalyst's mind.

Example: The abusing patient

The patient arrived for his analytic session very anxious about his work:

> Remembering a similar occasion, on which he had felt depersonalized over a weekend and dreamed that he had left his 'radar' set in a shop and would be unable to get it before Monday, I thought he had, in

phantasy, left parts of his 'good self' in me. But I was not very sure of this, or of other interpretations I began to give.

We note how the analyst is operating rather mechanically and without a depth of conviction. I think we could say he was interpreting symbolic content rather than incorporating it with some aspect of the countertransference. The problem, however, is what aspect of the countertransference; and that is difficult because at that stage the analyst has lost his own insight into what is happening to him. Thus his uncertainty could have been a signal that he had got 'stuck', but he could not feel it as anything other than that he was not doing very well and ought to try harder. Instead it was the patient who seemed more aware of the problem, unconsciously, than the psychoanalyst at that moment:

> And he, for his part, soon began to reject them all [the interpretations] with a mounting degree of anger; and, at the same time, abused me for not helping. By the end of the session he was no longer depersonalized, but very angry and contemptuous instead. It was I who felt useless and bemused.

The reader will recognize this interesting situation in which the patient's worry about his work has diminished, while the analyst's worry about *his* work has mounted. The analyst has been left in a stuck position – the introjective one – in which he is filled with the uselessness which the patient has projected into him, and which he has been unable to metabolize. From the patient's point of view, he came with a certain state of mind (anxiety about his work), and by the end of the session that very same state of mind had disappeared from him, and the analyst's work was in doubt. The analyst, unfortunately stuck with a part of the patient, had not grasped that experience at all. He had not put it into words which might then have formed a process of reprojecting, benignly, back into the patient. There are interesting aspects of how this happened, and important implications for further interpretations:

> When I eventually recognized my state at the end as so similar to that he had described at the beginning, I could almost feel the relief of a re-projection. By then the session was over.

Interestingly, the analyst did eventually manage to sort out ('metabolize') in his own thoughts what had happened, but not until after the session. Nevertheless, it was still a relief:

> But he [the patient] was in the same mood at the beginning of the next one – still very angry and contemptuous.

The patient returned to his next session still stuck in *his* projective phase:

> I then told him I thought he felt he had reduced me to the state of useless vagueness he himself had been in, and that he felt he had done this by having me 'on the mat', asking questions and rejecting the answers, in the way his legal father did.

So we see the psychoanalyst recovering and able to gather his words; but it is not the original situation he describes, it is now too late for that: 'it was useless to try to pick up the thread where I had dropped it. A new situation had arisen which had affected us both.' It was this new situation which had to be interpreted, the way the psychoanalyst had given the patient the opportunity to exploit his fumbling in order to express (communicate) something of the patient's own feeling of useless vagueness, and the way it had rendered the patient free of his unpleasant state of mind:

> His response was striking. For the first time in two days, he became quiet and thoughtful.

The reader is now accustomed to the importance of this response. The patient's demeanour changed abruptly to become quieter and more thoughtful. Please note also the change in the capacity for thought. Once the psychoanalyst could reflect on *his* experience and sort it out in words, the patient had gained a significant addition to his own capacity to think about his experience:

> He then said this explained why he had been so angry with me yesterday: he felt that all my interpretations referred to my illness and not to his.

I think it is clear that the patient has suddenly acquired a new power to capture his own view of the situation, rather than simply reacting to it with vehement protest against the analyst. We would find it difficult to contest the analyst's view that the interpretation struck a note of truth for the patient and restored some of his mental functioning.

This step-by-step, 'slow-motion' account describes how the patient's projection had fitted in with some problem of the analyst, who then began to identify with it and become disturbed by it. He could not handle the experience properly – at least, not at first – and, like the patient, he became overwhelmed by it. The analyst ended up simply stuck with the feeling of uselessness and vagueness. To retrieve the situation, he had to do

> a silent piece of self-analysis involving the discrimination of two things which can be felt to be very similar: my own sense of incompetence at having lost the thread, and my patient's contempt for his impotent self, which he felt to be in me.

This discrimination is a very crucial point. One aspect of the patient and another aspect of the analyst met together in the analyst, and the confusion of identity (who was ill?) needed disentangling, since in a sense, both were ill at that moment.

Let us consider this from another angle, one with which we are already familiar. It concerns the *quality* of the projection – the degree of violence involved. When the subject – patient or analyst – employs great violence in his unconscious phantasy, the result is more likely to be an entangling confusion within the mind of the other person. The aim, at least, is for the analyst to perform his reprojection with less violence than his patient originally used. If he succeeds, the whole bundle of mental qualities summarized in the Epilogue to Part II will be shifted a little to the right of the table (see p. 148).

THE MEETING OF MINDS

Not only does the psychoanalyst have human responses, however, but the patient may well surmise that he is bound to have them. He then wonders what the analyst is doing with them. All the time the patient is seeking out a *responding* analyst: for instance, 'the patient projects into the analyst's wish to be a mother' (Brenman Pick, 1985, p. 41). Indeed, being 'something like a mother'[17] is often a significant motivation to become a psychoanalyst or psychotherapist in the first place, and patients may correctly spot this. Then they can use it in certain ways: perhaps to gain the satisfactions of being mothered, which they have felt the lack of; or perhaps to find a way of giving good feelings to the analyst; or possibly to create a feeling of controlling the analyst's mind, and so on.

Irma Brenman Pick expanded this into a general property: 'If there is a mouth that seeks a nipple as an inborn potential, there is, I believe, a psychological equivalent, i.e. a state of mind which seeks another state of mind' (Brenman Pick, 1985, p. 35). As we noted above, at the psychological level the reality the patient relates to is the internal world of another, the psychoanalyst. When the analyst is affected by the patient's material and by the patient's state of mind, he or she is required to respond calmly. The dilemma of providing calm reflection when disturbed is one the analyst faces all the time: if 'we take in the experience of the patient, we cannot do so without also having an experience' (Brenman Pick, 1985, p. 35). To face it with calm reflection requires considerable emotional resilience and the powers to work it through:

> One great difficulty in our work is in this dual area of remaining in contact with the importance of our own experience as well as our allegiance to the profound value of our technique . . . I think this problem applies, for instance, to the controversial issue of interpretation versus response . . . the issue becomes polarized, as though one was all good, the other all bad. (Brenman Pick, 1985, p. 40)

The analyst constantly risks toppling off this knife-edge either into a method of cold rational automatism (the blank screen approach) or to *acting* upon his or her own responses to the patient 'because it felt right' (in the manner Heimann warned against – see above).

There is only one resolution to the controversy over interpretation versus response: the content of the interpretation must take account of the response in the analyst as well as the content of the patient's material:

> Unless we can properly acknowledge this [the analyst's anticipated or actual response] *in* our interpretation, interpretation itself either becomes a frozen rejection, or is abandoned and we feel compelled to act non-interpretatively and be 'human'. (Brenman Pick, 1985, p. 40)

So – merely 'being human' risks conforming to figures based on the splitting of objects into 'good' ones and 'bad' ones – a retreat from the painful mixtures of the depressive position. In the next example the bad aspects of mothering were relegated to family, spouse and past objects, and so on, away from the session and the person of the psychoanalyst. The analyst becomes the good satisfying mother – better than all the others. Both patient and analyst may enjoy that fiction. There is potential here for a stuck state, with the patient projecting a perfect mother into the analyst's wish to be one. Without this transaction ever reaching proper conscious and verbal articulation, the psychoanalysis, though enjoyable to both, is rendered stuck. The next example shows the analyst's struggle to think this through.

Example: The man who was sensible

Mr A, described by Irma Brenman Pick, had come to London after
a psychoanalysis abroad:

> He arrived for his session a few hours after having been involved in a
> car accident in which his stationary car was hit and badly damaged: he
> himself missed being severely injured. He was clearly still in a state of
> shock, yet he did not speak of shock or fear. Instead he explained with
> excessive care what had taken place, and the correct steps taken by him
> before and after the collision. He went on to say that by chance his
> mother (who lives in the same country as the previous analyst) phoned
> soon after the accident, and when told about it responded with 'I
> wouldn't have phoned if I had known you'd have such awful news. I
> don't want to hear about it'. He said that thanks to his previous analysis,
> he knew that he needed to understand that his mother could not do
> otherwise, and he accepted that.

We are presented, as is the psychoanalyst, with a very co-operative-
sounding patient who knows how to deal with a shock. The patient
is very aware of the impact of 'bad news' on his mother, who does
not want to listen to it, and how important his 'understandingness'
is to her and to his previous analyst.

> He was however very angry with the other driver, and was belligerent
> in his contention that he would pursue, if necessary to court, his
> conviction that he would have to pay for the damage.

Despite his understandingness he can also feel a quick, litigious
grievance:

> I believe that he conveyed very vividly his belief that he would have to
> bear alone or be above the immediate shock, fear and rage generated
> both by the accident and the mother's response to it. Not only did he
> believe that his mother did not want to hear the awful news, but that
> the analyst did not want to hear the awful news of there being a
> mother/analyst who does not listen to or share pain with him. Instead
> he felt he had been taught to 'understand' the mother or listen to the
> analyst with an angry underlying conviction that the mother/analyst will
> not listen to his distress.

The patient's protectiveness towards his mother is clear enough;
and that is why he is so understanding. But the analyst is also telling
us that the patient finds an analyst, too, who similarly will not want
to hear bad news. Do we follow Brenman Pick in this step? The

point is that the patient talks so calmly to this analyst when actually
he is distressed, and this must imply that he thinks she, too, could
not bear a distressed patient. One could say that, in effect, he does
not properly use the analyst to project the distress about the car
accident into. Like his previous one, this analyst will demand his
understanding rather than his grievance. But unconsciously, there
is another attitude:

> He went along with this, pulled himself together, made a display of
> behaving correctly, became a so-called 'understanding' person. He
> replaced the distress of bearing pain with competence in doing the right
> thing, but let us know that unconsciously he will pursue his grievances
> to the bitter end.

This patient is splitting his object: between the analyst he must
understand and protect, and the one whom unconsciously he will
grievously accuse:

> Now let us consider what took place in the session. The patient made
> an impact in his 'competent' way of dealing with his feelings, yet he
> also conveyed a wish for there to be an analyst/mother who would take
> his fear and his rage. I interpreted the yearning for someone who will
> not put down the phone, but instead will take in and understand what
> this unexpected impact feels like . . .

So the present psychoanalyst did feel some impact from the
patient – he made one kind of projection; it was to project not his
shock, but his loneliness. And she can tell us (now) that presenting
his loneliness through his stoical 'understandingness' did affect her
maternal feelings and sympathy:

> . . . this supposes the transference onto the analyst of a more
> understanding maternal figure. I believe, though, that this 'mates' with
> some part of the analyst that may wish to 'mother' the patient in such
> a situation.

She took in not just the situation in which a son felt hopelessly
lonely; more importantly she also took in a responsive kind of
'mother' who can feel for the patient's loneliness. And that 'good'
mother fused with her own maternal feelings. It seems natural
enough to respond like this; but Brenman Pick regarded her own
reaction a little suspiciously:

> I had been lured into either admiring the sensible, competent approach,
> or appearing to condemn it. I found that I was having the experience

of feeling superior to and judging the mother, previous analyst and his
own 'competence'.

She noticed from her own reactions that the patient had found a
particular aspect of the internal mother *in* the psychoanalyst to
project into – an aspect that can feel better than the others.
Brenman Pick noticed her own superiority: that she could mother
'better' than the patient's own mother; better also than his previous
psychoanalyst, who also seemed to imply that competence was
what was needed from the patient; and better than the patient's
internal mother, who demanded competence of him. Brenman Pick
found herself happily embroiled in a splitting between herself, a
thoroughly 'good' mother, and all those 'bad' ones:

> Was I being party to taking them all to court? . . . I then needed to show
> him that he believed, in presenting me with such an awful picture of a
> mother/analyst, he persuaded me to believe that I was different from
> and better than them.

She eventually realized that her superiority connected with the
patient's invitation to her to be the best of all mothers. In this way
the analyst had joined the patient in a pattern of interaction which
seemed perfectly sensible to him; and indeed, at some level, to her.
The problem is that it merely contributes to repeating the patient's
expectations. Those expectations, which derive from the use of his
splitting mechanisms in the transference, need to be understood
rather than repeated.

Brenman Pick believed that the patient could actively promote
this situation; that he would have some awareness of what a mother
will feel. He believed that his own mother did not want to hear bad
news, and froze off, and he seems to have been right about this.
Yet he also has some idea of an ideal mother, which he looks for
by seeking out the psychoanalyst's responses. Brenman Pick invites
the question: should she respond or interpret? When she responds
to his yearning to be listened to sympathetically, she claims, they
repeat his pattern of splitting. Moreover, she would claim that this
deeply buried enactment must be a transference pattern of a
habitual kind, and that the patient is better served by helping him
to understand that he can have a choice whether or not to persist
with projective manoeuvres in other people's minds.

The proper task, therefore, is to acknowledge this response *in*
an interpretation: 'The point is we have to cope with feelings and

subject them to thought' (Brenman Pick, 1985, p. 41). This
conforms to Heimann's injunction that the analyst *sustain* his
feelings as opposed to discharging them like the patient' (Heimann,
1960, p. 152). Both Money-Kyrle and Brenman Pick imply that
psychoanalysts (and therefore psychoanalysis itself) are not
perfect; they make mistakes, and have mixtures of feelings and
motives (the depressive position). Like the patient, they have
desires: 'to eliminate discomfort as well as to communicate and
share experience; ordinary human reactions. In part the patient
seeks an enacting response, and in part, the analyst has an impulse
to enact, and some of this will be expressed in the interpretation'
(Brenman Pick, 1985, p. 36). About her own slipping into her
motherly role, she says: 'If we cannot take in and think about such
a reaction in ourselves [i.e. the wish to mother], we either act out
by indulging the patient with actual mothering (this may be done
in verbal or other sympathetic gestures) or we may become so
frightened of doing this, that we freeze and do not reach the
patient's wish to be mothered' (ibid., p. 38). Brenman Pick has
amplified the moments of stuckness to which Money-Kyrle
pointed, with the details of 'mating' of a specific part of the analyst's
personality (which the patient gets to know extremely well) with
a certain aspect of the patient.

THE AVAILABLE PARTS OF THE PSYCHOANALYST

Brenman Pick, in asserting how a 'state of mind [which] seeks
another state of mind' as a mouth seeks a nipple, suggests a very
important model for understanding the transference/counter-
transference interactions; and for helping with the 'little piece of
self-analysis' that is required to disentangle stuck situations. The
psychoanalyst is required to know the parts of him- or herself which
are vulnerable and available to be projected into. Motherliness is
clearly one obvious possibility, since most psychoanalysts are in
the business of trying to feel for others and reducing their distress.
Every analyst will have a variant on this. Most will find themselves
becoming reassuring at times, or giving advice to their unhappy
patients. Every analyst will also have many other aspects with
which the patient will link in this way. Each one of us is a unique
personality, and will have unique aspects ready to respond. There
are certain common ones: the analyst's super-ego, for example; the

patient will expect, and often get, criticism, usually unintentional and unwitting, from the analyst. Another is the sexual aspect of the analyst, and perhaps this was the first of all these kinds of links to be noticed – Josef Breuer, in the treatment he conducted in 1882, froze over so completely when his patient, Anna O, fell in love with him that he backed out of the whole project of psychoanalysis altogether, leaving Freud to go on alone.

These problems obstructing the understanding of what is happening in the intrapsychic world of the patient arise from the psychoanalyst's mind becoming overrun by disturbance; the psychoanalyst's own disturbance mating with that of the patient. In a sense the analyst could be said to know about the disturbance, but is not able at such times to know about it usefully for the patient.

There may, however, be some aspect of the patient that aims specifically to disrupt this link of 'knowing' in the psychoanalytic pair. In subsequent chapters we will come on to the ways in which the patient may exploit the psychoanalyst's efforts to know. In the next two chapters I propose to take us through the very important developments in understanding the processes of knowing and thinking, and what goes wrong with them.

11 KNOWING AND BEING KNOWN

Some psychoanalysts proceed on the basis of an untroubled *treatment alliance* in which patient and analyst explore the patient's unconscious. Kleinian analysts view such an alliance as inevitably troubled. It is prone to conflict and disturbance, like all other aspects of the personality of the patient – and, for that matter, of the analyst. In Chapter 10 we saw the detailed emotional linking between the minds of patient and analyst, and how this is inevitably distorted by both. However, psychoanalysis has emerged from that discussion as an arena where another kind of link is offered. A psychoanalysis is an opportunity to know, and be known by, each other. This has come to be called the 'K'-link. It is formed within the fraught arena of the transference and countertransference and, as Chapter 10 attempted to show, the 'K'-link cannot be separated from the storms of emotional relating; the point is, we have to 'cope with feelings and subject them to thought'. Nevertheless, there is an impetus in patients – and, indeed in analysts – to separate knowing from the cut and thrust of emotional contact (see Chapters 13–15); and later we will consider certain patients who believe their psychic survival depends on separating out their knowing (Chapter 14).

First I want to begin with the important contemporary topic of symbolization. We considered the difficulty that thought-disordered schizophrenics have in knowing and thinking (Chapter 7), and their odd resort to the use of 'ideograms'. This led Hanna Segal to investigate symbol-formation and what goes wrong with it.

SYMBOL-FORMATION

To acquire the use of symbols entails the capacity for a dual recognition of an object: to recognize it as an object in its own right – a word, for instance; and also to know that it *means* something else. A word is a pattern drawn on a piece of paper, but it is *also* an entity that means something. A symbol is two things at once. The word 'apple' on the page is a black pattern of ink on white paper; it also means a fruit which can be eaten, looks green or red, and so on.

Segal advanced the view that the capacity for symbol-formation is affected by the operation of projective identification. In the more violent forms there is a loss of boundary between the self and the objects (see, for instance, *Occupying the object*, p. 122). Then, the object (symbol) becomes confused with the mental content of the subject (the meaning he or she wants to symbolize). Meaning and symbol become identical, equated: the symbol *becomes* the thing symbolized. Segal (1957) termed this 'symbolic equation', to contrast it with symbol-formation proper. Clearly this produces very pronounced effects on the capacity to think. If symbols are exactly the thing they symbolize, then they have to be used in the way the thing is used. Segal offered an exposition with the help of especially apt material from two patients.

Example: The patient with a violin

Patient A was a hospitalized schizophrenic:

> He was once asked by his doctor why he had stopped playing the violin since his illness. He replied with some violence, 'Why? do you expect me to masturbate in public?' . . .

The violin he held in his hand and the private – and perhaps shameful – genital were one and the same. The boundary between the symbol and the external object was eroded:

> For A, the violin had become so completely equated with his genital that to touch it in public became impossible.

This contrasts with the next patient, B, who could use symbols as representations, not equations.

Example: Another violin

Patient B created symbols differently:

> ... patient, B, dreamed one night that he and a young girl were playing
> a violin duet. He had associations to fiddling, masturbating, etc., from
> which it emerged clearly that the violin represented his genital and
> playing the violin represented a masturbation phantasy of a relation
> with the girl.

The violin *represented* a phantasy, it was not the reality of
masturbation. In this sense he could perhaps add some of the
enjoyment and excitement from what it represented (masturbation) to the expression of his actual musical skills.

The symbolic representation of masturbation by playing on a violin
is clearly quite different from the exact, concrete and embarrassing
equation of fiddling on the violin with masturbation. What makes
the real difference is the ability to see *in* the symbol some personal
or social meaning that the symbol is not. The process of putting
something personal into an external object (the symbol) depends
on whether that boundary between the self and external objects
remains intact. That, in turn, depends on the form of projective
identification a person habitually employs. If projective identification is accomplished with violence, with large transfers of parts of
the self, and with a consequent distortion of personal identity and
the identity of the object, then symbols become concretized into
being that person, or some aspect of him or her. Aspects of reality,
thought and truth are then seriously distorted.

On the other hand, the form of projective identification which
is much less violent and distorting of identity is a foundation for the
process of symbols proper, and for communication. At this
non-violent end of the spectrum, a charge of meaning is mildly
inserted into the symbol – the meaning is expressed by rather than
evacuated from the user. Such expression (unlike evacuation) does
not disturb the boundary between the subject (specifically his or
her meaning) and the symbol; the object (symbol) can retain its
true identity as something, while representing some other thing.
Thus communication and symbols are not simply shared agreement
on usage within a language culture, but require as an initial

precondition the capacity for a communicative form of projective identification.

THINKING

Disturbed symbolization leads to disturbed thinking. The thought disorder found in schizophrenics arises from the concrete kind of symbols formed by equation. Thinking is greatly enhanced once symbols proper can be achieved, especially words. To put it another way: this step from the concrete object to the symbol parallels the conversion of bodily sensations into psychological experiences; and is indeed part of that process. That achieved, thoughts are then generated which provoke the mind into developing the capacity for thinking. This conversion process – from sensations to experiences – contrasts with the other process of immediate discharge (evacuation) of feelings. For instance: hunger will be experienced in the tummy as 'hunger pains', say, and could merely be discharged as bodily pain to be treated with medicines, or simply screaming for help. Or those feelings could be held in mind and recognized as a condition which requires food – that is, represented mentally as hunger – to which appropriate thinking could then be applied, resulting perhaps in making a sandwich.

That sort of process of conversion from sensations to experiences was postulated (but never investigated) by Susan Isaacs when she described how 'Phantasy is the mental corollary, the psychic representative of, instinct' (Isaacs, 1948, p. 83). Bion and subsequent Kleinians have gone into this specific area to investigate the function involved in the generation of unconscious phantasy, experiences, meaning and thought out of bodily processes; and what happens when it goes wrong. Bion gave the term 'alpha function' to the conversion process and, as we have seen (Chapter 8), saw it in terms of a psychic or emotional container. Psychological symbols are containers for the bodily sensations. Sensations accumulate in the mind which, through reflection, makes some sense of them (i.e. gives them a meaning) and can then use them for thinking.

In the next example, this process goes wrong. Remember Segal's contention that symbol-formation is disturbed by violent forms of projective identification.

Example: Failure of meaning and communication

Segal described a patient in whom a problem of meaningful thought led to great difficulties in communicating. She had taken up philosophy, philology and modern languages in an attempt to help herself:

> Her verbal communications particularly early in her analysis were very difficult to understand. I often had difficulty in following the conscious meaning. She tends to misuse words, mix languages, etc. Often there is little connection between what she says, what she means to say and what she actually thinks. The unconscious meaning is often even more confused . . . in her the non-verbal clues are [also] lacking or misleading. For instance her tone of voice or her facial expression often bear no relation to her state of mind. Her symbolism is at times very concrete . . . She often responds to interpretations by physical sensation. Words are experienced as concrete things, often felt as a lump inside her . . . Sometimes she speaks for a long time and I realize she has said nothing concrete or real that I can get hold of.

Only with difficulty can we grasp this impediment of thought; and that seems to be the point. What is clear, however, is that the capacity to distinguish words (symbols) from sensations is disturbed. Words are so abstract that they seem to relate to nothing; at other times they seem to be equated with bodily sensations. The patient does not, in effect, have the use of a proper verbal container into which she can put her experiences so that they are adequately communicated (see Bion's example of *The man who stammered*, p. 112). In fact the reverse seems to happen: meaning disappears:

> At the same time, I can observe how she empties my words of all meaning, like listening to an interpretation and immediately translating it into some philosophical or psychoanalytical abstract term, often distorting its meaning completely.

We have come across an object that strips meaning away, a 'bizarre object' (see p. 133). We are using the idea of a container (Chapter 7), and we might question what sort of containing is going on. In contrast to the normal containing function of giving meaningful words to her experience, this patient appears to have an internal object that performs the reverse of containing. It strips meaning away from her words and her analyst's words:

> In those modes of functioning, one can see a disturbance between container and the contained. When she is over-concrete, the projected part is totally identified with the container. When she is empty of meaning, the container and contained have a relation of mutually emptying one another . . . this mutually destructive relation between the part she projects and the container seems mostly to be related to envy and to narcissism.
>
> Nothing is allowed to exist outside herself which could give rise to envy . . . She had several dreams characteristic of her, depicting her narcissism. For instance: *she was in bed with a young man, glued and fused to him, but the young man was herself.*

This omnipotent form of projective identification seems to operate in order to deny the separateness between herself and an object so that she denies that her object is someone else. Therefore (narcissistically) she does not have the pain of being aware of his separateness, his difference or his own valuable qualities which might arouse envy. We can be interested, with Segal, that this person habitually employs phantasies of union (projective identification) and exhibits gross distortion of symbols:

> Following several such dreams, she brought a different dream. *She was in a house, the attic of which was disintegrating. She did not want to take any notice because she lived in the middle floor between ground and top.* She had a number of useful associations to the dream. She owns a flat in a house which has three flats. The owner of the house wants her to participate in costs for repairing the attic. She is furious about it because she feels it isn't fair. It's true she signed a contract that she would, but she was foolish to agree to it. Her own flat is not in danger from the damaged attic, being in the middle, but she feels bad about it because of her friends who live in the top flat. Then she said that the middle must be her tummy and started complaining of her physical symptoms. The attic must be her head which is in a terrible disintegrated state. She can't think, she can't work. She thinks that her head should be entirely my concern.

The disintegrating attic conveyed that the patient had some awareness of the intellectual disintegration of her communications – that is to say, her head is full of the damaged communications. However, she split off her concern about it, and it appears projected into the psychoanalyst's (owner's) responsibility. We can see the projective identification – the patient's sense of personal responsibility is deliberately relocated into the analyst's responsibility for her:

> I have interpreted to her her repudiation of the analytical contract that we should both be concerned with her head and related the friends who live on the top flat to internal objects, thoughts and feelings that she did not want to concern herself with.

When the projective identification is interpreted, what happens?

> But somewhat later in the session I had noticed that, despite her complaints about the state of her head, there was something very superior in her attitude, particularly the fact that, though she complained in the session of how empty she felt and unable to communicate, she seemed to take quite a pride in her metaphors, which became more florid as the session progressed.

The interpretation brought out a change of attitude, a superiority, but also a recognition of an emptiness. I think we can understand from earlier examples how this emptiness represents the patient's experience of something having gone missing. With a further interpretation some clarity appears:

> When I interpreted that, she rather reluctantly said that, while she was speaking of the middle floor, she was in fact thinking of the first floor, an expression her family uses to denote 'upper class'.

The patient has become aware of her superior attitudes, the omnipotence she insists on sustaining through projective identification aimed at denying her dependence on the analyst's mind in order to think. Although she had originally been bothered by her difficulty in communicating, she became superior to the psychoanalyst, in whose hands she left the problem of keeping her mind and its internal objects in order; and thus superior to the process of making sense and giving meaning. Segal continues in her paper to describe the case of Helen Keller, who was deaf and dumb, learning speech from her teacher, because the patient had also read the Keller autobiography, but her reading was that Helen Keller had

> invented a sign language and taught it to her teacher . . . Helen Keller with all her handicaps having achieved a complete communicating with her audience, and my poor patient still struggling with the problem of

> communicating . . . She still had not accepted that she learned to speak from her parents.

The point of this case is to demonstrate how omnipotent projective identification severely interferes with symbolic communication. This patient was not psychotic, and her mind was not fragmented, but it is clear how the projective identification nevertheless interferes with her own identity – she felt empty, useful parts of her that could feel responsibility and concern went missing – and how it prevents a communicating 'K'-link in which analyst and patient work on knowing and being known to each other. The patient's internal object had not developed as a container that enabled her to understand more about herself and others. Instead, her own superiority had led to her installing a dreadful object that was superior to the work of knowing about herself.

We saw above (in Chapter 8) instances of patients who seemed to lack an adequate mother to assist with the conversion process of sensations to symbols (*The mother who could not understand*, p. 127; *The cheated patient*, p. 130; *The patient's failed container*, p. 131). This alpha function (conversion process) involves the containing of experiences; and in the first instance, when the infant is very young, that function has to be performed by an external object, 'mother'. And that function is repeatedly introjected to build up an internal object that establishes the infant's progressive capacity to 'know itself'. In the psychoanalytic domain it is the analyst's mind which replicates that 'maternal' alpha function for the patient to introject. Now we are in a position to see that problems of knowing can arise from two directions: first, the external object ('mother', psychoanalyst) may function badly, as Bion described with his patients who felt cheated of such an object; secondly, as with Segal's patient with whom we have just become acquainted, the patient has internal sources (envy) which place her in a superior position, refusing to recognize her dependence on an external object that can perform better than she can. In this case no internal understanding object can be introjected and develop within her.

The acquisition of the capacity to think and know entails the development of an internal object capable of giving meaning. Such a link, called a 'K'-link by Bion, is the experience of knowing, and of being known by, some other person. Brenman Pick, for instance (see *The man who was sensible*, p. 165), described this in the form of the *mutual* explorations going on in the transference/counter-transference relationship. Segal's patient dismantled this 'K'-link; she dismantled her contract and her thought processes. Bion called that '–K' (i.e 'minus K').

The ability to think about, to know and to be known depends on the development of the person through the early stages of the Oedipus complex, and particularly the capacity to sustain the wish to know about the parents and their activities. We will now consider this relation between thinking and the oedipal parents.

12   Oedipal Knowing

Normally, the Oedipus complex refers to links of loving and being loved – and hating and being hated – in the triangular situation, loving one parent and hating the other. These are sometimes referred to as 'L'- or 'H'-links (Bion, 1962b). It is also widely recognized that the Oedipus story is the account of the discovery of a dreadful hidden knowledge (a 'K'-link). Sophocles wrote his play almost like a modern detective story – the quest to find some wrongdoing and wrongdoer. Thus part of the core phantasy of childhood sexual life concerns finding out, curiosity, the acquisition of knowledge; and many disturbances to learning and knowing might therefore be rooted in the violence, fear and defences of the Oedipus complex.

Freud thought that knowing was an instinctual, epistemophilic component of the libido – a basic desire (thirst) for knowledge – and that it was inherent in the Oedipus complex in the form of the wish to know about the parents' sexuality in the primal scene. Klein added that the desire to know is partly driven by anxiety arising from aggression. The fear of harming others that arises from aggression leads to an anxious concern to look into reality to see if the phantasies about destroying objects are 'only' phantasies. Considerable reassurance is gained by finding that in external reality loved ones are still actually alive, remain (largely) loving, and are still available to be introjected. Thus enquiry into external reality can support a shaky internal world – as in the example of *The insecure internal object* (p. 82), when Richard was about to lose his psychoanalyst. However, the return of a good object does, as Richard reported in the earlier example (*Identifying with a* '*good' object*, p. 71), make a great difference to the internal world.

Bion added a further aspect to knowing, which concerned knowing about the internal world. His work with schizophrenics (see Chapter 8) led him to understand that the anxieties about the internal world could be dealt with by disrupting awareness, especially the awareness of one's own feelings and mind. He observed the infant's need to be contained by the maternal knowing of its internal states (see *The mother who could not understand*; *The cheated patient*; and *The patient's failed container*, pp. 127, 130 and 131); this led him to describe learning and knowing as activities that entail bringing things together in the mind: bringing together preconceptions (anticipations) with things as they actually are; bringing one idea together with another; putting two and two together, and so on. He likened such activities to the parents' coming together in their sexuality. Bion considered that things linked together in the mind may create reactions similar to parents linking together sexually. The experience of things coming together in the mind is a version of the combined parent figure, located internally (or internalized). We considered this in bodily terms (Chapter 5) in the examples *Attacked by worms* (p. 62) and *The man who assaulted his buttocks* (p. 66). Now we are concerned with this experienced within the mind rather than within the body.

We could, then, expect the tensions and aggression normally associated with the Oedipus complex to appear in the intellectual arena, as a thought disorder based in disturbance caused by the coupling of ideas – a mental intercourse. Such attitudes of superiority to an internal intercourse are also paralleled in the envy of the mental intercourse that goes on in someone else's mind. We will examine the way mental intercourse is refracted through oedipal excitement and aggression in the example in this chapter. We will be able to look at the evidence in more detail than Bion gives. First, however, I must describe some of the oedipal phantasies that occur, and the way the infant can try to deal with the most frightening of them.

Oedipal phantasies are a complex of a terror mitigated by other defensive phantasies. In effect the infant adopts phantasies of a defensive kind when it is overwhelmed by its terrifying feelings. To clarify this idea of *defensive phantasies* we can imagine a hungry infant who constructs a phantasy of some pain-giving object in its tummy. To rescue itself the infant may then elaborate a defensive phantasy that it evacuates that 'bad' object; and it may actually defecate in the extremes of its crying, living then in the distorted belief that the 'bad' object is outside. Sometimes in this state, when mother does come to feed, the infant believes that what has arrived is that very terrifying projected object that has caused the pain; and it can no longer accept the feed. Thus the terrifying phantasies derived from hunger pains are dealt with by other phantasies – in this case projection.

OEDIPAL PHANTASIES AND THE COMBINED PARENT COUPLE

We saw that some of Klein's child patients were preoccupied by worries and aggression towards the loved parents. In the first case of hers that we examined (*Inhibited play*, p. 39; and also in *Peter's naughtiness*, p. 139), Peter was anxious about the parental intercourse, its productive potential with which the birth of his brother confronted him, and his exclusion, which aroused murderous phantasies. When the child is very young, the parents' exclusiveness leads him or her to perceive them as a single joint figure, combined in an intimate structure known as the 'combined parent figure'. The emotional crises that attend upon this perception are seismic. Erna (see *Erna's Oedipus complex*, p. 53), as well as Peter, was tortured by persisting paroxysms of aggression and fear.

From an early age, children take evasive action. They defend themselves by engaging in other phantasies (see *The little girl with the elephant*, p. 55) that will mitigate the intensity of this situation. In the example *Damaged parents* (page 85), for instance, a phantasy, revealed in the patient's dream, was that he had separated his parents and controlled their activity with his superior potency. He was thus protected from experiencing further aggression – though he did feel that he was then burdened with parents he had to look after.

The next example offers material from a patient whose experiences were organized around a specific core phantasy. In her case it seems that experiencing a couple impelled her to push, or crash, her way into their intercourse. This in turn led to a view of intercourse itself moulded by this phantasy – one person crashing into another. The anxiety provoked by that disastrous picture had then to be coped with. She did this by constructing, and attempting to realize, another phantasy situation, one in which two people never come together at all; a barrier intervenes. This saves the partners in the intercourse; it saves the patient from feeling the crisis of intrusive aggression; but it creates a bleak world in which the patient has great difficulty in sustaining contact with anyone else. This case is particularly instructive in showing how curiosity is regarded as a crashing, intrusive *mental* intercourse in exactly the same way as the patient feels a violating sexual intercourse to be.

She has another method of protecting herself too: to force her knowledge, and her wish to know (curiosity), into the psychoanalyst, and thus to be rid of such a dangerous thing herself; then the dangerous crashing intrusion might be controlled – by him. In that way she can obliterate her worries; except that, in the course of making that projection into the psychoanalyst, she is engaged in another instance of an aggressive crashing intrusion (a violent projective identification).

This manifold array of phantasies had a powerful effect actualy in the psychoanalysis. The analyst had to struggle a good deal with his reactions to being 'put under pressure'. Segal's patient in *Failure of meaning and communication* (p. 174) also avoided knowing (and avoided the contract with the analyst to investigate) in the same projective way. Be alert to the manner in which knowledge and self-knowledge in the psychoanalysis are hampered in this example.

Example: The projection of understanding

Michael Feldman's patient, a woman, was deeply involved in her psychoanalysis but could rarely know it. She had presented with quite severe sexual difficulties, which led to panic when there was any prospect of intimacy. She evaded the psychoanalyst, too; and in order to protect herself from curiosity about her anxiety and pain, she also avoided speaking about connections she could make and know for herself in her own mind:

> Just before the session I wish to describe, the patient had recalled, for
> the first time, an incident from her childhood . . . When she was five
> years old and already attending school, a truck carrying a boiler had
> gone out of control, had crashed through the tall thick hedge in front
> of the house and come to rest just in front of the living room, where her
> mother and grandmother were sitting at the time . . . [This reflected] an
> anxiety that expressed itself in her problems with any intimacy. There
> was an object that intruded in a violent and uncontrolled manner . . . It
> illustrated the need for a protective barrier.

The patient has brought to her analyst a vivid image. It impressed
him, quite clearly, as a terrifying experience for her. He was aware
that it linked with the experience she also suffered when he tried
to get close to her in an understanding way:

> Shortly after this she arrived for a session ten minutes late and slightly
> out of breath. She said she was sorry she was late, she had a number of
> things to attend to before she left the flat, and she should have left more
> time. She was then silent. I found myself feeling a bit frustrated and
> thinking ruefully that after years of analysis she accounted for her
> lateness in such superficial and un-insightful terms.

Notice the analyst's reaction: Feldman seemed to think that she
could have some more thoughts and feelings about being late, but
that she either was not aware of them or did not connect with him
about them. For instance, the patient may have been held up for
quite valid reasons; even so, she could have said more about her
feelings *about* being late. Her reaction could have been many
things – disappointment, perhaps, at missing some of her time;
pleasure at keeping him waiting; relief at keeping a distance – there
are many possibilities. The analyst is left in the dark, not knowing;
but he also feels frustrated because he knows that there is
something to know, but he cannot get at it. His view is that he
carries all the wish to know – that is, any interest the patient had
seems to have been projected into him:

> As she began to speak again, I suddenly recalled something I had
> forgotten – that this was the day her parents were making a rare visit to
> this country and were due to stay with my patient in her flat. Her remark
> about having a number of things to attend to contained an implicit
> reference to this.

In fact the analyst *does* begin to function as the one who knows
things about the patient. She certainly has remembered because

her parents' visit was preoccupying for her, but she has chosen not to speak about it. A certain amount of knowing is going on, but no link between them – no 'K'-link. By this time, she had overcome her protective barrier and was now telling him:

> She was intensely preoccupied with what her parents might learn about her private life – particularly about her sexual life, and also about her analysis.

I think it is clear to the reader that the patient experienced the parents' visit as an intrusion. But it also has a particularly sexual implication:

> ... she described the elaborate precautions she intended to take to hide any evidence of her sexuality such as hiding suspender belts and a frilly nightgown she had received as a present in a locked cupboard, or in the loft above her flat. She was equally secretive about her analysis, and when they visited her and she was unable to account for her absence, she unhesitatingly missed the session.

She hides her frilly nightgown and she hides her psychoanalysis – there is a clear link between her sexual activity and her psychoanalysis: both have to be hidden. Of course it is possible that she was anxious about her sexual feelings towards her psychoanalyst, and concealed them. And though this may be true, the slant of the session concerns curiosity as much as sexuality:

> there is a phantasy that both parents, in different ways, are intensely curious, and rather intrusive, particularly about her sexual life.

So what the analyst remembered about the patient's preoccupations was right, but it had seemed that the patient felt they could not be addressed. She could not come and say that she was late because she was anxiously making her flat ready for these prying parents. In effect she was bundling things out of the way in her mind as well as her flat. It was as if the analyst, too, had prying interests that would be intrusive:

> These matters [sexual] could never be openly referred to in the family, although she conveyed that there was a highly charged atmosphere, with each member of the family having suspicions and fantasies about what was going on . . . [In the analysis] it proved difficult to find ways of speaking about any intimate matters.

The atmosphere of frustrated interest pictured in her family was re-created with her 'prying' psychoanalyst:

There was, on the contrary, a pressure to tolerate any situation in which derivatives of these early configurations were present in my patient's mind, and in mine, but could not be addressed in any direct or open way.

I think that Feldman is indicating that for this frightened patient enquiry is dealt with in exactly the same way as physical intrusion – by protective barriers. Now observe the pained interchange between the patient and her parents:

After a silence, the patient said she had telephoned her parents the previous evening to check that everything was all right and to confirm arrangements for their arrival. She spoke to her father, who was preoccupied with the sleeping arrangements during their stay – in particular that he might have to share a double bed with her mother. The patient reassured him . . . and said he should not worry, he would have a single bed to sleep in; she would sleep in the double. Father said, 'What! have you got a *double bed?* What for? I didn't know you had a double bed!'

What do we find? First, that Father too, like the patient, is worried about pairing up – the fear of the parents sleeping together. But we also have another sort of linking up here, the telephone contact; when that contact is made, the patient conveys that an intrusive enquiry bursts in – in the form, here, of father's explosive curiosity. She reassures father, and herself, that all can sleep alone – the protective barrier of being alone:

She thought mother was probably kicking father by now, and he did not say any more.

So the intrusive telephone intercourse is also dealt with by an opposing force to restore the protective silence.

She was then silent for a long time. I thought it was clear that she was expecting me to take up the material that she had brought, and she had no intention of saying anything further about it herself.

Once more the analyst feels subjected to carrying the curiosity and the investigative push, and to doing so without her as a partner, since she was too frightened to join him:

I said I thought that she showed an anxiety similar to her father's about being too close to something, and she behaved as if it was important for her, too, to be in a single bed, apparently not really engaging with me or with the things she had spoken about. We knew that there was more that did go on, but it had to be kept hidden . . .

What do we think of the link now made between the fear of coming together with a partner sexually and coming together psycho-analytically? It seems to be an interesting parallel, but how did the patient take it?

> She was then silent for a very long time.

That was not very promising. It left the analyst in a quandary. He was pressed to carry the effort to make the 'K'-link, but then she was silent. He could be right that she had retreated to her 'single bed' because he was attempting to link up with her:

> I was familiar with the process whereby the patient reported some material to me and then seemed to withdraw to a single bed, as it were, leaving me to address the material, which was often potentially exciting or disturbing for her. It never seemed to be useful for me to accept the responsibility for all her thinking and verbalizing in the session and yet I felt I had to do something . . . I had thought carefully about my interpretation, and it had seemed a reasonable approach.

The analyst had no partner to work with – there was no 'K'-link between them. It is not that the patient is in a negative state of feeling towards the analyst (negative transference); it is actually a non-contact. Although her wish to link up with him in the work of curiosity had survived, he believed he was pressed to be responsible for it – to accept it as a part of him. Her projected wish mated with his own. It is not that she lacks a psychoanalytic curiosity; rather, it does exist, but is located in him, locked up in a cupboard (her analyst's mind). The analyst then suffers the patient's dilemma: to restore the 'K'-link would be to 'become' a violent curious intruder; to remain silent would re-create the family atmosphere of locked-up, frustrated but unspoken curiosity.

Eventually he conveyed his feeling that he had been put in the position of an intrusive father who had taken too close an interest in her sexuality; while he, the analyst, had shown too much curiosity about her mental intercourse. Although there was another period of silence, this interpretation did eventually enable the patient to make a response:

> After a further long silence she said with an anxious note in her voice that she suddenly remembered that she had not put away her contraceptive pills. It would be O.K. unless people started looking in drawers . . . After a short silence she said she was getting in a bit of a panic. It was then the end of the session, and she left in a slightly disorganized way, looking very anxious.

This anxious response suggests that she feels someone (could it be the psychoanalyst?) has discovered her means of making things sterile. Such a reading would suggest that the interpretation had been correct, had established a genuine 'K'-link, but in so doing had also re-enacted the fearful and disorganizing intrusion, leaving her panicky. It may be that when she referred to 'drawers' the patient felt a serious embarrassment, like Segal's *The patient with a violin* (p. 171), as if she was actually exhibiting her underwear to her psychoanalyst. In that case Feldman intruded not just into her but, she felt, right into her secret 'drawers' that contained her means of keeping out of fertile contact. It really is a very painful process for both of them.

This patient uses the analyst's mind as a space into which to project the wish to establish a link with another person. Again we can see the potentially violent phantasy behind this projection into the analyst. I have used this material to show the conjunction between a violent projective identification and the failure to distinguish between a bodily and a mental or symbolic level of contact. The disturbing violent reaction to being excluded from a united couple is an oedipal anxiety which disastrously wrecks the capacity to make the 'K'-links within herself or with another mind which will enable her to learn.

The cases we have considered in this chapter and the previous one have demonstrated how the research accomplished with the thought disorders of schizophrenic patients has alerted Kleinian psychoanalysts to disturbances in less seriously troubled patients. The notion of a 'K'-link and the subtle, as well as blatant, disruptions of it have been extremely fruitful concepts. Such a notion speaks directly to the psychoanalytic enterprise of knowing and learning, and of how that specifically is interfered with by transference – or, to put it the other way round: much finer detail of the transference relationship is now possible given the understanding of the relationship of knowing (the 'K'-link) and what disrupts it. In the next chapter we will consider some more of these situations, but more explicitly in the context of the technical problem of encouraging patients who are particularly slippery to engage in a link with the analyst – certain 'difficult-to-reach' patients.

13   BEING MOVED

The dedication to not knowing displayed in somewhat similar ways in Segal's and Feldman's cases makes these patients 'difficult to reach'. Considerable recent research has gone into working with such patients. The results have drawn attention to the nature of the immediate contact between patient and psychoanalyst, which was so disrupted in these two cases. The moment-to-moment emotional contact as it appears in the psychoanalyst's experience (counter-transference) is followed in detail. The particular patients who shelter from emotional contact use very subtle methods of moving out of reach. Such patients try quite desperately to create a stasis, an emotional equilibrium, which is never disturbed by emotional contacts with others.

A special focus on the whole setting of the psychoanalytic treatment has developed. Klein asserted that 'it is essential to think in terms of *total situations* transferred from the past into the present, as well as of emotions, defences, and object-relations' (Klein, 1952, p. 55). We have seen already, in the example of *The man who assaulted his buttocks* (p. 66), how a masochistic perversion seemed straightforward on the surface, but when a wider view of the transference situation was taken, an extremely complex entangled identity emerged. The contemporary reading of this principle has been influential in the development of the newer approaches to practice, especially through Betty Joseph's paper 'Transference: the total situation' (Joseph, 1985), which follows Klein's recommendation. What is transferred to the psychoanalyst in the present is not exactly the patient's 'mother' from babyhood. Instead it is the *way the baby related* to its mother.

The man who was sensible (p. 165), for instance, did not just relate to his psychoanalyst as a mother, but used her to accomplish the same splitting of the object into 'good' and 'bad' mothers for specific defensive reasons.

Joseph described a number of patients who were apparently difficult to reach and related in a particular, odd way. They maintained a self-protective effort to create an emotional distance, out of the psychoanalyst's reach. This often entailed getting the analyst to enact a kind of *pseudo*-analysis. Thus the patient made it seem as if a psychoanalytic treatment was going on, as if understanding was accumulating; but in fact the patient retained, behind that front, a remoteness from the analyst, and a defensiveness against being emotionally moved by any under-standing. There was a subtle situation which looks like a 'K'-link, but it is not; it is the antithesis, and it actively prevents such a link. Often the patient's communication was aimed at projecting into the psychoanalyst's curiosity and thus linking in such a way that the analyst was the one who carried the impulse to enquire, as in the examples in the last two chapters. The patient appears to remain passive and unmoved. Real learning does not then happen.

Example: The twisted carrots

This patient, described by Joseph, was a rigid, controlled and anxious person in his early twenties, married with a young baby. He knew some of the analytic literature.

> When he had been in analysis over three and a half years . . . he started a session saying that he wanted to talk about his problems about clearing out his cupboards. He was spending so much time on them. He described how he had got to clearing things out and how he did not seem to want to stop. This was put forward as if it were a problem with which he needed help.

The reader will find this unexceptional, but for the psychoanalyst something felt not quite right about it, apparently, and she waited to try to understand why.

> He added that he did not want to go to friends in the evening because he wanted to go on with his clearing out.
> He paused as if he expected something from me. I had the strong impression that I was expected to say something about his clearing out his mind or something rather pat, so I waited.

How should we take these later comments? It seems that he is
drawing back from some meeting; he would prefer to remain
self-absorbed (involved in his cupboard). So when he seemed to
expect the analyst to say something, there could indeed be
something suspect. In the countertransference the analyst had a
definite reaction, a discomforting sense that she could find herself
drawn into something rather superficial. She continued to wait
until she could disentangle this – which, with the help of further
associations, she began to do:

> He added that, anyway, he did not really like going to these people in
> the evening, because the last time they went the husband was rude. He
> had turned to watch the TV while my patient and his wife were there
> and subsequently made dictatorial statements about children's school
> difficulties. I suggested to him that I got the impression that he had been
> waiting for me to make some pseudo-Kleinian interpretations about the
> clearing out of his mind and inner world, and when I did not, I became
> the rude husband who watched my own TV and was somewhat
> dictatorial in my views as to what his difficulties were, that is to say, I
> did not refer to his preconceived remarks.

We can follow how the interpretation brings the countertransference feeling (the patient wanted some definite unthreatening
response) together with the content (the friend's/analyst's rude-
ness and a turning away from him). When the analyst declined to
enter into the expected role with the expected interpretation, he
felt her to be the rude friend who watched his own TV. He felt her
to be withdrawing from his own purpose – to assist in keeping him
safely unmoved in a predictable sort of analysis. There could be a
slightly hard or critical edge to such an interpretation. It certainly
challenged any wish he might have had for a bland predictability.

> At first he was angry and upset, but later in the session he was able to
> gain some understanding about his touchiness.

What do we discern in his response? It is definitely emotional – he
is angry and upset; therefore, a contact with the patient had been
provoked, though it would seem it was not of the kind he wanted.
Nevertheless, despite the apparent disagreement over the degree
of contact, the patient did apparently gain some further understanding – and the analyst reported that it was some insight into
his competitive controlling. It is the next session that discloses the
interesting aspect of this material:

The following day he said that he felt much better . . .

He might have felt better because of the understanding he gained in the previous session; but it might also be that he retreated into a similar false situation. A dream threw some light on this question which confronted the analyst:

> . . . and had had a dream. *He dreamed that he and his wife were in a holiday cottage. They were about to leave and were packing things in the car but for some reason he was packing the car further down the lane, as if he were too modest to bring it to the front door or the lane was too muddy and narrow.*

What do we make of the car keeping a distance down the lane? It seems possibly as if the patient is conveying that the analyst is on the right lines in interpreting, the day before, his wish to keep out of contact:

> *Then he was in a market getting food to take home, which was odd: Why should he take food if he were going home?*

The dream prompts us to something odd – as, indeed, the analyst's countertransference did the day before: getting food for himself connects with his wish the day before to remain absorbed in himself (his cupboards), to decide on his own interpretations. In effect he refused to depend on food from the home, including food from the psychoanalytic 'home':

> *He was choosing some carrots – either he could take Dutch ones which were twisted or some better French ones which were young and straight, possibly slightly more expensive. He chose the Dutch twisted ones and his wife queried why he did so.*
>
> His associations led to plans for the holidays . . . his preference for France over Holland.

An odd situation again: he prefers France but, perversely, chose Dutch carrots!

> Carrots led to his memory of the advertisements during the war of carrots as good cheap food and a help against night-blindness.
>
> Briefly I suggested . . . his attempts on the previous day to force me to interpret in a particular way, as well as the understanding he had gained about it, had become linked with attempts to pack my interpretations inside himself, not to use for himself but for other purposes, as, for example, to use for a lecture which he was actually giving that evening. This then becomes food which he himself buys to take home, not food he gets from home-analysis. He chooses carrots which should help his

night-blindness, which should give him insight, but what he actually
selects are the twisted ones.

Here is a full interpretation which sets out the processes involved
as the patient deals with knowing and being known – a response
to the work of the day before. In fact there is a complex narrative.
Yesterday's work (the food he chooses) could, in the light of the
dream, be taken in two ways: one nourishing, one twisted. His
choice is for the twisted way, but this is odd; and in fact he realizes
this, and wonders why, though that curiosity is projected into his
wife. The response to the challenging interpretation of his wish for
pat interpretations, in fact, comes in the form of a dream in the next
day's session.

We have several main elements here: there is some interest in
having a nourishing analysis which can help with his blindness (i.e.
increase his insight); that is met by another odd, or twisted, part of
him which will use the analysis to retreat out of contact (down the
lane) and into a self-involvement and self-nourishment. The means
by which he frustrates proper nourishment is in the twisting of
analysis into this 'pseudo-analysis' which avoids real learning and
knowledge. Joseph points to the importance of the way in which
the psychoanalyst could be drawn into making pseudo-interpreta-
tions which are used for completely different purposes – to keep a
distance and avoid a disturbing emotional contact. The patient
engages with the psychoanalyst in a link with the analyst's desire
to know about the material. It is a link that does a number of things:
it dissolves the boundary between patient and analyst; prevents
thought; disturbs both identities; and abolishes the sense of a
contact with another separate person; but perhaps above all for this
patient, it achieves a sense of success over the analyst as a
competitive rival, rather than learning from her (a 'minus K'-link).
The analyst attempted, as best she could, to resist this debilitating
call to a bland pseudo-analysis while maintaining the effort to know
about what was happening. Thus the analyst exhibits an interest in
knowing and learning, but it is precisely this interest that becomes
useful for this patient to link up with (to 'mate' with) and to project
into defensively.

The transference, then, is the patient's *use* of the analyst. The
analyst performs a function for the patient – to have her own
curiosity, which can be made to contain the patient's projected

curiosity for him and render it ineffective. He is not just transferring the figure of a containing mother; he transfers the specific kind of containing function that is performed by the analyst (or the wife in this material) – a 'mating' of curiosities, rendering them ineffective. Joseph's (1985) idea of transference as the 'total situation' is not simply restricted to isolated references to the analyst about which patient and analyst converse. The very function of co-operation between them, the arena in which the psychoanalysis works, is a fulcrum of the patient's conflicts (sometimes in conjunction with the analyst's). The alliance between them is the arena of greatest transference vividness and conflict:

> Strachey (1934) . . . showed that what is being transferred is not primarily the external objects of the child's past, but the internal objects . . . [The transference] must include everything that the patient brings into the relationship, how he is using the analyst, alongside and beyond what he is saying. Much of our understanding of the transference comes through our understanding of how our patients act on us to feel things for varied reasons; how they try to draw us into their defensive systems; how they unconsciously act out with us in the transference, trying to get us to act out with them; how they convey aspects of their inner world built up from infancy. (Joseph, 1985, pp. 156–7)

In everyday social contact, people say things 'for effect', and this is no less prevalent in the fraught world of the psychoanalytic consulting room. What the patient does to the analyst, the effect his words have, have a long history in the patient's life with his objects. In this sense there is 'always something going on'. And so we are more concerned with the kind of use to which the patient puts the object in order to still anxieties and conflicts. The method for that will have been transferred from the past. The patient's use of the analyst replicates the use of objects in infancy and childhood.

I want to move on now to look at more of these processes which avoid contact and which thereby establish a stony impasse in the psychoanalytic process. We can ask: what is going on when it seems that nothing is going on? The stilling of lively contact by the patient – perhaps with the analyst's collusion – can be understood as a protective endeavour to remain afloat among flooding anxieties. In the next chapter we will explore a slightly different organization of the personality, one that is not just arranged to protect against the pain of living, but one in which the deadening of lively contact may be sought for itself. The satisfaction achieved by deadening the self in this way is now regarded by Kleinian psychoanalysts as a subtle form of satisfaction of the death instinct (see Chapter 9). It becomes a deadening repetition of the old, as Freud (1920) revealed. Much clinical effort has been directed by Kleinians towards the careful discrimination between the patient's defensive efforts in deadening pain and the patient's efforts to 'enjoy' death. We will see how far Kleinian psychoanalysts have been able to understand these odd personalities that can paradoxically or perversely enjoy deathliness for its own sake.

14 Impasse and the Organization of the Personality

In Chapter 13, we met a competitive, controlling patient who could take in (pack in) the psychoanalyst's interpretations, but did so for twisted purposes (*The twisted carrots*, p. 189). He took certain actual features of the personality of his analyst – her wish to learn through the psychoanalytic process – and could control her through them. He was gifted in relating to his object, very sensitive to the processes going on in her mind. He used his gifts to provide himself with the kind of help that made sense to him – to prevent a good, or deep, personal contact developing. In that way his life was deadened, and the analyst was engaged to help deaden the analysis. It is unclear from the clinical report whether Betty Joseph's patient was simply defending himself against intolerable experiences, or whether he was in some measure enjoying defeating her.

The satisfaction in destroying others' work and their creative effort is perhaps present at times in all of us. Freud (1920) noted how some patients reacted negatively to the therapeutic efforts of psychoanalysis. Instead of gaining understanding and some resolution of their early phantasies and traumas, they merely continued to repeat them. They did not get better. He attributed some of these 'negative therapeutic reactions' to the death instinct; in fact they were part of his evidence for postulating such an instinct. We have also seen this spoiling impulse in envy (Chapter 9); and in psychotic patients we saw the working of the death instinct as a self-directed destructiveness (Chapters 7 and 8).

Mostly people struggle successfully with such self-defeating impulses, but there are some patients for whom the struggle cannot be properly won. That antagonism becomes the centre of their personalities. Their world is not so completely destroyed as that of a psychotic patient; they relate to others in a more realistic way. In the example *The twisted carrots* (p. 189) the patient was not psychotic; unlike a psychotic, he was very much aware of the analyst as a person. Instead of destroying his own mind in order to avoid his painful emotional life, as the psychotic patient does, he sought out aspects of his object's mind in an endeavour to subdue emotional contact.

Contemporary Kleinian interest has moved from the analysis of psychotic patients to investigate these inaccessible personalities. It has been found that they organize their defensive systems around the use of objects in order to subdue life – in particular emotional life. This kind of personality is now termed a 'pathological organization' (see, for instance, Steiner, 1987, 1993). This interest has added a new dimension to the understanding of the more subtle forms of destructiveness; but the subtlety in no way diminishes its effectiveness. Rich personal relationships are greatly hampered; and the psychoanalysis itself is pervaded by a sense of emotional debility.

There are various features of these personalities which we shall consider in this chapter: (a) the analysis gets stuck in a non-progressing condition, an impasse, as the analyst is implicated in an organized system which protects against the pain of living; (b) the personality is defensively organized around the destructive impulses (death instinct); (c) evidence suggests an internal domination by anti-life attitudes – for instance, an 'internal mafia gang'; and (d) such attitudes are sustained by an internal 'propaganda' that death is superior to life, so that truth and honesty, as well as liveliness, succumb.

IMPASSE

The dominance of aggressive parts of the personality has a crucial quality – it keeps the patient in an entrapped position, and, typically, it restricts the analyst to a limited purpose as well. The psychoanalysis continues – in form; but it works *against* real insight rather than as a help to self-understanding. The analysis becomes an impasse. There is a kind of contrariness, a perversity, about attending for an analysis and then using it to support a continuing lack of insight. Such a perversity, however, is understandable when we recognize the patient's continuous need of an object for his or her own purpose – a quite different one from the analyst's. The patient wishes to subdue emotional life; the analyst to know it. It is difficult for the psychoanalyst to enter into the patient's world in a significant (non-perverse) way when she or he seems constantly to be recruited to support the status quo internally. In the following case, described by Betty Joseph, the patient had already developed some feelings of despair about being stuck. He felt stuck *in* something, in his awful state of mind; he might never get out of it.

Example: The patient imprisoned in a cavern

This patient had missed his previous session (Tuesday) because he overslept, and was puzzled because he had become aware of his appreciation of the psychoanalysis. Then:

> When he was describing the pain and misery of the Monday night [when his girl-friend had not returned his phone-call], he said that he was reminded of the feeling that he had expressed at the beginning of the Monday session, the feeling that perhaps he was too far into this awful state ever to be helped out by me or to get out himself. At the same time, during and immediately after the session there had been feelings of insight and hope.

The analyst presents this case to us because the patient is conveying something strange, as if he is trapped, almost as if he were addicted, in his pain and misery.

> He then told a dream: *he was in a long kind of cave, almost a cavern.*

The internal situation:

> *It was dark and smoky and it was as if he and other people had been taken captive by brigands. There was a feeling of confusion, as if they had been drinking. They, the captives, were lined up along a wall and he was sitting next to a young man. This man was subsequently described as looking gentle, in the mid-twenties, with a small moustache. The man suddenly turned towards him, grabbed at him and at his genitals, as if he were homosexual, and was about to knife my patient, who was completely terrified. He knew that if he tried to resist the man would knife him and there was tremendous pain.*
>
> After telling the dream, he went on to describe some of the happenings of the last two days. He particularly spoke first about K [the

girl-friend who had not telephoned]. He then spoke about a meeting he had been to, in which a business acquaintance had said that a colleague told him that he, the colleague, was so frightened of my patient, A, that he positively trembled when on the phone to him. My patient was amazed, but linked this with something I had shown him on Monday, when I had commented on a very cold, cruel way in which he dealt with me when I queried a point about another dream. This association was connected with the idea of the man in the dream looking so gentle but acting in this violent way, and so he felt that the man must somehow be connected with himself, but what about the moustache? Then suddenly he had the notion of D.H. Lawrence – he had been reading a new biography of Lawrence and remembered that he was enormously attracted to him in his adolescence and felt identified with him. Lawrence was a bit homosexual and clearly a strange and violent man.

Before going on to the analyst's interpretations, let us look at the content of the dream and the associations. A series of elements emerges: the inside situation (the cavern); being the brigands' captive in this violent place; being captivated by a homosexual violence (D.H. Lawrence); his adjacence to the violent, perverse and castrating man; the misery over being out of contact with his girlfriend.

I worked out with him that it seemed therefore that this long, dark cavern stood for the place where he felt he was too far in to be pulled out by himself or by me; as if it was his mind, but perhaps also part of his body. But the too-far-in seems to be linked with the notion that he was completely captured and captivated, possibly, by the brigands. But the brigands are manifestly associated with himself, the little man linked with Lawrence, who is experienced as part of himself.

The idea seems to be that he seduces, but also destroys, *himself* – and he is captured because it is that self-destructive state which is so seductive.

We can see that the giving-in to this brigand is absolutely terrifying, it is a complete nightmare, and yet sexually exciting. The man grabs his genitals.

Being imprisoned in the cavern by violent brigands appears to be a captivity to some violent part of himself in which he is imprisoned. But the imprisonment is connected with a sexual excitement – he is captivated – despite the fact that this excitement is terrifying:

So, I think the dream is clearly a response, not just to the girl-friend K being out on the Monday night and A lying in bed getting more and more disturbed about it, of which he was conscious, but to the fact that he had felt better, knew he had, and could not allow himself to get out of his misery and self-destruction.

I have chosen this patient to exemplify the stuckness of these patients. His analysis has progressed sufficiently for him to become aware of the impasse. He is captured by a violent, self-destructive (castrating) part of himself; but this is both sexually exciting, and also a satisfaction of a self-directed aggression. There is a lot of satisfaction in this position, sunk in misery and excited fear. We must also note his attempt to engage the analyst's sympathy for his unhappiness about his girlfriend: it is a move to recruit the analyst into supporting the misery, and thus to slide away from the contact which had felt better.

DEATH OVER LIFE

The problem for the psychoanalyst, then, is the extremely difficult task of disentangling the patient's pain (for which she or he might require understanding) from a sadomasochistic use of it (which demands that the psychoanalyst plays a part in maintaining the gratification in being stuck in misery, or in an emotional deadness). The next example describes a patient's dream which illustrates the advantages of death over life; the patient is persuaded that the best medicine is death.

Example: Perverse internal relations

John Steiner described a patient who was restricted in his activities and profession; and a particular dream demonstrates a perverse and deadly cruelty that seems to dominate his more sensitive feelings. The patient dreamed that he

> . . . was a tourist in Nepal, and was shown a boy who had swollen eyes and was weeping. A Nepalese doctor was called but the treatment consisted of putting the boy out of his misery. The doctor asked the boy if he wanted to die and he said he did.

Help is represented in the dream by death. Death is a panacea for the pain of living – like Martin Eden's desperate final musings in Jack London's novel (see Chapter 9).

> *The doctor tried to kill him with blows on the head, but when this*
> *failed he began sawing through the neck in a very painful way. The*
> *patient wondered why as a tourist he was watching all this and he*
> *felt quite powerless to intervene, but when he tried to turn away he*
> *was unable to stop himself watching.*

The analyst has reported this dream to show us how the patient is persuaded of the advantages of death. We must note, too, that attempts to dissociate himself from the cruelty (he tried to turn away) failed. The patient's attention is riveted to some death-inducing activity. His unacknowledged fascination was with a drama which proved that death is the best cure. The dream conveys that the emotions the child represents – tears, sadness, perhaps feeling dependent – are best not felt at all, but deadened; in this connection we might recall the example of *The wicked child* (p. 103), in which a child is also killed. This patient is caught in a fascination which very probably derives from a part of himself which looked for Nepalese-style psychoanalysis – that is, destruction of his curiosity and his thinking (blows to his head).

> The dream reminded him of a film involving a battle between Americans
> and Chinese. A Chinese boy befriended an American, but was
> discovered and was tied to a tripod and tortured in full view of the
> American ship. They were slowly cutting his body with a sword, and
> he screamed out, pleading to be killed, until his American friend finally
> shot him from the ship.

This gruesome cruelty repeats the dream: a child (again representing feelings of love and perhaps separation) was tortured for having feelings (friendship), and finds relief in death (and in a friend who agrees to death as the cure).

> . . . he was demonstrating how he felt imprisoned by a cruel destructive
> part of himself. If he admitted that he felt he was an ill, weeping boy he
> was afraid I would collude with his cruelty and that he would receive
> Nepalese medicine, but if he attempted to befriend me [the perverse
> part of him] threatened him with terrible cruelty.

This is the desperate entrapped position again. It offers no way of properly coping with, or expressing, the weeping but friendly child inside him. The only way out is death to it all. Death is advanced as the most reliable way out of the miseries of life, but in this context it is rivetingly fascinating in its own right as an enjoyable cruelty.

THE INTERNAL MAFIA GANG

Rosenfeld (1971) used the term 'negative narcissism' to indicate this odd situation where the destructive aspects of the personality gain the upper hand and achieve the highest status. It is 'narcissistic' in the sense that the focus of the negative feelings is turned towards the self. It contrasts with the turning of libido to the self in ordinary narcissism – which, as we have seen (Chapter 1), leads to a belief in a person's goodness. In many of these personalities the highest valuation is given to the person's aggressive, domineering and brutal (anti-life) qualities. Destructiveness is idealized; it is like the state of mind which seems to overtake gangs of hooligans. They espouse callousness and brutality as their highest group ideal, and may engage in violent and vicious fighting with great pride – and, indeed, often with a great excitement that is quite overtly sexual. Their own tenderness and capacity for compassion are completely overwhelmed, and remain in a wholly latent state. Such people not only engage in actual brutal fighting with others, they are also the scene of an internal battle within themselves in which their own destructiveness has taken over and dominated their capacity for more humane, loving and honest attitudes.

Rosenfeld described these personalities as if a battle has been lost and the person finally gives in to a demand from the destructiveness within. This internal conflict and internal defeat can appear as a scene

> . . . in dreams of being attacked by members of the mafia or adolescent delinquents and a negative therapeutic reaction sets in. This narcissistic organization is in my experience not primarily directed against guilt and anxiety, but seems to have the purpose of maintaining the idealization and superior power of the destructive narcissism. (Rosenfeld, 1971, p. 249)

Personalities of this kind demonstrate an internal dominance by a part of themselves that demands the idealization of destructiveness. In the next example that part of the personality is clearly identified with a bodily part, the patient's hands.

Example: The man who was nine feet tall

Rosenfeld's patient was a businessman who had to leave London occasionally on short trips and often returned too late on Mondays for his psychoanalytic session. Instead, during his trips, he spent the weekends with women he met and his psychoanalysis concerned his problems with them. Rosenfeld states that this was clearly an acting-out – that is to say, seducing women was an activity that discharged his feelings. A form of action replaced any anxiety or tension that might make him aware of his underlying distress at being distant from the analyst and missing sessions.[18] His vulnerable side, anxious about separating or missing, was excluded from his awareness, evacuated in the form of an action (his brief affairs) instead of remaining an awareness:

> . . . but only when he regularly reported murderous activities in his dreams after such weekends did it become apparent that violently destructive attacks against the analysis and the analyst were hidden in the acting out behaviour.

So the psychoanalyst is telling us that the patient is doing more than fitting a substitute figure into the gaps and absences – the seduced women to fill in for the psychoanalysis. It is a more alarming problem, which concerns an unconscious phantasy of mounting destructive attacks on his analysis. It seems that he has an affair with destructiveness as much as with women:

> The patient was at first reluctant to accept that the acting out of the weekend was killing, and therefore blocking the progress of, the analysis, but gradually he changed his behaviour and the analysis became more effective and he reported considerable improvement in some of his personal relationships and his business activities. At the same time he began to complain that his sleep was frequently disturbed and that he woke up during the night with violent palpitations which kept him awake for several hours.

This recalls a similarity with the night terrors of some of the child patients discussed in the early chapters – for instance, Erna (see *Erna's Oedipus complex*, p. 53), who had elaborate night-time rituals to combat her night terrors and help her to sleep. Interestingly, the problem of this patient's destructiveness is expressed in terms of a part of himself:

During these anxiety attacks he felt that his hands did not belong to him; they seemed violently destructive as if they wanted to destroy something by tearing it up, and were too powerful for him to control so that he had to give in to them.

We are shown a clear conflict within the patient's personality in which a part of him that seems uncontrollably destructive takes him over. An unconscious communication then appeared in a dream:

He then dreamt of a very powerful arrogant man who was nine feet tall and who insisted that he had to be absolutely obeyed. His associations made it clear that this man stood for part of himself and related to the destructive overpowering feelings in his hands which he could not resist. I interpreted that he regarded the omnipotent destructive part of himself as a superman who was nine feet tall and much too powerful for him to disobey . . . He had disowned this omnipotent self, which explained the estrangement of his hands during the nightly attacks. I further explained this split-off self as an infantile omnipotent part which claimed that it was not an infant but stronger and more powerful than all the adults, particularly his mother and father and now the analyst. His adult self was so completely taken in and therefore weakened by this omnipotent assertion that he felt powerless to fight the destructive impulses at night. The patient reacted to the interpretation with surprise and relief and reported after some days that he felt more able to control his hands at night.

We are interested in that relieved response. It seems to confirm the interpretation of this internal state.

In common with other similar patients, there seems to be an irresistible compulsion to submit to (absolutely obey) the destructive grandiose (nine feet tall, etc.) part of the self. In this case the internal quality of the dominating agent was very concretely expressed by its identification with his own hands. The identification of his hands is rather like the example of the man whose buttocks were beaten as a way of chastising his domineering father, who had become that part of him (see *The man who assaulted his buttocks*, p. 66).

In ordinary narcissism, libido (love) is turned towards the self (see Chapter 1). But here destructiveness, rather than love, is focused on the self. What emerges are omnipotent, grandiose and domineering attitudes which insist that the subject should idealize destructiveness and untruth. In this destructive (or negative) narcissism, the more usual valuation of life and death is challenged. In so far as those normal values are life-affirming, challenging them – as the negative narcissism does – is a manifestation of the death instinct. It is against life, and a subtle subversion of normally accepted values (a perversion). There is then a topsy-turvy system in which what is felt as 'good' is denounced by the patient as 'bad'; and what the patient feels as 'bad' is proclaimed 'good'. There is a profoundly perverse quality in this; and true sexual perversions may be connected with these moral systems, which acquire a sexually excited charge.[19]

PROPAGANDA

The belief in the superiority of death over life is not easily held; a continual pressure is needed to assert this attitude. It is one which is coerced, and may require the collusion of others (incuding a psychoanalyst) to support that coercion. The internal domination may be wrought through an internal seduction of one part of the personality by another rather than an internal intimidation. In our next example the need to keep up the idealizing attitude towards the destructive part of the mind is displayed as a kind of permanent internal propaganda war, winning the personality over. The casualty here is not merely the richness of emotional life but, especially, truth itself. These personalities seem to be committed to untruths or to twisted truths – propaganda.

Example: The patient with a 'foxy' part

This piece of clinical material, reported by Donald Meltzer, describes a personality that is clearly structured around 'good' and 'bad' parts; and the 'bad' has a capacity to take over (seduce) the whole personality, despite the fact that some other part of the patient has an awareness that it is not what he actually wants:

> Although this cultured and intelligent man in his late thirties entered analysis because of somatic symptoms, extensive character pathology was soon revealed. Early in analysis the narcissistic structure expressed itself clearly as in the following dream. He was walking uphill on a lonely woodland track and saw another man about his age, a former business client of very paranoid disposition, ahead of him. When the track divided, instead of going to the right as he had intended, he followed the other man, going down onto a beach . . .

Here is another dream (as in the other examples in this chapter) in which the patient's mind is taken over. In this case a 'colleague' induces the patient to descend into a paranoid state. It is a strong pressure that does indeed succeed in leading him astray:

> . . . On the beach he listened with admiration as the other man declaimed at length about his income and importance, how even on holiday he had to keep in constant touch with his office, as they could do nothing without his advice.

Because the figure is a colleague, the analyst begins to regard it as part of the patient's own personality. It is a grandiose and complacent part, and seemingly persuasively convincing with its imposing claims. Meltzer described this as propaganda. This part of his patient's personality often appeared as a fox, and was recognized as sly and seductive; it was also connected with a perversion and with a fear, a terror, that derived from dead babies (an early memory of the patient):

> This destructive part prevented him from admiring or respecting anyone by its slander, its omniscient propaganda. It kept him in a state of impotence by its denigration of the female genital, while it threatened him with homosexual desires by presenting penises as delicious, suckable nipples. But above all 'foxy' offered him protection from the terror of the dead babies – or so it claimed.

Meltzer concluded that the patient was drawn down by an omnipotent and devious part of the self. Its hold over the patient is to offer protection from an underlying terror; and this terror is connected with the death of babies. However, the protection is of a particular and odd kind: it lies in a submission to the seductive power of its propaganda. It is the seduction of believing in what you want to believe in, not in the truth:

> Only in the transference . . . did he come to realize that this 'foxy' part had never protected him, that in fact he had been protected all along by an external good object, fundamentally his mother; in the transference by the analyst . . . Where dependence on internal good objects is rendered infeasible . . . the addictive relationship to the bad part of the self, the submission to tyranny, takes place. An illusion of safety is promulgated by the omniscience of the destructive part.

Meltzer has concluded with an important point concerning the nature of the internal good object with which we might now be familiar. When such a resource (the internal support of a good and understanding internal object) is not available, the personality is vulnerable to its destructive part and the seduction of a perverse view of dependency. Instead of a true awareness that as a baby he lived because of his mother's care, he supports an illusion about the omniscience of his destructive attitudes. A seductive propaganda about his own antagonism (paranoia), his perverse wishes (he enjoys penises more than nipples), and his self-constructed truth (penises are in fact believed to be nipples) has won his allegiance. The propagandizing self takes over the more honest, modest and realistic part of the personality. Propaganda exemplifies this topsy-turvy domination. Deceit has to be idealized as good, death as exciting, despite a submerged (unconscious) awareness that it seems to be against something in the patient – against the truth that certain other feelings exist. Although these conditions, called perverse, are indeed often connected with sexual excitement, the perversion is at root a perversion of truth.

The four cases to which I have drawn attention in this chapter have illustrated several aspects of these borderline personalities: their stuckness; the organization of defences to support death as superior to life; the internal domination by destructiveness; and the propaganda seducing an idealization of destructiveness. In a way these personalities are, like psychotic patients, victims of their self-directed aggression. However, they have achieved the destruction of their lives through a sophisticated level of relationships for organizing their objects as supporting assistants.

Patients are driven to relinquish their search for emotional 'truth', and end up by subverting (or perverting) the course of the psychoanalysis into a substitute satisfaction of a grandiose and self-destructive kind. The term 'perversion' has grown in usage and now alludes primarily to distortions of truth and knowledge; while sexual perversion is, psychoanalytically, a perversion of the subject's knowledge about his or her sexual objects, as Freud described (Freud, 1927).

LOVE AND HONESTY

One difficulty in following the journey into the experiences of these kinds of people is that we seem to enter a moral universe –

or, indeed, an immoral one. It can be very difficult for the psychoanalyst, and for his reader, to refrain from his own judgements about this topsy-turvy set of moral standards. The thrill of exalting 'badness' can so easily elicit a tut-tutting response; and such tut-tutting can in turn provoke its own dismissal as intolerance. Yet it cannot be that analysts should maintain a morally neutral position, since we then do a violence to ourselves by freezing off our reactions, and slip away to a distance remote from our patients' experience. It is important that the reader, like the psychoanalyst, should note his or her reactions to the assertions that 'good' is good; or, conversely, that 'bad' is good. And indeed, we might ponder that we are none of us really so far removed from turning our own moral world upside down. Few of us can really be immune from that sort of moral madness, as we shall now see.

'NORMAL' MADNESS

There is a kind of madness involved in being drawn down into some disturbed and untruthful part of the personality which operates on the basis of propaganda rather than sincerity. In that state of mind, accomplished by a dominant self-idealizing part, the subject does not need truth or, therefore, a real psychoanalysis. Money-Kyrle suggests that there is a general cultural response to this kind of insanity – a fascinated fear of it:

> Most people fear contact with the insane . . . But some primitive cultures have felt them to be especially wise or holy, and even civilized nations have sometimes chosen them as leaders.
> This ambivalent attitude can be analytically explained on the assumption that there is always a mad part of the self – though in different degrees in different individuals – for which actually insane persons can easily come to stand. Moreover the mad part is often felt to be more powerful than the sane part. (Money-Kyrle, 1969, p.434)

He suggests that a potential for a destructive part of the personality (an insane part) to become dominant occurs in most of us, though on the whole it is kept at bay. If, however, it is externalized (projected) into society – or into a political leader – it makes sense of the historical fact that certain *cultural* developments can bring out in enough ordinary people such an allegiance to destructiveness that they create or passively tolerate odiously oppressive social and political systems. The oppressive society comes to represent the potential for internal oppression and insanity – the triumph of destructiveness over honesty and life.

The idea of internal oppression has led to a development in the practice of contemporary psychoanalysis. Psychoanalysts pay attention to the subtle and complex levels of emotional contact and how they may be dissipated, or dominated and overwhelmed with alternative propaganda. It is to these developments in practice that we will move on in the last chapter.

15   Change and Development

We have just met patients who avoid honest contact and, in fact, cultivate a belief in something greater than their emotional life – the destruction of it. Not all patients operate to deaden emotional life, just for the sake of it. But now that analysts have been alerted to the 'fine grain' of the emotional texture in the immediate here and now, the technical practice with these patients has become modified for use with all patients. Much greater emphasis is now placed on interpreting the process; less on the interpretation of symbols. The next example is just one of these tiny but intensely felt movements towards and then out of contact.

Example: Projecting envy

This example of Betty Joseph's illustrates one of these 'microscopical' shifts in the emotional contact as the patient retreats from a brief moment of painful feeling. This is an envious man, who speedily removed himself from a momentary disturbance by projecting envy into those around him:

> To give a minute example: one Monday, T really seemed to become aware of exactly how he was subtly taking the meaning out of what I was saying and not letting real understanding develop. For a moment he felt relief and then a brief, deep feeling of hatred to me emerged into consciousness.

We witness this precise moment when a real emotional contact – hatred – emerged. But:

> A second later he added quietly that he was thinking how the way that he had been feeling just then towards me, that is, the hatred, must have

been how his fellow students had felt towards him on the previous day when he had been talking and explaining things to them! So, immediately that T has a real experience of hating me because I have said something useful, he uses the momentary awareness to speak about the students, and distances himself from the emerging envy and hostility, and the direct receptive contact between the two of us is again lost.

The analyst presents a precise moment: before it the patient felt a deep hatred; afterwards he began to talk quietly again. The patient's shift was smooth and swift. He accomplished an immediate questioning of his disturbance, and he did it in a particular way: he turned his new insight into an understanding of others. A kind of understanding does survive; indeed, an understanding of others could be useful to him. However, it appears from his demeanour (he talked quietly again) that he used his new knowledge to abolish his own hatred and envy as he talked of others'. This shift – away from his brief emotional disturbance – is so subtle that it looks like something else altogether; in fact, it looks like insight and understanding. For this patient a sustained emotional quietness seems to be essential; he needed to restore that monotone.

Viewed in this way, a psychoanalytic session is a kaleidoscope of emotional shifts. These shifts take three forms:

Flux: First of all, every interaction between people leads to an emotional response, some movement of their mental state. There is a continual flow of feelings, a shifting flux. In the course of this disturbance anxieties may begin to build up; then defences emerge; and the atmosphere shifts towards a return to some point of equilibrium. The person always struggles to redress his balance of mind.

A static balance: Then, secondly, as we saw in Chapter 14, certain people move as best they can to abort this fluid kind of emotional responding (flux), and develop a means of sticking in a deadened state – a stasis. The balance is rigid. If they are emotionally moved for a moment it is quickly abolished, usually through rather primitive and violent methods of defence. These shifts are out of contact altogether, as in the patient described above (*Projecting envy*).

Long-term psychic change: Thirdly, there is a longer-term change which modifies the psychic structure. This has a degree of permanence about it. It does not abolish these continual shifts of emotional state; it is indicated in evidence of new (or added) structure within the internal world.

We will look at examples of each of these three kinds of shift, which I shall call flux, stasis and long-term psychic change.

FLUX

The first example, of a child patient, is described by Betty Joseph. The child's anxieties and defences are freely open to view, and there is a very fluid movement of feelings, reactions and defences.

Example: The child who pulled hair

An anxious and demanding boy of three and a half (referred to as C) illustrates a significant emotional movement over the course of a few sessions:

> . . . he suddenly flung himself at me, dragged at my hair, and pulled out a very small fistful; he opened his hand, looked at the hairs with horror, got hold of the rug, and covered my head with it, so that I was in a tent. I tried to help him to understand his anxieties about what he might see if he looked at me, and about what he felt he had done. Slowly he came up, peeped under the rug at my head, then pulled away. When I tried to emerge to talk to him more easily, he ran at me with the pillow and covered my head with that.

We meet C in a desperate situation: he damaged his analyst but then had to cope with his feelings about that. His defence is to ensure that he cannot see what he has done. The child is struggling with the balance of his passions: his remorse and his rage, to see or not to see, to come close or to retreat. There is a flurry of competing emotional currents in him.

> I again spoke about his anxieties. He then specified things, saying very clearly, 'you'll pull my hair', and retreated further from me. When it came to the last minutes of the session, he ran away from the playroom a minute or two before time.

Despite the patient's generally uncontained state, the analyst continues to try to speak, contain in her words what she thinks is happening to him. Eventually the child had some words of his own – 'you'll pull my hair'. But then he still needed to run to safety.

> . . . a few weeks later C came to a session very wild and apparently disturbed. There were a number of references to me, the analyst, as being a 'naughty boy', and one to my being 'a nuisance'. I thought that he was in this way showing me, in this session, great anxieties about himself being bad and a trouble and a nuisance to his parents, particularly as his mother had been unwell. As the session went on he became calmer, and standing at the table holding things together with rubber bands, he said quietly, as if out of the blue, 'I pulled your hair, remember?' I simply commented on his worry and guilt about what he felt he had done to me, and he added, 'I kissed, remember?' This is of course from one angle, clearly a denial, he did not kiss, he fled. But I think there is something more dynamic to be understood here. C was able to bring into the session a memory showing the burden of guilt and anxiety that he was carrying around inside himself – but also now affection.

The psychoanalyst is showing us how the child continued to rework the experience, bringing it to life in some pocket of memory and, indeed, managing, anxiously, to repair it with a phantasied kiss. It was not dead and gone.

> It suggests that within this second session there was relief at his being able to tell, and my being able to accept, the memory of his 'bad' actions, and this may have, in part, prompted the idea of the kiss.

The content of the material has an end result which is a positive attempt to make up in an emotional way – a kiss. Despite the late response we are considering (in a session several weeks later), we can see that C is eventually relieved. But in all that there remains a profound sense of contact between child and analyst; and it was felt deeply by the analyst herself, judging by how moved she felt by the boy's phantasied kiss. Both the analyst and C are alive to powerful currents of feelings. Both seem to accept those disturbing currents. This level of relief has a very different quality from the deadening process that abolishes disturbance. The example implies that a fluid shift took place over the period between these sessions. Despite the defence of denial, the experience is not deadened as it might be in more pathological organizations, where such contact is swiftly dissolved. It had remained an active moment in C's mind, one that he could continue to bring to life as he worked at it. These moment-to-moment emotional ups and downs are the stuff of human relations, and contrast with the stuck positions. They are of crucial therapeutic importance:

> I think that one of the main aims of our therapy is to work with such shifts, to enable them to happen less blindly and automatically, to make them and their elements more conscious and more manageable to the ego in a more healthy, flexible and realistic way . . . If we were to believe that we could eliminate them, we should be encouraging splitting. (Joseph, 1989, p. 201)

In a sense the analyst's composed non-judgemental knowing needs to become the patient's. It is important that we relate to these shifts rather than make judgements about them. The patient struggles as best he can to deal with his difficulties and anxieties. A judgemental attitude does not help the patient to understand, nor does it help the analyst to keep a clear mind to accommodate the experiences the patient wishes her to understand.

STASIS

The child C's emotional contact contrasts with the deadening quality of the evasive patient in the previous example (*Projecting envy*, p. 209) who goes immediately out of contact. In the next example we have a patient who has been similarly stuck in the past in a pathological organization, and this shows in the case material; but he is in fact more able now to emerge from that stuck position. So this example demonstrates nicely the contrast between the monotonous return to his pathological organization and the fluid emotional life when he emerges.

Example: The to-and-fro contact

This man, treated by Betty Joseph, was anxious because the psychoanalysis was ending:

> The session was a Friday. My patient, N, arrived saying that he felt bad and anxious, as if too much was going on. He and his wife were currently selling their house and there were important changes going on in his work.

N is troubled. He is in touch with a degree of disturbance in himself – perhaps too much so; and he is putting it across to the psychoanalyst. However, there is a distance between the changes at home and work, and those in the immediate experience of his psychoanalysis:

> I clarified that it seemed that the anxiety was more focused round the issue of stopping the analysis. This he agreed but went on to describe in detail his feelings of discomfort as if he was angry and resentful. I thought at that point, and suggested, that it was partly that he had not really been able to believe that I could let him go, but that now he was having to face this aspect of stopping.

We can see the analyst working at the patient's distancing manoeuvre, and why she does so. And she gets a formal agreement from him. However, she suddenly finds that the patient is really not with her:

> My patient responded, however, to my remark by going back to discussing his difficulties, his resentments, his coldness, and so on. I thought, and showed him, that he was sinking into a kind of anger and misery – shown by his settling into and stressing all the difficulties and getting caught up into it, in order to avoid the specific feelings about actually leaving and what it really meant to him at that moment.

The patient responds, but reverts and creates a relief for himself that comes from deadening a lively and involved response. This is the typical retreat from contact that we have seen in the pathological organization.

> In other words I thought that he was sinking into a kind of bog of misery as a defence, so that the anger was part of the bog and was not anger in its own right.

But is the analyst right in thinking that he used the anger to avoid contact? What is the response to the interpretation?:

> N became silent – a pause – and then he said he had the thought, 'clever old bag'.

In fact the patient *had* responded to the interpretation. He had felt, but only later conveyed, a sharp moment of real anger – not a self-involved misery, but an anger which has a punch that makes real contact. When his retreat was then interpreted he responded by re-establishing emotional contact:

> He explained he thought I was right and that he was aware when he made the remark that he resented my being right, so he went quiet.

Now we could both agree to the misery being used actively as a kind of masochistic defence, and he himself had clear insight into his resentment about my being right.

So we learn that the original interpretation had indeed achieved a response of a momentary anger, but this had not been reported at the time. Instead the patient enacted a deadening descent into his 'bog'. Only now, after a further interpretation, can he come back into a contact where he can report what had happened. And now the session (and emotional contact) takes off in another direction:

> They had been invited to the Xes where the wife is a very poor cook, so his wife had a brilliant idea. She would offer to make a summer pudding, which the patient just adores, and they would take it with them to the supper. He would help his wife by topping and tailing the fruit. This was said in a very positive and warm manner.

N's association is now about an obviously good contact with his wife, whom he helps to make up for bad cooking. In the psychoanalyst's view the bad cooking represents his own poor efforts in his psychoanalysis as he retreated, and he is conveying, through the mutually helping contact at home, his pleasure and gratitude that a similar helping contact has been restored in the session. The last piece of material has a richer, more lively feel; we might be reminded of Peter, in one of our very first examples, whose play suddenly went forward in a more imaginative, creative way (see *Inhibited play*, p. 39).

During this session the patient moved out of contact after an envious moment, and into a 'bog of misery' in which he could maintain himself in an emotional statis. In fact, however, there is a great deal more movement in this material than in his old habit of deadening. It is worth noting the sequence of movement:

–He moved out of the bog of misery; he was swept by envy of the 'clever old bag'; in that he moved towards an integration of this painful envy;

–then he returned to his bog;

–but subsequently, moved by the interpretation, he could agreeably report to her what had happened;

–they could then discover what they had learned together; his 'brilliant idea' of the summer pudding then indicated a movement towards having a good experience, and it is a sensual as well as an emotional one.

There is a movement, too, into a dependent relationship towards his feeding wife; a movement, as well, towards a symbolic level of satisfaction, and a wider recognition of his capacity to help in a creative endeavour. All these shifts – which I list from Betty Joseph's account – contrast a rigid, static equilibrium with a more fluid content.

DEFENSIVE STRUCTURES

Pathological organizations are composed of a tight structure of defences which attempt to keep a deadened stasis in the emotional life, quite different from the frantic and anxious movement of the child in *The child who pulled hair* (p. 211). Although there are many varieties of these defensive structures (O'Shaugnessy, 1981; Steiner, 1987), and indeed each individual has his own idiosyncratic methods of attaining an emotional stasis, they seem to form certain clusters. The narcissistic group allow little room for the analyst to be effective, cannot let the analyst help, and tend to take over the interpretations as their own to create what amounts to a self-analysis in the presence of the analyst. Perhaps we might include the patient we will encounter at the end of this chapter (see *Academic reconstruction*, p. 225). A more phobic group manage with a series of avoiding and distancing defences, perhaps rather in the manner of the last example. A further group (we have seen a number of examples) operate through twisting the truth, often excitedly in a perverse fascination with good being bad, and vice versa (*The twisted carrots*, p. 189; *Perverse internal relations*, p. 199; *The patient with a 'foxy' part*, p. 204).

Indeed, there is a question to be answered in future research about the relation between the deadened stasis and a masochistic excitement. It seems that, somehow, the profound deadening which Kleinian psychoanalysts attribute to the death instinct can become eroticized. In that process the whole manoeuvre becomes masochistic and appealing (or addictive) for its own sake. This greatly complicates any simple account of the defensive nature of these personalities; consequently, the term 'pathological organization' has come to be preferred to 'defensive organization' for these patients.

LONG-TERM PSYCHIC CHANGE

In the next two examples, we will see the beginnings of a structural change in the ego; in the first of them, the establishment of a relationship committed to planting and tending life and growth represents the internalization of a good internal object clearly derived from the analyst; in the second, we will witness evidence of an internal repositioning which widens the scope of internal vision to scan more of the personality.

Example: The man who planted sweet peas

The next illustration is a man whom Betty Joseph had already treated for some time; considerable progress had been made, albeit often lost. On a Friday he came anxious,

> saying he was afraid of going backwards again, which meant into his cold, rather perverse behaviour.

The patient gives us a glimpse of the way his mind works. He is feeling better, though not yet sure of himself, and in particular he may be 'tempted' to feel worse again:

> I had the impression that this remark was not just a statement about anxiety related to the weekend but more of a threat to himself and to me to drive himself backwards.

In a way this seemed a helpful, insightful warning.

> This I worked through with him in the next part of the session and slowly he seemed in contact and insightful again, and then, as he put it, something quite different came into his mind. Yesterday evening he planted the sweet pea plants that he had got over the weekend, a friend who was staying at his house came out and helped him – although it was raining a bit it was very pleasant.

We can understand here how the patient wants to convey something to his analyst. As he continues we can see that he senses in himself that he has planted something in his mind which can grow – his understanding of himself (his insightful warning); or rather, an internalized version of his understanding analyst:

> He laughed lightly, saying of course he knew that his getting the sweet peas was connected with my having sweet peas in my front garden. Also when he was a child, there were sweet peas in a wild part of the garden at home and he loved them, they meant a great deal to him.

Here is a poignant expression of appreciation and gratitude. The patient's reference to childhood is an acknowledgement of his dependency and need for help. This help is specifically sought from his psychoanalyst (the sweet-pea garden) whom he internalizes (plants the sweet peas in his own garden). She enables him to achieve his own warning understanding (about going backwards).

> Here we have what might look like . . . an idealization in the transference as a defence. But I do not believe it is so: indeed the reference to the rain suggests it is not all ideal.

Because the rain represents something amiss – we could say it is his tears and sadness – this is the depressive position, sadness and achievement in a poignant mixture:

> . . . the defensiveness has lessened and he has been able to discover a sweet analyst whom he can introject, plant inside himself, and identify with.

This material has indicated a growth of something of a valued sweetness, despite being in the midst of the 'wild' garden. It appears to be a significant change in which the capacity for the loving, valuing and understanding has been planted *within him*. It could thus be recognized as an internal object that has been established. This object is identified with the analyst. It seems very poignant and moving for the patient, and indeed for the analyst too.

In this material we have a sense of permanence – planting and growing – not a hasty and perhaps temporary movement away from something painful, as would be the case in one of the defensive manoeuvres. This is palpable – the analyst feels a solid change – but it is also expressed in the material as the planting of the sweet growth. Thus we have various ingredients: the growth of understanding and of conscious loving feelings; acknowledgement of dependency and depressive mixed feelings; content expressing a structural change (the new structure growing); and the psychoanalyst's emphatic countertransference experience of some depth to the patient's feelings (not idealization).

It is important to have full evidence of structural change. It is not enough that the patient feels better, as this may be a defensive relief; nor is it enough for the analyst to feel satisfied, as this may be a countertransference reaction that merely proceeds from the patient's seductiveness, as Irma Brenman Pick showed (*The man who was sensible*, p. 165). The clinching confirmation is when the analyst's experience (countertransference) meets a corresponding pattern in the content of the material. In this case the analyst's countertransference was of a deep and poignant moment in the session; it is a pattern of change expressed as a loving planting in the rain (sweetness amid the wild). Structural change is often expressed very concretely like this. In the dream in the next example, progress in the psychoanalysis (in this case a degree of integration of the personality) was vividly presented in the material as a change of perspective on the internal world.

Example: The man who came to face himself

This man, also described by Betty Joseph, had constantly projected his worries and disturbance into his wife:

> ... [he] came into analysis worried about his relationship with his wife – or, to be more accurate, worried that she was worried that their relationship seemed poor and unsatisfactory to her; he did not see anything particularly wrong with it.

The patient uses his wife to do the worrying, a projective solution that avoids having to feel worried himself.

> Slowly I gained the feeling that I was supposed to follow him, almost pursue him with interpretations, but he did not seem interested in trying to understand or actively to use the analysis – it was as if it was I who wanted him to use individual interpretations or the analysis in general.

The patient had come to use the psychoanalyst to get a bit worried for him too:

> B was anxious but also rather relieved as he began to feel himself coming more alive sometimes during the sessions. I have not the space here to give details of such a session with a dream, just before a holiday, when B became very clear about simple feelings of jealousy and anger linked clearly with his early and current family experiences. He was unusually moved by this dream and our work on it, and as the session was coming to an end, said in a happier voice: 'I must tell you my grandiose idea. I think that car manufacturers should build a front passenger seat so that

it can turn round and the passenger join in with and face the children sitting in the back, or a child could sit in the front and turn to the others.

So I showed him, by his tone and the way he spoke to me, as well as by what he said, the pleasure in the session of getting into touch with his childhood, the experience of being really able to love and feel jealous, that what he had been talking about had brought him contact with the child in himself, which he was beginning to turn to and face . . .

In his phantasy of the turning car seat the patient is indicating his willingness, and now his ability, to change – to move his psychological position – and to face his child needs, feelings and anxieties. It is a vivid picture of actual internal change (inside the car), to relate now to more of his internal objects and parts of the self. A real, albeit painful, addition has occurred to this man's personality: he has begun to form a link with a loving/jealous child part of himself (inside the car – i.e. inside himself). The scope of his internal vision has widened, and that widening involves integrating what he now sees (a similar move towards integration occurred in the example of *The man who split off his aggression*, p. 125). It is an addition to the function of understanding himself. As in the preceding example, this is both satisfying (his 'happier voice') but also painful, as it entails acknowledging his childlike jealousy and anger – again a mixed state indicative of the depressive position.

INDICATIONS OF THERAPEUTIC CHANGE

Therapeutic change does not aim to create a pain-free life. Not all lively contact, when it happens, is necessarily pleasant. Life, as we noted in Chapter 9, is painful as well as enriching. It stirs the heart emotionally. Such stirring contact may be hatred as well as love; but it is all lively, part of life itself. What deadens and dampens such contact – even dampens anger or hatred – is antipathetic to life.

We have attempted to distinguish between three things: the moment-to-moment emotional flux; the stalling of emotional life altogether in a stasis; and the longer-term change in structure which psychoanalysts would regard as therapeutic benefit. It appears from experience that when the analyst has sustained a persistent contact with the patient's shifts (including a close contact with the patient's methods of avoidance of contact) over a period of time, then that understanding analyst becomes an influence towards a more self-understanding patient. The patient can sustain more moments of contact with the analyst; and this becomes a structural change that has some permanence.

I want to stress one important difference between the to-and-fro changes from moment to moment of the clinical session, and the overall development which the analyst regards as beneficial. As we noted in the example of Richard *Identifying with a 'good' object* (p. 71) there is a sense of permanence in the establishment of an internal security. Later we saw (in the example of *The patient's failed container*, p. 131, and many subsequent examples) that the good internal object has a very specific function: of containing the patient's experiences in understanding and words. This is the hallmark of a real development of the personality which Kleinian psychoanalysts seek – an internal understanding object contributing an internal vision of a more whole self.

The widening of the scope of personal insight will result from the installation within the self of that understanding object that is embodied, externally, in the analyst. As she or he makes all these moment-to-moment observations of the patient's flux (or stasis), the analyst promotes the possibility of an internal self-understanding object within the patient. In summary, the elements of a therapeutic movement include the internalization of an internal object capable of understanding; and thus a wider awareness of the personality; and therefore the integration of hitherto split-off (and projected) disowned parts of the self. Furthermore, it includes withdrawal of projections; the capacity to take more responsibility for oneself and one's impulses, especially impulses one feels are bad ones; the emergence of guilt and concern (the depressive position); the capacity to face the state of one's objects; and an acknowledgment of the separateness of the object.

BALANCE

There is no steady state towards which the psychoanalyst must work. There is always a state of flux; that is the burden and the thrill of life. And the patient will always be endeavouring to steady his emotional state against the disturbances imposed by the stimuli and incursions of his external world and his bodily sensations, while continuing to experience life to the maximum he can tolerate.

There is only a balance point, an emotional equilibrium, around which he will tend to swing as he is swayed this way and that.

Example: Pain and retreat

In the next case, also one of Betty Joseph's, a patient swings back and forth around a position of more emotional contact with himself, and with his psychoanalyst. A contact is succeeded by a retreat; but he is also buttressed, to some extent, against that retreat by an internal object, based on the introjected analyst who resists the retreat, and he approaches contact again:

> The background of this session was that on the previous day, Wednesday, I had been showing my patient his way of dealing with his difficulties by trying to force despair into me instead of trying to contact his own depression and understand it. In this session, Thursday, he came in saying he was depressed. He told me a dream. The dream was *that he was standing at the corner of a well-known central London street with someone, a woman. They were standing in the gutter, perhaps surrounded by clothes, old clothes to sell. His elder sister went past in the road with some men friends; he called to her; she nodded but went on. There was something about burglary.*
>
> I briefly linked this dream with what we had been speaking about on the previous day; that is, how he tries to force despair into me. . . . which then drags me down into the gutter . . . But now, as if there is unconscious insight into this, in the dream, he knows about it, it is an old problem. It is the old clothes which he is trying to sell me, but I am not buying it – I am also the sister, who goes past with her own friends, her own life, and is not dragged down by despair.

The psychoanalyst is claiming that the patient has some insight, but that he turns it into 'old insight', and thus makes the analysis predictable and unmoving – a retreat from his contact. But he is also aware (in the dream) that the analyst won't buy that. In this moment we have two kinds of change: first, the change from real insight to old predictable insight that leads to deadening things; but second, a new understanding has begun to develop – an unconscious insight – associated with the person of the analyst. Internally there is a struggle between retreating into the gutter, and not buying that. As in many of our examples, an internalization of an object that understands the self, the psychoanalyst, is a significant internal change which has the potential to enlarge the awareness of internal reality – what the patient is really like. The patient is able to become more aware of himself in the following material:

> My patient, as we discussed this, got a real feeling about the pull and masochistic attraction of being himself dragged down.

The psychoanalyst's understanding has achieved some contact:

> After some contact, relief, and understanding had been established about this session, my patient remarked that he felt at that moment as if he had got something in his eye; was it just a hair or was it that old scratch that he had ages ago? Did I, the analyst, remember the scratch? I did indeed, and queried with him if he remembered how it happened. He replied, of course, that it was when he was dancing with a woman friend called Hope and her fingernail scratched his eye so badly. So I could show him that when we could see and feel why he has to be dragged down into the gutter of misery, in identification with me, and in his masochism, and he begins to emerge from it again, then there is pain in his eye, his natural vision, the pain that is caused by hope.

The hope causes pain. It is the pain of life; it is also the pain of having to forgo his excited fascination with misery and death. His unconscious communication about the pain of hope is a real self-understanding.

The development of hope, successful work and understanding is painful; the ambiguity is very apparent, and he oscillates back and forth. In a sense he wants to make contact with the analyst (calling to his sister in the dream). At the same time this hope and progress hurt; insight (expressed in his associations as his sight, or his eye) hurts; he prefers old insight and complains about hope:

> . . . psychic change is not just an end, a final state, but is always going on in treatment . . . we as analysts need to be able to find and follow the moment-to-moment changes in our patients, without concerning ourselves as to whether they are positive, or signs of progress or of retreat, but seeing them as our patient's own individual method of dealing with his anxieties and relationships in his own unique way . . . Indeed, our capacity to listen fully and stay with our patients must help them increasingly to be able to observe, tolerate, and understand their own habitual ways of dealing with anxiety and relationships and this is part of the process of changing these habitual ways and becoming what we would call psychically 'more healthy'. (Joseph, 1989, p. 192)

There is a delicate balance to be observed for the analyst too. The instruction not to be concerned whether the shifts are positive signs of progress or the reverse may seem paradoxical, as the analyst has an overt purpose: to bring about therapeutic change. In this extract, however, Joseph points out the importance of respecting the individual's need to operate his own defences in his own way, at the moment when he needs to, as he protects against his anxieties and struggles with his difficulties. In this she is alluding to the challenging injunctions pronounced by Bion:

> What is known about the patient is of no further consequence: it is either false or irrelevant. If it is 'known' by patient and analyst, it is obsolete . . . The only point of importance in any session is the unknown.
>
> . . . do not remember sessions . . .
>
> . . . the psychoanalyst can start by avoiding any desires for the approaching end of the session (week, or term). Desires for results, 'cure' or even understanding must not be allowed to proliferate.
>
> . . . The psychoanalyst should aim at achieving a state of mind so that at every session he feels he has not seen the patient before. If he feels he has, he is treating the wrong patient. (Bion, 1967, pp. 18–19)

These are now famous aphorisms, summarized as the command to 'abandon memory and desire'. The wish for progress, and the search over time to locate signs of it, cloud the psychoanalyst's capacity to listen in to what the patient is saying *now*. The down-to-earth version of this is to listen meticulously to what is going on from moment to moment.

THE 'K'-LINK

The understanding object supports interest and enquiry, a 'K'-link. The capacity to hold in view and know a more complete picture of the self indicates a greater acceptance and integration of hitherto unacceptable parts of the person. As an internal function, the 'K'-link and the understanding internal object stand against the splitting of self-directed attacks which emanate from the death instinct, and thus stand for integration. In the Kleinian view a profound motive for withstanding pain is the thirst for something true, including an internal truth, the sense of an '*aha!*' moment. And that in itself is enhanced by the possession of the internal object that understands and promotes a growth of self-knowledge, however wretched, painful and fragile this may often feel. The thirst for 'knowledge' led Bion to believe that truth for the mind was like food for the body. Thus the psychoanalyst is intent on finding in his patient a part of the ego that is engaged in an investigation of himself ('K'-link) despite any internal sabotage of that ('minus K'). This is not all: the psychoanalyst also seeks out a part of the patient's ego which can tolerate pain – the pain of concern and guilt, or the pain of envy (perhaps envy at the analyst's hope, as in the last example). The patient must take responsibility for various parts of himself, his feelings and his impulses, which he may regard as bad and negative. Integration implies this wider view of an inclusive picture of good with bad, together with the attendant psychic pain.

In the next example we have a complex interplay between the psychoanalyst's attempts to establish a 'K'-link and the patient's unconscious tendency to subvert the analyst's intention by projecting into his interpretations so that a sterile form of insight results.

Example: Academic reconstruction

Eric Brenman described this unmarried woman – aged twenty-eight, the daughter of successful academic parents – as seeking help for her state of suicidal depression, helplessness and total inability to work:

> Her parents maintained a keen academic interest in psychoanalysis and were alleged to have 'analyzed' the patient with 'sweet reason' as far back as she could remember . . . There was a history of succeeding academically and then dropping out at the last moment . . . She changed career studies a few times and repeated the pattern. She was almost married on a number of occasions and broke off at the eleventh hour. The potential careers of the patient were felt to be not her own choices but those of her parents.

This history paints a recurring pattern to this troubled patient's life as she attempted to gain her freedom from other people (representing parents) closing in on her. It will no longer surprise the reader that this pattern of brief involvement, followed by its quick interruption, recurred in the analysis as well:

> She formed a precarious intense attachment to me in her desperation, but became more remote when crisis was not pressing . . . [She was] someone who could become engaged but not married . . . From early

on in the analysis when I interpreted to her what I believed to be her feelings, she would interrupt, analyze herself and demonstrate that she knew that her feelings were irrational and that she had to educate herself as to what was sensible and logical, so that no real experience of what she was feeling was allowed to develop.

Part of her life pattern was clearly an 'academic interest' in her own feelings which she had adopted from her parents. It interrupted emotional contact.

It is important to bear in mind that at this stage in the patient's life 'the parents' are still the internal parents constructed from her experiences and perceptions; and that this is an amalgam of the parents' own personalities, of the patient's distortions of them through her own use of them as external objects to project into, and indeed of the parents' own reactions to being perceived by their child in that way.[20]

The contact with the analyst as someone who could help to understand her feelings in a different way could become distorted:

She 'got in' first . . . In other words the patient was making constructions designed to avoid meeting her real feelings and experiences.

The analyst is faced with an interesting problem. If he makes interpretations, he finds a willing patient who can energetically go along with him, but she has thereby evaded both him and her own feelings. The emotional contact between patient and analyst is immediately broken.

This suggested that perhaps she was reliving in the analysis a life style in which 'educators' had made constructions to obviate feelings.

Thus, the analyst's interpretations could themselves be made a re-enactment of a childhood experience. It repeats past experience with parents; but an experience she has adopted for herself, because it offers a successful method of avoiding being emotional moved. It has therefore become more than repeating a past experience; it remains currently a useful one, repeated through recruiting suitable figures in the present, and for particular purposes that are active now. The psychoanalyst, unfortunately, offers himself as the perfect person to enact a situation that has been internalized:

. . . internal objects who, far from helping her to know herself and her rightful place, confuse her with ostensible kindness . . . This links with an experience in the transference of feeling "analyzed" by me with sweet reason.

Internally it is as if she continually says to herself, 'This is the way to deal with your feelings, make academic interpretations about them and rule them out as "irrational".' Then she finds an external object who seems to say things near enough in line with that internal dialogue to make her feel that she has an exact external counterpart. This is a difficult situation for the analyst:

> The patient occupied my mind with her 'sweet reason' analysis and I formed the impression that I was supposed to admire it and abandon my own views . . . I found myself making more extra-transference interpretations than usual, but it seemed to be the only means of reaching her. I formed the opinion that what was being relived was a parent/infant relationship which strongly conveyed that on no account were we to interact with real feeling since we both appeared to be too frail to do so.

The analyst is trying to show us how he has himself been caught up with the patient's internal object, but we must recognize that there is a serious anxiety behind this situation. The patient seems to be convinced that she and her object – external, but presumably also the internal object – are too frail to cope with feelings. The analyst is recruited to this role of defending them both against something neither of them could cope with: strength of feeling. It is no good, therefore, making interpretations of the type 'You see me as your father'. What is transferred from the past is not just the father, nor just the defence (projective identification), nor just a relationship (daughter helping father to put up with dangerous feelings). What is transferred is a particular way of using the object that serves a function right now – the function it served then. The patient uses her object idiosyncratically, and needs the object to go along with her way of managing the situation. The means are borrowed from the past, resemble the past, but are in service to the present.

The patient had herself learned that her parents would readily co-operate with this defensiveness; probably because it matched their own. Similarly she could find in the analyst a sufficiently academic part of him, too, with which she could mate and reconstruct the elaborate defensive activity for them both. In this case we see how the patient not only linked with the analyst's curiosity to discover things ('K'-link) but also projected into the analyst's own curiosity ('minus K'). And she projected precisely into his psychoanalytic function of making interpretations and reconstructions. The lesson is that such projection has to be elucidated, and its function for the patient must be clearly recognized by both patient and analyst before there can be any useful understanding of how the patient has adopted it very early in life and in co-operation with obliging objects who were also helped (defensively) by that kind of projection.

HERE AND NOW VERSUS THE INFANTILE PAST

Psychoanalysis has traditionally endeavoured to unearth, in the form of the transference, the traumas of the past. The figure of the psychoanalyst, in the transference, *is* the past figure who created the traumatic situation for the patient. We see in the present a new version of the old figures that patient and analyst dramatize between them; thus the infant's past experience can be reconstructed and presented back to the patient in words. The psychoanalytic work is thus to move from a dramatization (the enactment in the transference) to knowledge of the past.

So much for the accepted view of transference. Now, the current change of emphasis appears to make a radical break with this tradition. By emphasizing how the transference retains a key function in the present, we seem to sideline knowledge of the actual infantile past. There is a current debate about where the emphasis should lie. It is a question of timing:

> These differences concern the technical problem of how and when to interpret explicitly the unconscious phantasy and infantile experience which is being enacted in this interplay between patient and analyst. There is general theoretical agreement that such linking should be done only when it is emotionally meaningful to the patient, but in practice analysts can vary in their assessment of when the right moment has come. (Segal, 1989, p. ix)

Constructing the past could raise problems with those patients who distort the psychoanalytic search away from a more emotionally immediate contact and insight – then it is a useful diversion, with effective defensive results. Another way to put this is that what is transferred is current, active unconscious phantasy, not replicas of the past – bearing in mind that although the unconscious phantasies which stock the patient's adult experiences with meaning are generated from the experiences with figures who were important in childhood and infancy, they are nevertheless the stuff of active experience now.

Many other aspects of the psychoanalytic process are interestingly discussed in Meltzer (1967), but I have emphasized the increasing focus on the contact with the psychoanalyst as the most important ongoing point of development in Kleinian psychoanalysis. It is a search for the truth about patient's and analyst's contact with each other in the transference and countertransference interaction. This recent concentration upon the emotional movements and evasions that occur in the consulting room has thrust them to the foreground in the technical handling of psychoanalysis. We have needed to distinguish the relief that comes from avoiding emotional contact from the relief of having the psychoanalyst as a containing object that can give shape to pain and disturbance. The psychoanalyst's task is to make this distinction.

Psychoanalysis is this process. It is often unfinished – just as the progress of ideas and practice continues forever unfinished. It may finally be apparent that despite the elaborate journey we have made, there are many ongoing themes left hanging at the end of Part III: (a) the development in the theory of learning and symbol-formation (the 'K'-link in the early Oedipus complex); (b) the manifestation of self-directed deathly impulses in certain personalities and their pathological organization; (c) the understanding of the *intrapsychic* interactions that make up the transference/countertransference interaction; and (d) the technical observations of the detailed state of emotional contact between patient and analyst, and how true psychic development can occur in psychoanalytic treatment.

The human mind is surely the most fascinating thing in the universe. Perhaps the only greater fascination is two human minds struggling on to discover what is happening between them. Psychoanalysis is thus one version of the greatest human hunger: to master what happens in our experiences with one another.

EPILOGUE TO PART III:
THE EVOLUTION OF KLEINIAN
TECHNIQUE

At present Kleinian psychoanalysts can look back on a long thread of development punctuated by phases in which different kinds of patient have been at the focus of research: children; patients with depressive states; schizophrenic patients with fragmented minds; and recently, the difficult-to-reach borderline patients in impasse. Each phase has prompted new theoretical ways of thinking; then a refinement of technique; and in turn, new clinical problems have advanced towards the centre of the clinical stage to form the next phase.

To some extent, Kleinian psychoanalysts could have been criticized for inconsistency. They were originally notable for deep-going interpretations of very early phantasies in the infant – heroic, intrusive and grandly speculative. Now, they advocate a meticulous sensitivity to the microscopic, fine grain of the patient's reactions to interpretations. To clarify the developments in clinical practice, and to highlight the current style, I shall briefly summarize the three stages.

1 The infant's objects Melanie Klein was justifiably proud of her play technique with children. It had served her well in establishing child analysis, and in some of the major theoretical breakthroughs. In Chapter 4 we saw in detail how Klein applied Freud's dream interpretation to the play of children. At that time she was particularly rigorous over the paradigm of the process in the session: **associations–interpretation–response**. It was Klein's clinical strength to be able to observe this process in such detail, and it gave a particular clinical emphasis to the writings of British psychoanalysts, especially those who were close to Klein.

Children in general, and not least those in psychoanalytic treatment, conceive their experiences (and therefore their play) in terms of parts of the body which they are discovering and feeling anxious about. Klein adopted a concept used by Abraham, the 'part-object'. This designated a function rather than an actual identified being. When a mother feeds her infant, she is restricted simply to a feeding 'mother' – often termed the 'breast' – in the infant's mind. Another object would be another version of mother as a separate function – for example 'the lavatory' mother, into whom the infant discharges its noxious experiences and/or bad objects. So the infant's world is populated by objects that have single functions which, in an objective sense, are only part of the whole person. Abraham distinguished part-object love – a love for something which performs a single satisfaction for the infant – from whole-object love, where the infant can experience complex figures with multiple functions, some good for it and some bad. Such a mixed 'whole' figure is the focus of the depressive position, and of those mixed feelings. The infant then loves the object, the whole object, for itself, not simply for what it does for it.

As a result, there was extensive interest in interpreting the unconscious phantasies that concerned part-objects, such as the 'breast' or the 'penis' – and, typically, their functions. This kind of approach culminated in the notions of the depressive position, in which parts begin to come together and mix, and the internalized objects are absorbed into the ego as part-objects. During this phase, too, Klein remained under the consistent shock of how much destructiveness there was in children, so interpretation rested on exposing the negative impulses which generated such anxiety for the child. As we have seen, this had a remarkable effect in many cases. Although Klein was still writing about her play technique in 1955, Kleinian technique was by then about to change.

2 Psychotic process The interpretation of part-objects was modified somewhat during the 1950s and 1960s when Kleinian psychoanalysts were working with schizophrenic patients. Following Klein's paper on schizoid mechanisms (1946) there was a sudden awareness of parts of the self which were also related to in a variety of ways, as we saw in Chapters 7 and 8. In addition, there was a massive increase in awareness of the processes by which the infant mind is regulated, especially the destructive processes. Splitting and projective identification were means for organizing the patient's experience through direct alteration of the structure of his or her mind. At the same time the work of Klein and that of Rosenfeld, Segal and Bion demonstrated that the subject was aware of these processes (albeit unconsciously) and could communicate worries about them to the analyst, who could interpret to the patient what was happening to him or her. Very far-reaching interpretations of patients' capacity to split and project parts of the self into objects, both internal and external, were elaborated, and patients were subjected to blunt expositions of their destructive impulses. Their seeming madness was commensurate with the madness of their patients. The intensity of this malignant destructive process was as startling as the aggression in children. It was highlighted in 1957 by Klein's description of envy as lucid further evidence of primary destructiveness. The interpretation of these forms of destructiveness, especially of envy, led Kleinian psychoanalysts to err on the side of rigidly combating apparent resistances to the analyst. The sense of Kleinian psychoanalysis as an intra-analytic dispute or battle then began to become legendary. This, however, has now changed, perhaps quite radically.

3 Countertransference Not only were colleagues often shocked by the adventurous depth of interpretations of part-objects and of psychotic attacks upon the self; it is possible that patients, too, were highly disturbed by them. But perhaps more than anything, the centrality of destructiveness in interpretations tended to provoke, in non-psychotic patients at least (and in non-Kleinian audiences to papers), a sense of an adversarial approach between analyst and patient. More recently there has been a major redirection of attention towards the adversaries *within* the patient's world. In any case, the recent trend has been 'to talk to the patient, especially the non-psychotic patient, less in terms of anatomical structures (breast, penis) and more in terms of psychological functions' (Spillius, 1988, p. 9).

To some extent this represents a return from the work with psychotic patients to further research with non-neurotic ones, particularly borderline personalities. The gradual appreciation among the whole of the psychoanalytic community that the analyst has an emotional life with the patient has led Kleinians to formulate the transference/countertransference interaction in their own terms – notably in terms of the relocation between individuals of significant elements of their mental make-up: projective identification. The recognition of more benign forms of projective identification has led to a modification of the emphasis on destructiveness, and an attempt to formulate balanced interpretations which has given equal emphasis to loving feelings as well.

Indeed, this balance was recommended a long time ago in Joan Riviere's paper which was perhaps the first Kleinian contribution to the pathological organizations: 'the love for the internal object must be found behind the guilt' (Riviere, 1936b, p. 151). Love is as powerful a spring of phantasy life as destructiveness.

The legacy of the work with psychotic patients has been a fascination with the here-and-now processes that occur in the patient's mind, the way the interplay between love and hate is resolved and struggled with. It was found that the psychotic patient's problem is not so much his neurotic difficulties and the way he defends against them – far worse: he deals with his neurotic problem by destroying that part of his mind which contains those experiences and could become aware of them. Those attacks go on before the analyst's eyes. Although – with a few notable except-ions – Kleinian psychoanalysts no longer regularly treat psychotic patients, attention to the state of mental functions (and the integrity of the self) has survived alongside the attention to the content of those functions. Another legacy of the work with psychotic patients has been the study of knowing, thinking and learning, and this has tended to shift the view of the psychoanalytic process. Instead of the analyst as a kind of feeding breast, another version has slid in: the psychoanalyst, as an understanding object, provides a form of truthfulness that acts as the food for mental nourishment and development.

Bion's injunction to abandon memory and desire (Bion, 1967), deriving from his work with the thought disorders of schizo-phrenics, has had a powerful and lasting influence in loosening Kleinian psychoanalysts from a too slavish attention to the derivatives, and re-enactments, of the past. This has set up a tension between working with the immediate process of the present on the one hand and, on the other, interpreting the recapitulation of the past in the transference. Different members of the Kleinian group of psychoanalysts take different stances on this.

THE TOTAL SITUATION

Transference relationships arise to enact specific gratifications (narcissistic, sadomasochistic, etc.) and defensive functions, as well as to embody characteristic objects and relationships. In this sense it is the 'total situation' that is transferred, not simply a repeat of some past event which can be reconstructed. The anxieties, defences and relationships have a real meaning and function currently, in the present – this is not merely an empty repetition of the form of the relationship. Klein argued that these forms of intricate but desperate manoeuvrings with the analyst sustained the continuing functions of the infant–mother interactions:

> . . . the patient is bound to deal with conflicts and anxieties re-experienced towards the analyst by the same methods he used in the past. That is to say, he turns away from the analyst as he attempted to turn away from his primal objects; he tries to split the relations to him, keeping him either as a good or as a bad figure: he deflects some of the feelings and attitudes experienced towards the analyst on to other people in his current life, and this is part of 'acting out'. (Klein, 1952, pp. 55–6)

In this passage, Klein is concerned particularly with the defence of splitting the object. But the other primitive defences – projection, projective identification, introjection and identification, employed with similar degrees of force and omnipotence – will also appear in the present transference situation. Transference is generated from the present use of historical defences; in other words, the adult personality's unconscious phantasies (which underlie all these defence mechanisms) is transferred from the present unconscious into the analytic relationship – although, to be sure, the unconscious phantasy of the adult has been progressively elaborated out of the infant's relations with objects. Close attention to the immediate present is not inconsistent with a similar attention to the reconstructed past; it is merely that the desperate function it now serves should not be overlooked in the calm search for its function in the past.

If full reference is made to the total situation of the active object relations, then an expanded understanding of the transference can rapidly open up. We saw this in the example *The man who assaulted his buttocks* (p. 66), in which a simple sadomasochistic transference could be understood in vastly greater depth once the intricate object relations were allowed to clarify the confusing identifications.

Fundamental principles Despite these vast changes in Kleinian practice, and the unresolved issues that still remain, there has been a striking continuity of fundamental principles of technique which have endured throughout. In particular there seem to me to be four principles that permeate all the phases.

First, the *process*: the close attention to the response to interpretation, visible in the fine grain of the transference enactments, is a constant feature of Kleinian practice.

Second, there is continuing emphasis on the centrality of interpreting the *transference*, expanded as the total situation including the function of the enacted object relations as well as the symbolic meaning of the analyst.

Third, Kleinian psychoanalysts have remained firmly rooted in the patient's *infantile level* of functioning – it has been said that whereas Freud discovered the child in the adult, Klein discovered the infant in the child.

And fourth, the pervading spectre of destructiveness is kept in a balanced focus with the loving person. If ever an epitaph for Kleinian psychoanalysis has one day to be written, it will surely refer to the relentless hunting down of all the forms of destructiveness that so spoil the greatest human aspirations.

Although members are engaged with disparate themes, and there are differences of emphasis, the group of Kleinian psychoanalysts remains a coherent whole, more like a research team than a competing group of individuals each advancing his or her own name.

REFLECTIONS:
PROGRESS AND HISTORY

As I have found myself stressing again and again, the Kleinian fascination is a taste for very remote forms of experiencing. So much has derived from patients who are called 'psychotic' that it often seems wilfully contrary to write publicly outside the technical confines of the psychoanalytic circle. There is a genuine belief among Kleinians that a whole separate layer of mind has been revealed beneath the familiar preoccupations of the ordinary Oedipus complex – which itself lies well below the awareness of ordinary conscious daily experiences. In the course of infantile life that earliest layer disappeared, subducted under the tectonic movements of development. The psychoanalytic exploratory route has travelled via the analysis of children to the analysis of psychotic patients: the former are closer to that early and infantile mode of experiencing; the latter have not properly slid from view behind the mature forms of mind. This path was traversed in the three decades from 1934 to the mid 1960s. Re-emerging, psychoanalysis has not come back to the same old daylight. The old problems that were once ordinarily oedipal, symbolic, and so on, now have quite different connotations after our sojourn in the underworld. We no longer diagnose the hysteric, the obsessional, and so forth. Instead we are concerned with those who are not quite psychotic – we diagnose 'borderline personality' very widely indeed. We are concerned with different conceptions – debility of thought and learning ('minus K'), organized internal tyranny, and so on. These rewrite the Oedipus complex in new versions. The world of mental process has been forever redefined for Kleinians by the detour through those primitive levels.

What emerges from our investigations as distinctively Kleinian?

First is the central theoretical notion of the death instinct. This is more or less completely excluded by other schools of psychoanalysis – certainly its clinical manifestations as envy and the subtle interplay between love and aggressive derivatives of the death instinct.

Second is the clarity of distinction between internal and external worlds, and thus between internal and external objects. The concreteness of internal objects is to be contrasted with the 'transitional objects' described by Winnicott (1971), and with the idea of mental representation, a sort of internal symbolization (see, for instance, Sandler, 1987).

Third, meaning is an experience contributed from the subject's state of mind rather than a property inherent in external objects which the subject learns to apprehend. Of course social meanings are learned, but on the basis of common inherent unconscious phantasies which are elaborated personally and socially.

Fourth is the elaboration of unconscious phantasy and meaning into thoughts, and then into a mind with which to think them.

Fifth, the Kleinian view of countertransference is an intrapsychic one, a property of the active internal world of the analyst resonating with the intrapsychic world of the patient.

Sixth, Kleinian psychoanalysts particularly stress that interpretations should address the immediate here-and-now reverberations of the transference in the sessions. Interventions that do not can be in danger of being defensive against the disturbance of the countertransference, or at least in danger of being experienced by the patient in that way.

Seventh, and related to the first, is the recent conceptualization of the pathological organization as the personal institution within the personality of a self-directed destructiveness derived from rather unmodified derivatives of the death instinct; and the precise, subtle but enduring impasse in the psychoanalysis to which these organizations give rise.

The clinical reports selected in this book have at times made much of the **association–interpretation–response** formula, though this conception is not especially Kleinian. Even so, the examples I have offered have not always adhered as closely as they might to this evidential clinical process. Many accounts which I have found myself using have not always been such a meticulous record of that intimate process as I would have liked.

Many other aspects of the psychoanalytic process are interestingly discussed in Meltzer (1967), but I have chosen this one as especially important in the clinical verification of concepts. That Kleinian psychoanalysis will turn out to be a 'scientific' cul-de-sac has often been predicted by many people – some hopefully! The future of psychoanalysis, they say, will lie elsewhere. Nevertheless, whatever the future story, many of these gains in the past will have been absorbed – the notion of the mixed feeling states of the depressive position, widely accepted as the source of varied subtle emotional responses, and of the poetic imagination; the specific terrors of fragmentation and splitting; the containing experience of the interpersonal relatedness of intrapsychic worlds; and the underpinning of the concept of projective identification. Gratefully or otherwise, these notions are currently in widespread use in many quarters in psychoanalysis – on the continent of Europe, in South America and elsewhere, as well as among many non-Kleinian psychoanalysts in Britain.

Psychoanalysis can never be the same after these strange and difficult discoveries. Some have concluded that Kleinians have taken leave of reality as we know it, and swum off into the detached freedom of their patients' wild phantasies – or, as some would believe, into the world of their own unsupported phantasies. This sense of remoteness from the world we live in as adults does not, however, mean that Kleinians actually live in a world of phantasy, or that they believe their patients do. The problem is to capture the blend of the two – the external and internal worlds; especially since, throughout the early stages of life, that blend constantly changes and emerges in confusingly varied proportions. The 'world' outside the infant is strikingly different from the 'world' outside the adult. The infant's is an animistic world in which sensible, physical properties are probably apprehended only in mentalistic terms – that is to say, the infant sees motivations in everything around (and, indeed, inside) it. The external world of the infant is therefore first of all 'social'. It apperceives other minds that are, like its own, motivated, impulsive and desiring. In the beginning the infant relates to just such a psychological object as itself, and does so through curiosity, hating and love.

Thus, at the level of mind at which Kleinians think the

unconscious works, the external world is a social world, not a material factual one. In fact there have been strong traditions within Kleinian psychoanalysis which apply theoretical concepts to social settings (e.g. Menzies Lyth, 1988, 1989).[21] However, a 'social' reality is a flux. Both subject and object vary with each other. That shifting world reverberates with the subject – quite unlike the concrete external environment which normally attends the experience of conscious adults. What we can see now, in contemporary psychoanalysis, however, is that the patient is not really giving us a view of the deepest workings of his or her mind, but instead a view of what she or he is doing with another person's mind – projecting into it or receiving projections from it. It is the patient's own perception of the interaction – a perception, to be sure, deeply impregnated with his or her own methods of perceiving.

The focus on the individual's own perceptions and self-descriptions of their minds advocated by Abraham does not leave much room for analysts themselves to describe how minds work – beyond recording the patient's views. And some have objected to this; they have complained that in effect such an approach rules out the whole of psychoanalytic metapsychology. Metapsychology is the body of theories that have been built up on the basis of many individual psychologies found in each patient to create, by induction, a set of generalized notions about human psychology. In fact there has always been a tension within psychoanalysis between looking carefully at how the mind of an individual works (the work of each psychoanalytic treatment) and the development of a general system; Freud's earliest work was founded on the view that each person's symptoms and each person's dreams had to be decoded every time for their idiosyncratic, individual meaning. Of course this soon gave way to attempts to systematize his results into a general theory, which he called metapsychology.

In fact the idea of decoding (interpreting) was itself a general theory about meaning and mental contents. This had remained a continuing polarity within psychoanalysis: to analyse individuals or to create metapsychological theories. It has been cast as a debate between an objective view of the topic – to build theories of sufficient general scope to which individuals, in all their variation, conform, rather as a natural science such as physics seeks ever more general theories about the nature of matter – or alternatively a subjective approach, laying emphasis on the individual's own experiences. Kleinians were very much part of that debate when the controversy over Klein as a dissenter from psychoanalysis was at its height during the 1940s. Such a contrast is not necessarily so conflictual; in principle, at least, there is no reason why subjective individual experiences should not have more general patterns and properties. When it came to the practice of gathering the *subjective* data, however, a problem did indeed arise. There are no properly worked out principles for gathering such subjective (or intersubjective) data as the natural scientist gathers objective data, and it is an urgent need within psychoanalysis to find such principles, which will make the gathering of more subjective data a rigorous exercise comparable to gathering objective data.

Increasingly throughout the twentieth century, human beings have been understood as psychological beings. Their difficulties have therefore been increasingly seen as psychological, and less as moral. The impetus for this change has comprised many elements, but psychoanalysis has figured prominently among them. In very large measure, across the whole of our culture, the general apperception of mental illness and disturbance has been moulded by psychoanalysis itself. As psychoanalytic ideas have spread, so the presentation of psychological difficulties has become permeated by a psychoanalytic sophistication. This has created a particular situation for psychoanalysts. They face a moving target. New kinds of patients mean new ideas, which in turn mean new ways of working, but they also mean patients with new ways of presenting themselves, and thus a new target for the psychoanalytic probe.

This is disconcerting for psychoanalysts. As scientists – often medical scientists – we are accustomed to think of ourselves as investigating eternal truths – in our case, eternal truths about the human being. There is then the temptation to resist the kind of mutual interaction I have discussed in this book. Sometimes psychoanalysts resort to discrete categories (often called diagnoses) in the pulsating interpersonal flux. In this there is a blind endeavour to mimic medical science: to have consistent, well-defined categories that give a sense of permanence and stability, when in fact we should not be looking for such categories. There is a painful lack of charity to the patient in reducing his or her interactive potential to a diagnosis; the patient becomes a pathological entity rather than a striving agent. After all, it is the patient as a feeling, struggling colleague who is the substance of the subjectivity the psychoanalyst seeks, and this is the hallmark that makes psychoanalysis a science of the subject.

NOTES

1 A note on the third-person pronoun: I have tried wherever possible to avoid a gender bias. The penalty is at times a ponderous inclusiveness, and just occasionally I have given way to a smoother style using 'he', 'him and 'his', to stand for both genders.

2 At this time the majority of experimental subjects for these new therapies seem to have been women, and Breuer's only patient was a woman, Anna O.

3 For fuller accounts of the discovery of the unconscious, see Ellenberger (1970); Whyte (1978).

4 In this case the loved object was lost through an oral activity of butchery, and contrasts with the anal loss (through elimination) in the example on p. 21.

5 The question of whether the infant has a psychological nature at all at birth is a vexed one. Margaret Mahler (1975), for instance, put the psychological birth of the human infant at around nine months of life, and this is accepted as the orthodox view among many psychoanalysts in the United States. However, this often seems unrealistic to mothers, and to anyone acquainted with babies; there does in fact *seem* to be a world of experience going on in the little organism right from birth. Daniel Stern (1985) disputed Mahler's claim on the basis of experimental psychology, which tends to suggest very much early psychological experiencing.

6 Both Petot (1982) and Grosskurth (1985) have considered the strong evidence that the observations reported in Klein's earliest paper were observations on her children, made in the manner that other psychoanalysts at the time were adopting with their own children.

7 At this point Klein added a footnote to explain that she was explicit about sexual matters with her child patients, that she was careful to use the words the child himself used for the anatomical parts and functions. She would discover these from her initial interview with the parents.

8 In this phantasy the child displays her homosexual, ('reverse') Oedipus complex – i.e. love for the parent of the *same* sex, and therefore rivalry with the parent of the opposite sex. This contrasts with the direct Oedipus complex – love for the parent of the opposite sex and rivalry with the same-sex parent. Freud considered that all people are bisexual, and have both a direct and a reverse Oedipus complex. We all have the same propensity for developing both a homosexual love and a heterosexual love, although in most – but not all – cases the homosexual love tends to become desexualized.

9 Here, I am not elucidating *why* the unconscious achieves distorted representation in consciousness, merely indicating some phantasies found in the unconscious and the perceivable forms they take. We considered the why-question very briefly in Chapter 1; to take it further, the reader might start with Freud's *Interpretation of Dreams* (Freud, 1900).

10 The original but briefer version of this paper was published in 1952 and is included in Paula Heimann's collected papers (1989), *About Children and Children-No-Longer*.

11 At the risk of introducing confusing extra detail at this point, it might nevertheless be borne in mind that hostile relations do not lead only to introjective problems of an unassimilated object, because later (in Chapter 7) we will have evidence that identity can be greatly distorted by hostile forms of projection as well.

12 The sense of the internal object's permanence which was stressed in the example *Identifying with 'good' object* (p. 71) does not mean that it *is* permanent, only that the subject feels it to be so for the time being. Although, as good experiences accumulate throughout infancy and later life, the sense of permanence becomes actually more enduring, something adverse can happen, and the permanence and security can always be shaken.

13 It has been noted that Klein reported this case not long after the sudden death of her own son.

14 There is a potential complication here in that if internal objects are identified with (assimilated into the ego), attacks on an object could be identical to attacks on the self. There is, however, a sharp distinction in practice: the experience of an object inside that is attacked (like a tapeworm eating into the stomach (see *Attacked by worms*, p. 62), or Richard's anxiety about collisions with the internal psychoanalyst/mother (see *The insecure internal object*, p. 82) differs from the sense of oneself in pieces – losing one's feelings (the example we have just considered) or the capacity to think, as we shall see in later examples.

15 The peculiarly concrete form of symbolization typical of these disturbed kinds of patients will be discussed in the Appendix to this chapter.

16 The child sometimes played the full game with a cotton-reel on a piece of string which allowed him to bring the reel back as well as throw it away. When it returned, he said '*da*'. Perhaps this '*fort–da*' game is to be compared with the psychotic preoccupations of Abraham's patient who repeatedly expelled and introjected objects (*Anal holding on*, p. 21); or with the little girl, Ruth, who played with things falling out of a tumbler, and so on (*Anxious Ruth*, p. 47).

17 Specific gender stereotypes of 'mother', or of 'father', are misleading when one is considering the infantile level of experience. These terms tend to indicate functions rather than persons. At one time Kleinian analysts tried to accommodate this by finding other terms; notably 'breast' and 'penis'. However, because of a depersonalizing quality, and because they seem mistakenly to overeroticize these functions, these terms have tended to fall from use (cf. Spillius, 1988). Such functions, as opposed to people, are called 'part-objects'. The issue arises because the infant experiences mother extremely intensely, but largely empty of the set of social meanings and connotations that will be supplied as the infant enters the wider social world. Of course the *way in which* the actual mother is experienced as a 'mother' by the infant is partly determined by the mother's own socialization. But for the infant those social stereotype elements of its mother are not yet appreciated as such – instead they and she are apprehended only according to the functions of unconscious phantasy.

18 'Acting-out' is the term used by Freud to mean the discharge of mental energy in the form of action in order to prevent it being used in thought and awareness – if such awareness would be painful. In the terms we have adopted in recent chapters in this book 'acting-*out*' is linked to Bion's idea of the evacuation of feeling states or of parts of the mind (see Chapters 7 and 8).

19 These Kleinian observations lead to quite important implications for moral philosophy. The systems of normally accepted values and perverse values seem to derive some of their intensity from the life and death instincts, respectively. In this view, there appears to be direct evidence for some inherent and biological factor in morality and ethics.

20 In fact, as Brenman himself commented in a personal communication about this case: 'When I refer to parents I am referring to"internal parents" – the picture of the parents inside the analysand's mind. This may approximate to the nature of the actual parents but has gone through such transformation that it is, at the point of this example, impossible to differentiate the actual parents from transferences that change the picture of the past by various dynamic interactions – that differentiation work is done by the analysand later when helped by the analysis' (Brenman, 1993).

21 The social relations of the Kleinian group itself outside the British Psycho-Analytical Society in British political and intellectual life is interestingly debated by Rustin (1991) and Frosh (1991).

REFERENCES

Quotations are from those editions marked *; otherwise quotations are from the first or only edition. Place of publication is London unless otherwise indicated.

Abraham, Karl (1911) 'Notes on the psycho-analytic treatment of manic-depressive insanity and allied conditions', in Abraham (1927*) *Selected papers on Psycho-Analysis*, pp. 137–56. Hogarth; reprinted (1979) Karnac.

—— (1924) 'A short study of the development of the libido, viewed in the light of mental disorders', in Abraham (1927*) *Selected Papers on Psycho-Analysis*, pp. 418–501. Hogarth; reprinted (1979) Karnac.

Berman, Leo (1949) 'Counter-transference and attitudes of the analyst in the therapeutic process', *Psychiatry* 12: 159–66.

Bion, Wilfred (1957) 'The differentiation of the psychotic from the non-psychotic personalities', *Int. J. Psycho-Anal.* 38: 266–75; reprinted (1967*) in Bion, *Second Thoughts*. Heinemann, pp. 43–64, and (1988) in Elizabeth Bott Spillius, ed. *Melanie Klein Today. Volume 1: Mainly Theory*. Routledge, pp. 61–78.

—— (1959) 'Attacks on linking', *Int. J. Psycho-Anal.* 40: 308–15; reprinted (1967*) in Bion, *Second Thoughts*. Heinemann, pp. 93–109, and (1988) in Elizabeth Bott Spillius, ed. *Melanie Klein Today. Volume 1: Mainly Theory*. Routledge, pp. 87–101.

—— (1962a) 'A theory of thinking', *Int. J. Psycho-Anal.* 43: 306–10; reprinted (1967*) in Bion, *Second Thoughts*. Heinemann, pp. 110–19.

—— (1962b) *Learning from Experience*. Heinemann; reprinted (1984) Karnac.

—— (1967) 'Notes on memory and desire', *The Psycho-Analytic Forum* 2: 272–3, 279–80; reprinted (1988) in Elizabeth Bott Spillius, ed. *Melanie Klein Today. Volume 2: Mainly Practice*. Routledge, pp. 17–21.

—— (1974) *Brazilian Lectures 1*. Rio de Janeiro: Imago Editora; republished (1990) in *Brazilian Lectures*. Routledge.

Brenman, Eric (1980) 'The value of reconstruction in adult psycho-analysis', *Int. J. Psycho-Anal.* 61: 53–60.

—— (1993) Personal communication.

Brenman Pick, Irma (1985) 'Working through in the counter-transference', *Int. J. Psycho-Anal.* 66: 157–66; reprinted (1988) in Elizabeth Bott Spillius, ed. *Melanie Klein Today. Volume 2: Mainly Practice*. Routledge, pp. 34–47.

Ellenberger, Henri (1970) *The Discovery of the Unconscious*. New York: Basic.

Feldman, Michael (1989) 'The Oedipus complex: manifestation in the inner world and the therapeutic situation', in Ronald Britton, Michael Feldman and Edna O'Shaughnessy, *The Oedipus Complex Today: Clinical Implications*. Karnac, pp. 103-28.

Freud, Anna (1926) *Four Lectures on Child Analysis* (original English translation as *Introduction to the Technique of Child Analysis*). New York: Nervous and Mental Disease Publishing Company; reprinted (1974) in *The Writings of Anna Freud. Volume 1*. New York: International Universities Press, pp. 3-69.

Freud, Sigmund (1900) *The Interpretation of Dreams*, in James Strachey, ed. *The Standard Edition of the Complete Psychological Works of Sigmund Freud*, 24 vols. Hogarth, 1953-73, vols 4-5, pp. 1-627.

—— (1905) 'Fragment of an analysis of a case of hysteria'. *S.E.* 7, pp. 1-122.

—— (1909) 'Analysis of a phobia in a five-year old boy'. *S.E.* 10, pp. 5-149.

—— (1910) 'The future prospects of psycho-analytic therapy'. *S.E.* 11, pp. 141-51.

—— (1911) 'Psycho-analytic notes on an autobiographical account of a case of paranoia'. *S.E.* 11, pp. 9-82.

—— (1914) 'On narcissism: an introduction'. *S.E.* 14, pp. 69-102.

—— (1917) 'Mourning and melancholia'. *S.E.*14, pp. 243-58.

—— (1918) 'From the history of an infantile neurosis'. *S.E.* 17, pp. 7-122.

—— (1920) *Beyond the Pleasure Principle. S.E.* 18, pp. 7-64.

—— (1923) *The Ego and the Id. S.E.* 19, pp. 12-66.

—— (1927) 'Fetishism'. *S.E.* 21, pp. 151-7.

—— (1940) *An Outline of Psycho-Analysis. S.E.* 23, pp. 144-207.

Frosh, Stephen (1991) *Identity Crisis: Modernity, Psycho-Analysis and the Self*. Macmillan.

Gitelson, M. (1952) 'The emotional position of the analyst in the psycho-analytic situation', *Int. J. Pyscho-Anal.* 33: 1-10.

Grosskurth, Phyllis (1985) *Melanie Klein: Her World and Her Work*. Hodder & Stoughton.

Heimann, Paula (1942) 'A contribution to the problem of sublimation and its relation to processes of internalization', *Int. J. Psycho-Anal.* 23: 8-17; reprinted (1989*) in Heimann, *About Children and Children-No-Longer*. Routledge, pp. 26-45.

—— (1950) 'On counter-transference', *Int. J. Psycho-Anal.* 31; 81-4; reprinted (1989*) in Heimann, *About Children and Children-No-Longer*. Routledge, pp. 73-9.

—— (1955) 'A combination of defences in paranoid states', in Melanie Klein, Paula Heimann and Roger Money-Kyrle, eds *New Directions in Psycho-Analysis*. Tavistock, pp. 240-65. Original version (1952) 'Preliminary notes on some defence mechanisms in paranoid states',

Int. J. Psycho-Anal. 33: 208–13; reprinted (1989*) in Heimann, *About Children and Children-No-Longer.* Routledge, pp. 97–107.

—— (1960) 'Counter-transference', *Br. J. Med. Psychol.* 33: 9–15; reprinted (1989*) in Heimann, *About Children and Children-No-Longer.* Routledge, pp. 151–60.

Isaacs, Susan (1948) 'On the nature and function of phantasy', *Int. J. Psycho-Anal.* 29: 73–97; reprinted (1952) in Melanie Klein, Paula Heimann, Susan Isaacs and Joan Riviere, *Developments in Psycho-Analysis,* pp. 67–121. Hogarth; reprinted (1989*) Karnac.

Joseph, Betty (1975) 'The patient who is difficult to reach', in P.L. Giovacchini, ed. *Tactics and Techniques in Psycho-Analytic Therapy.* New York: Jason Aronson, pp. 205–16; reprinted (1988) in Elizabeth Bott Spillius, ed. *Melanie Klein Today. Volume 2: Mainly Practice.* Routledge, pp. 48–60, and (1989*) in Joseph, *Psychic Equilibrium and Psychic Change.* Routledge, pp. 75–87.

—— (1981) 'Defence mechanisms and phantasy in the psycho-analytical process', *Bulletin of the European Psycho-Analytical Federation* 17: 11–24; reprinted (1989*) in Joseph, *Psychic Equilibrium and Psychic Change.* Routledge, pp. 116–26.

—— (1982) 'Addiction to near death', *Int. J. Psycho-Anal.* 63: 449–56; reprinted (1988) in Elizabeth Bott Spillius, ed. *Melanie Klein Today. Volume 1: Mainly Theory.* Routledge, pp. 311–23, and (1989*) in Joseph, *Psychic Equilibrium and Psychic Change.* Routledge, pp. 127–38.

—— (1983) 'On understanding and not understanding: some technical issues', *Int. J. Psycho-Anal.* 64: 191–8; reprinted (1989*) in Joseph, *Psychic Equilibrium and Psychic Change.* Routledge, pp. 139–50.

—— (1985) 'Transference: the total situation', *Int. J. Psycho-Anal.* 66: 447–54; reprinted (1989*) in Joseph, *Psychic Equilibrium and Psychic Change.* Routledge, pp. 156–67.

—— (1987) 'Projective identification: some clinical aspects', in Joseph Sandler, ed. *Projection, Identification, Projective Identification.* Madison, WI: International Universities Press, pp. 65–76: reprinted (1988) in Elizabeth Bott Spillius, ed. *Melanie Klein Today. Volume 1: Mainly Theory.* Routledge, pp. 138–50, and (1989*) in Joseph, *Psychic Equilibrium and Psychic Change.* Routledge, pp. 168–80.

—— (1988) 'Object-relations in clinical practice', *Psychoanal. Q.* 57: 626–42; reprinted (1989*) in Joseph, *Psychic Equilibrium and Psychic Change.* Routledge, pp. 203–15.

—— (1989) 'Psychic change and the psycho-analytic process', in Joseph, *Psychic Equilibrium and Psychic Change.* Routledge, pp. 192–202.

King, Pearl and Steiner, Riccardo, eds (1991) *The Freud–Klein Controversies 1941–1945.* Routledge.

Klein, Melanie (1926) 'The psychological principles of early analysis'. *Int. J. Psycho-Anal.* 8: 25–37; reprinted (1975*) in *The Writings of Melanie Klein. Volume 1: Love, Guilt and Reparation.* Hogarth, pp. 128–38.

—— (1927) 'Criminal tendencies in normal children', *Br. J. Med. Psychol.* 7: 177–92.

—— (1929) 'Personification in the play of children', *Int. J. Psycho-Anal.* 10: 193–204; reprinted in (1975*) in *The Writings of Melanie Klein. Volume 1: Love, Guilt and Reparation.* Hogarth, pp. 199–209.

—— (1932) *The Psycho-Analysis of Children.* Hogarth; reprinted (1975*) as *The Writings of Melanie Klein. Volume 2: The Psycho-Analysis of Children.* Hogarth.

—— (1933) 'The early development of conscience in the child', in Sandor Lorand, ed. *Psycho-Analysis Today.* New York: Covici-Friede, pp. 149–62; reprinted (1975*) in *The Writings of Melanie Klein. Volume 1: Love, Guilt and Reparation.* Hogarth, pp. 248–57.

—— (1935) 'A contribution to the psychogenesis of manic-depressive states', *Int. J. Psycho-Anal.* 16: 145–74; reprinted (1975*) in *The Writings of Melanie Klein. Volume 1: Love, Guilt and Reparation.* Hogarth, pp. 262–89.

—— (1940) 'Mourning and its relation to manic-depressive states', *Int. J. Psycho-Anal.* 21: 125–53; reprinted (1975*) in *The Writings of Melanie Klein. Volume 1: Love, Guilt and Reparation.* Hogarth, pp. 344–69.

—— (1946) 'Notes on some schizoid mechanisms', *Int. J. Psycho-Anal.* 27: 99–110; reprinted (1975*) in *The Writings of Melanie Klein. Volume 3: Envy and Gratitude.* Hogarth, pp. 1–24.

—— (1952) 'The origins of transference'; reprinted (1975*) in *The Writings of Melanie Klein. Volume 3: Envy and Gratitude.* Hogarth, pp. 48–56.

—— (1955) 'The psycho-analytic play technique: its history and significance', in Melanie Klein, Paula Heimann and Roger Money-Kyrle, eds *New Directions in Psycho-Analysis.* Tavistock, pp. 3–22; reprinted (1975*) in *The Writings of Melanie Klein. Volume 3: Envy and Gratitude.* Hogarth, pp. 122–40.

—— (1957) *Envy and Gratitude.* Tavistock; reprinted (1975*) in *The Writings of Melanie Klein. Volume 3: Envy and Gratitude.* Hogarth, pp. 176–235.

—— (1961) *Narrative of a Child Analysis.* Hogarth; reprinted (1975*) as *The Writings of Melanie Klein. Volume 4: Narrative of a Child Analysis.* Hogarth.

Laplanche, J. and Pontalis, J.-B. (1973) *The Language of Psycho-Analysis.* Hogarth.

Little, Margaret (1951) 'Counter-transference and the patient's response to it', *Int. J. Psycho-Anal.* 32: 32–40; reprinted (1981) in Little, *Transference Neurosis and Transference Psychosis*. New York: Jason Aronson.

Mahler, Margaret (1975) *The Psychological Birth of the Human Infant*. Hutchinson.

Meltzer, Donald (1967) *The Psycho-Analytical Process*. Heinemann.

—— (1968) 'Terror, persecution, dread – a dissection of paranoid states', *Int. J. Psycho-Anal.* 49: 396–400; reprinted (1973) in Meltzer, *Sexual States of Mind*. Perthshire: Clunie, pp. 99–106, and (1988*) in Elizabeth Bott Spillius, ed. *Melanie Klein Today. Volume 1: Mainly Theory*. Routledge, pp. 230–38.

Menzies Lyth, Isabel (1988) *Containing Anxiety in Institutions: Selected Essays Volume 1*. Free Association Books.

—— (1989) *The Dynamics of the Social: Selected Essays Volume 2*. Free Association Books.

Money-Kyrle, Roger (1956) 'Normal counter-transference and some of its deviations', *Int. J. Psycho-Anal.* 37: 360–66; reprinted (1978) in *The Collected Papers of Roger Money-Kyrle*, Perthshire: Clunie, pp. 330-42, and (1988*) in Elizabeth Bott Spillius, ed. *Melanie Klein Today. Volume 2: Mainly Practice*. Routledge, pp. 22–33.

—— (1969) 'On the fear of insanity', in (1978) *The Collected Papers of Roger Money-Kyrle*. Perthshire: Clunie, pp. 434–41.

O'Shaugnessy, Edna (1981) 'A clinical study of a defensive organization', *Int. J. Psycho-Anal.* 62: 359–69; reprinted (1988*) in Elizabeth Bott Spillius, ed. *Melanie Klein Today. Volume 1: Mainly Theory*. Routledge, pp. 293–310.

Petot, Jean-Michel (1982) *Melanie Klein: premières découvertes et premier système 1919–1932*. Paris: Bourdas; English translation (1991) Madison, WI: International Universities Press.

Racker, Heinrich (1949) 'The counter-transference neurosis', *Int. J. Psycho-Anal.* (1953) 34: 313–24; reprinted (1968) in Racker, *Transference and Counter-Transference*. Hogarth.

Reich, Annie (1951) 'On counter-transference', *Int. J. Psycho-Anal.* 32: 25–31.

Riviere, Joan (1936a) 'On the genesis of psychical conflict in earliest infancy', *Int. J. Psycho-Anal.* 17: 395–422; reprinted (1952) in Melanie Klein, Paula Heimann, Susan Isaacs and Joan Riviere, *Developments in Psycho-Analysis*, pp. 37–66. Hogarth; reprinted (1989*) Karnac, and (1991) in Riviere, *The Inner World and Joan Riviere*. Karnac, pp. 272–300.

—— (1936b) 'A contribution to the analysis of the negative therapeutic reaction', *Int. J. Psycho-Anal.* 17: 304–20; reprinted (1991) in Riviere, *The Inner World and Joan Riviere*. Karnac, pp. 134–53.

Rosenfeld, Herbert (1947) 'Analysis of a schizophrenic state with depersonalization', *Int. J. Psycho-Anal.* 28: 130–39; reprinted (1965*) in Rosenfeld, *Psychotic States*. Hogarth, pp. 13–33.

—— (1949) 'Remarks on the relation of male homosexuality to paranoia, paranoid anxiety and narcissism', *Int. J. Psycho-Anal.* 30: 36–47; reprinted (1965*) in Rosenfeld, *Psychotic States*. Hogarth, pp. 34–51.

—— (1952) 'Notes on the anlysis of the super-ego conflict in an acute schizophrenic patient', *Int. J. Psycho-Anal.* 33: 111–31; reprinted (1955) in Melanie Klein, Paula Heimann and Roger Money-Kyrle, eds *New Directions in Psycho-Analysis*. Tavistock, pp. 180–219, (1965*) in Rosenfeld, *Psychotic States*. Hogarth, pp. 63–103, and (1988) in Elizabeth Bott Spillius, ed. *Melanie Klein Today. Volume 1: Mainly Theory*. Routledge, pp. 14–51.

—— (1971) 'A clinical approach to the psycho-analytic theories of the life and death instincts: an investigation into the aggressive aspects of narcissism', *Int. J. Psycho-Anal.* 52: 169–78; reprinted (1988*) in Elizabeth Bott Spillius, ed. *Melanie Klein Today. Volume 1: Mainly Theory*. Routledge, pp. 239–55.

Rustin, Michael (1991) *The Good Society and the Inner World*. Verso.

Sandler, Joseph (1987) *From Safety to Superego*. Karnac.

——, Dare, Christopher and Holder, Alex (1973) *The Patient and the Analyst*. George Allen &Unwin.

Segal, Hanna (1957) 'Notes on symbol-formation', *Int. J. Psycho-Anal.* 38: 391–7; reprinted (1981*) in *The Work of Hanna Segal*. New York: Jason Aronson, pp. 49–64, and (1988) in Elizabeth Bott Spillius, ed. *Melanie Klein Today. Volume 1: Mainly Theory*. Routledge, pp. 160–77.

—— (1964) *Introduction to the Work of Melanie Klein*. Hogarth.

—— (1978) 'On symbolism', *Int. J. Psycho-Anal.* 59: 315–19.

—— (1989) Preface to Betty Joseph, *Psychic Equilibrium and Psychic Change*. Routledge, pp. vii–ix.

—— (1993) 'On the clinical usefulness of the concept of the death instinct', *Int. J. Psycho-Anal.* 74: 55–61.

Spillius, Elizabeth Bott (1988) 'Developments in technique: introduction', in Elizabeth Bott Spillius, ed. *Melanie Klein Today. Volume 2: Mainly Practice*. Routledge, pp. 5–16.

Steiner, John (1982) 'Perverse relations between parts of the self', *Int. J. Psycho-Anal.* 63: 241–52.

—— (1987) 'The interplay between pathological organizations and the paranoid-schizoid and depressive positions', *Int. J. Psycho-Anal.* 68: 69–80; reprinted (1988) in Elizabeth Bott Spillius, ed. *Melanie Klein Today. Volume 1: Mainly Theory*. Routledge, pp. 324–42.

—— (1993) *Psychic Retreats*. London: Routledge.

Stern, Daniel (1985) *The Interpersonal World of the Infant*. New York: Basic.

Strachey, James (1934) 'The nature of the therapeutic action of psycho-analysis', *Int. J. Psycho-Anal.* 15: 127–59; reprinted (1969) *Int. J. Psycho-Anal.* 50: 275–92.

Whyte, L.L. (1978) *The Unconscious before Freud*. Friedman.

Winnicott, D.W. (1947) 'Hate in the counter-transference', in Winnicott (1958) *Collected Papers: Through Paediatrics to Psycho-Analysis*. Hogarth, pp. 194–203.

—— (1971) *Playing and Reality*. Tavistock.

INDEX

INDEX OF EXAMPLES